The Politics of Distinction

Christopher Beach

The Politics of Distinction

WHITMAN AND
THE DISCOURSES OF
NINETEENTH-CENTURY
AMERICA

THE UNIVERSITY OF GEORGIA PRESS

Athens & London

© 1996 by the University of Georgia Press
Athens, Georgia 30602
All rights reserved
Designed by Walton Harris
Set in 11/14 Bulmer by Books International

The paper in this book meets the guidelines for
permanence and durability of the Committee
on Production Guidelines for Book Longevity
of the Council on Library Resources.

Printed in the United States of America

00 99 98 97 96 c 5 4 3 2 1

Library of Congress Cataloging in Publication Data

Beach, Christopher.
The politics of distinction : Whitman and the discourses
of nineteenth-century America / Christopher Beach.
p.   cm.
Includes bibliographical references (p.) and index.
ISBN 0-8203-1834-5 (alk. paper)
1. Whitman, Walt, 1819–1892—Knowledge—America.
2. Politics and literature—United States—History—19th
century.   3. Literature and society—United States—
History—19th century.   4. United States—Civilization—
19th century.   5. Discourse analysis, Literary.
6. Intertextuality.   7. Poetics.   I. Title.
PS3242.A54B43   1996   95-43303

British Library Cataloging in Publication Data available

for Carrie and Julian

CONTENTS

Acknowledgments   *ix*

Abbreviations   *xi*

Introduction: The Logic of Distinction   *1*

1 Intertextuality and the Poetics of Distinction   *18*

2 The Invisible Discourse:
   Slavery and Subjectivity in *Leaves of Grass*   *55*

3 The Aesthetics of "Indifference":
   Whitman and the American City   *102*

4 Figuring the Body in Leaves:
   Whitman and the Discourse of Corporeality   *152*

Notes   *185*

Works Cited   *205*

Index   *213*

 ACKNOWLEDGMENTS

There are several people whose help has been invaluable to me in writing this book: John Norman helped me in the early stages of the book to formulate its central ideas; Priscilla Wald, M. Wynn Thomas, and Robert Ferguson each read portions of the manuscript and offered valuable suggestions; Virginia Carmichael read and commented insightfully on the entire manuscript; and Stuart Culver gave a careful reading of the introduction. I would also like to offer special thanks to Molly Thompson of the University of Georgia Press, who has been unusually supportive throughout the reviewing and revising process.

Finally, I could not have written the book without my family. My parents, Northrop and Myrtle Beach, have been a constant source of support and encouragement. My wife, Carrie Noland, has helped more than anyone to guide me through the book's many stages of writing and revision. And my son Julian, whose arrival in this world coincided almost exactly with the beginnings of this project, has been a wonderful companion as well as a source of inspiration.

A section of chapter one has been published in *Walt Whitman Quarterly Review* 12.2 (Fall 1994), and a section of chapter two has been published in *Canadian Review of American Studies* 26.2 (Spring 1995).

ABBREVIATIONS

Abbreviations for the most frequently cited sources of Whitman's writings are as follows:

Corr   *The Correspondence,* ed. Edwin Havilland Miller

CP1855   *Complete Poetry and Collected Prose,* ed. Justin Kaplan

DN   *Daybooks and Notebooks,* ed. William White

EPF   *The Early Poems and the Fiction,* ed. Thomas Brasher

GF   *The Gathering of the Forces,* ed. Cleveland Rogers and John Black

IR   *In Re Walt Whitman,* ed. Horace Traubel, Richard M. Bucke, and Thomas Harned

IS   *I Sit and Look Out: Editorials from the "Brooklyn Daily Times," by Walt Whitman,* ed. Emory Holloway and Vernolian Schwarz

LG   *Leaves of Grass: Comprehensive Reader's Edition,* ed. Harold Blodgett and Sculley Bradley

N   *An 1855–56 Notebook Toward the Second Edition of "Leaves of Grass,"* ed. Harold Blodgett

NUPM   *Notebooks and Unpublished Prose Manuscripts,* ed. Edward Grier

NYD   *New York Dissected,* ed. Emory Holloway and Ralph Adimari

PW   *Prose Works, 1892,* ed. Floyd Stovall

UPP   *The Uncollected Poetry and Prose of Walt Whitman,* ed. Emory Holloway

WOT   *Whitman in His Own Time,* ed. Joel Myerson

WWC   *With Walt Whitman in Camden,* Horace Traubel

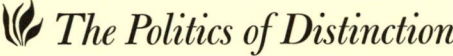 *The Politics of Distinction*

 INTRODUCTION

The Logic of Distinction

> *There is something wild in everything specifically American, something*
> *that has not known the glossy, high-flown rhetoric and theatricality of*
> *our bourgeois cultures, that has not been kitted out in the gaudy finery of*
> *cultural distinction.*
>
> —Jean Baudrillard, *America*

> *American literature must become distinct from all others. American*
> *writers must become national, idiomatic, free from the genteel laws—*
> *America herself appears in the spirit and the form of her poems, and*
> *all other literary works.*
>
> —Walt Whitman, Notebooks

> *As to the general question of Mr. Walt Whitman's poetical achievement,*
> *you will think that it savours of our decrepit old Europe when I add that*
> *while you think it is his highest merit that he is so unlike anyone else, to*
> *me this seems to be his demerit; no one can afford in literature to trade*
> *merely on his own bottom and to take no account of what the other ages*
> *and nations have acquired: a great original literature America will*
> *never get in this way, and her intellect must inevitably consent to come,*
> *in a considerable measure, into the European movement.*
>
> —Matthew Arnold, letter to W. D. O'Connor

Whitman's poetry has always elicited dramatic, at times even hyperbolic responses, responses in keeping with his own inflammatory rhetoric. Early commentators like Matthew Arnold were shocked by Whitman's sudden and audacious appearance in literary circles; indeed, Whitman's transformation from journalistic writer and editor to major poet remains one of the most surprising phenomena in American literature. How could a poet hope to create, in Arnold's terms, a "great original literature" by merely "trad[ing] on his own bottom"? With no national poetic tradition of any note, how could an unconnected and self-educated writer like Whitman expect to establish one? With no existing poetic medium or discourse within which to frame his project, how could Whitman create new ones? C. Carroll Hollis states most succinctly the problem with which every critic of Whitman has had to come to terms: "In the late 1840's and early 1850's there was no way a man with a prophetic message like Whitman's could ever have been heard in or through any artistic medium open to him. . . . It seems incredible that an un-educated . . . misfit, thirty years old, could produce within six years a volume that changed the history of American poetry."[1]

The explanations for the phenomenally sudden growth of Whitman as a poet have always been of two essential kinds: biographical and stylistic. The first approach is represented by books like Paul Zweig's *Walt Whitman: The Making of the Poet*, which examines in detail the decade prior to the first publication of *Leaves of Grass* in 1855.[2] Hollis, on the other hand, represents the opposite strain in Whitman criticism: in eschewing biographical explanations as well as intertextual ones, Hollis views the emergence of *Leaves of Grass* as a fortunate fusion—achieved largely unconsciously—of journalistic rhetoric, metonymic style, performative speech acts, and foregrounding devices such as the *cursus*. Hollis claims that "we do not know enough about the great mystery period (1848–1855) to trace the birth and growth of the persona, its role, its language, its message, its form, but we do know the end result" (237). Biographically oriented critics like Zweig, Justin Kaplan, Floyd Stovall, and Gay Wilson Allen are more willing to speculate about this period of "birth and growth," but although each of these commentators has added considerably to our understanding of Whitman's life and its relationship to his work, none has provided a fully satisfactory account of Whitman's poetic development in these years.

My goal is not to attempt an explanation of Whitman's genesis as a poet. Instead, I want to propose a model from which we can derive at least a partial motivation both for Whitman's difference from his poetic contemporaries and for his unique poetic evolution. What I posit is a phenomenon I call Whitman's "logic of distinction." I argue that his poetic negotiation with the various discourses of nineteenth-century America represented a double logic, whereby he differentiated his poetry from previous literary models while at the same time articulating a poetics that could *not* be marked as culturally distinct with respect to social class or cultural orientation. Whitman's project, as he articulates it both in the poems of *Leaves of Grass* and in various nonpoetic writings, involves a complex balancing act that reveals a great deal about the dynamic between literary modes and class relations in nineteenth-century America.

The theoretical implications of such a dynamic have been most suggestively explored by the cultural sociologist Pierre Bourdieu, whose work is largely concerned with the field of cultural production and the role of "cultural capital" within an economy of sociocultural relations. More specifically, Bourdieu's writings articulate a logic of cultural "distinction" that contributes both to the production of cultural goods (such as literature) and to the socially inflected systems of cultural value, or "taste," which determine the reception and circulation of literature within a given society.[3] I will use Bourdieu's theory strategically in my discussion to help illustrate aspects of Whitman's relation to "high" or "literary" culture, his attempts to subvert that culture even while participating in it, and his more specific ambivalence concerning his aesthetic relationship to the traditions, canons, and conventions of Anglo-American poetic culture. Where Bourdieu maps out the complete set of strategic possibilities available to writers and artists, the field where cultural distinctions emerge, I want to examine one particular figure, Walt Whitman, who traverses such a field in ways that disrupt and reconfigure the circulation of cultural values. Whitman's curious collapsing of high and low is at once typical of an American middle class improvising its cultural status and yet also radically defamiliarizing, even antagonistic, within the context of literary production. As my discussion moves from specifically literary culture to other areas of sociocultural discourse such as those surrounding slavery, urbanism, and the body, the logic of cultural distinction will be seen to operate on the social level as well: issues of race, class, gender, and sexual orientation can usefully be seen as inscribed, in different ways, within a larger politics of distinction that informs all of Whitman's writing. It was Whitman's interaction with these various discursive fields, as well as with specifically literary writings, that helped him to articulate a theory of distinction as it operated on different social and cultural planes. Whitman's own poetic project was formulated as part of the larger project of an American national literature that would be "distinct from all others"; yet this distinction, like Whitman's, would declare itself in terms of a "free[dom] from genteel laws" and an "idiomatic" expression. In other words, American poetry would be nationally distinct as a result, paradoxically, of its *lack* of (high) cultural distinction, and would participate in the idiomatic register of daily life (the sociolect) rather than the literary register of the educated elite.

Whitman's gesture was a highly self-conscious one. He was hardly the isolated primitive he is often portrayed as being; on the contrary, he was a poet operating consciously within the system of literary intertexts and within a cultural field of production that was determined largely by the avenues of publication and cultural promotion available at the time. In each of the chapters that follow, I focus both on the way in which particular poems in *Leaves of Grass* evolve from the use of different societal discourses and on self-conscious literary attempts by Whitman to address those discourses. The first chapter addresses in general terms the issue of cultural distinction in Whitman's work, using contemporary sociocultural theory (Bourdieu) and nineteenth-century sociocultural thought (Veblen) to place *Leaves of Grass* within the context of its literary and cultural environment in mid-century America. The second chapter involves the issue of slavery. The discourses surrounding slavery were among the most significant components of Whitman's sociolect; I examine the intertextual and social contexts of Whitman's relationship to race and slavery as worked out both in his poems and in his notebooks and other prose writings. In the third chapter I explore Whitman's relationship to the city and to the multiple discourses of the new metropolis; I read Whitman's New York as a site of Bakhtinian heteroglossia (an extreme manifestation of the sociolect), as opposed to the idiolectic mode suggested by the pastoral lyric. The fourth and final chapter treats Whitman's unique and complex interaction with discourses of the body; informed by Roland Barthes's notion of the body as the primary site of idiolectic expression and by Bourdieu's idea of "bodily hexis" as a class-defined language of the body, my readings engage Whitman's efforts to articulate a new textuality of the body amidst the various discourses surrounding women, sexuality, and health.

In order to explore Whitman's relationship to this cultural context, I have adopted a method that is neither traditionally biographical nor purely stylistic. Instead, I propose to examine Whitman's particular logic of distinction by focusing on two basic levels of discourse that alternate in his poems: the sociolectic and the idiolectic. Since these terms occur with some frequency throughout this study, let me briefly define the way in which I use them.

I use the concept of the *sociolect* to define more closely the historical and cultural circumstances in which a given text is produced, a particular configuration of the available discourses surrounding a given subject and constituting a society's communal or mythic understanding of that subject. Thus while transhistorical discourses exist for such sociocultural phenomena as slavery, commerce, or technology, it is the translation of those general discourses into terms of a more immediate range of concerns that constitutes the sociolect of midcentury America, a sociolect that informs Whitman's poems. The act of distinction by which Whitman appropriates these sociolects and then seeks in turn to express their historical and ideological content in a language that comprises his *idiolect* is of central importance to the making of his poems; it is an act that has both aesthetic and ideological implications.

Just as discourses can be either literary or nonliterary, the sociolect can be considered either in the more general sense of (nonliterary) social utterance or in the more specific sense of a general period style of writing. A helpful analogy in this case is Bakhtin's distinction in "The Problem of Speech Genres" between primary genres (those that take place in everyday, unmediated uses of language) and secondary genres (those that occur in more complex and organized forms of cultural communication such as literary texts and specialized academic and scientific research).[4] When I speak specifically of a literary sociolect, such as that of Romanticism in the first half of the nineteenth century, I refer to a mode of literary writing so widely disseminated and accepted as to be a virtual period style, rather than the style of a particular author.

The idiolect has been defined as "language in as much as it is spoken by a given individual."[5] Clearly, however, such a simple definition is problematic. In the case of a literary idiolect, what is to differentiate the language of a writer who makes no attempt to depart from the standard idiomatic speech of his or her day and one who, like Whitman, is constantly pushing the borders of language, attempting to create a new language or idiolect that would be recognizably his own? In fact, the borders between idiolect and sociolect, even in poetic texts like those of Whitman, are constantly shifting in accordance with developments both in literary practice and in societal practice. In the case of Whitman, who was a professional journalist during the seminal period of his development as a poet, the poetic process was never far removed from its immediate cultural and historical context. Yet, at the same time, Whitman's most successful poems cannot be explained in reference to a given source, either in previous works of literature or in the larger social realm. Instead, we continually discover a personal register of language use that eludes sociohistorical categorization.

The concept of the sociolect that I have mapped out here is crucially interwoven with that of the intertext as it has been explored by Michael Riffaterre and others. For Riffaterre, the poem's language is defined semiotically rather than referentially; the poetic text is a self-sufficient artifact apart from the codes of normal or extraliterary discourse, one which "rests upon so many intricate relationships that it is relatively impervious to change and deterioration of the [nonliterary] linguistic code."[6] The poem does not simply incorporate various discourses or codes, Riffaterre claims, but it in fact transforms them so that they become part of the poem's new logic, a redefined textual space in which language is "playing a complex game" in defiance of normative rules of grammar, meaning, and verbal combination. Thus the poem has its own idiolectic system, its own private lexicon, while it also interacts with and transforms the sociolect, the normative or commonplace usage of a particular linguistic code. Riffaterre does grant that the "idiolect is inseparable from the sociolect . . . that it challenges," but he is less interested in this extrapoetic relationship than he is in the way the text's "closure" is finally established through "the relation between the text and its intertext."[7] The poet "expels the sociolect, replaces the commonplaces of language and preexistent, pertinent (i.e., comparable) texts with the idiolect" ("Textuality," 10). This notion of the sociolect as a general system of verbal activity to be systematically excluded, expelled, or replaced in the text is as far as Riffaterre will go in admitting the possibility of an outside world of culturally and historically differentiated language use that might affect the writing or reading of poems. To posit a relationship between the poetic text and the world outside the literary is to commit the "referential fallacy" of a belief in the relationship between the poem's logic and the "logic of the sociolect"; thus the only appropriate reading of the poem, for Riffaterre, can be a semiotic one that will assume that there can be no meaning save in the relationship between a sign and a complex of other signs. Riffaterre's sense of the poem's relationship to history, then, includes only literary history, and his notion of culture is an equally literary one.

In this study, I will put pressure on Riffaterre's notion of the sociolect by admitting into my reading of Whitman's poetry the cultural and historical intertexts that define the poet's experience. In fact, a greater attention to the sociolect can itself provide a useful alternative to more narrowly intertextual or semiotic readings by providing a broader framework for an understanding of the poet's manipulation of linguistic and symbolic systems. If the poet's deviation from the historically current norm of language use differs substantially from the deviation of other poets from that same norm, we can conclude that the poet in question has created a new code, an original or at least highly differentiated idiolect, out of his or her interaction with the sociolect. Such a radical departure from what we can identify as standard poetic practice of the time—that practice exemplified by the work of the "fireside" poets, for example—is certainly characteristic of Whitman's poetry. At the same time that Whitman's poetic writing is highly idiolectic—highly differentiated from the work of his contemporaries—it is also engaged, more directly than the work of Bryant, Longfellow, and other contemporaries, with the sociolectic language of everyday speech and sociohistorical event. Much of the resonance of Whitman's poems comes from their immediate reference to the sociolect, a sociolect that often enters the poems in a form that is less heavily mediated by the strictures of poetic convention that inform the work of other writers.

Riffaterre's intertextual semiotics—applied primarily to the canonical texts of nineteenth- and twentieth-century French poetry—is less obviously relevant to the works of an American poet like Whitman. Despite Harold Bloom's attempt to define all subsequent American poetry in terms of certain Emersonian tropes, it is clear that the types of recurring motifs and shared allusions that characterize the highly intertextual French poetic tradition, and to some extent those of all European literatures, are far less predominant in American writing. Various reasons can be given for this American difference: greater geographical diversity, less centralized institutions of educational and cultural dissemination, a different ideological stance regarding the function of literature, and a historically much shorter tradition involving far fewer canonical poets. The concept of an American Renaissance, albeit a twentieth-century critical invention, denotes the seminal role of Whitman and his contemporaries in the *creation* of a national literature, rather than in the continuation or continual rewriting of one. The notion, shared by such authors as Emerson, Thoreau, Melville, and Whitman himself, of the American writer of midcentury as self-made and self-reliant, is markedly different from the self-image of nineteenth-century French poets (and British poets), who were attempting to insert themselves into a firmly defined and well-respected tradition. Whitman represents the extreme of such a self-reliant stance, not only in his auto-originary claims to write a "song of myself" but also in his background as a cultural autodidact and professional journalist.

Whitman's rhetorical move, and the gesture that distinguishes him most clearly from poetic contemporaries like Bryant, Whittier, and Longfellow, is to define himself and his poetic language in terms of a social interdependence that would be separate from any literary interdependence (tradition, canon, or literary intertextuality). Immediately following his claim to "sing myself" in the first line of his longest poem, Whitman proposes for himself not the narcissistic or solipsistic independence we might expect from the poem's title but a complete identification with the addressee, whether reader or listener: "And what I assume you shall assume / For every atom belonging to me as good belongs to you." Thus Whitman immediately projects himself into a democratic social space, one that can be understood either in terms of interpersonal and interbodily relations (the merging of social and physical selves) or in terms of a shared linguistic matrix, a common sociolect.

The word *assume,* which Whitman emphasizes by using it twice in the second line of "Song of Myself," contains within it a complex set of meanings that correspond to different levels of human interaction: a linguistic assumption (a statement accepted as true without the necessity for proof or demonstration), a bodily assumption (either of the body into heaven after death or of food into the body), and a social assumption (of a possession, a property, a degree, or an employee). All of these meanings are included within the larger rubric constituted by the more general sense of the word's Latin root, *assumptio*—a taking up, or adoption. Whitman simultaneously adopts and is adopted by his readers at the beginning of *Leaves of Grass.* If the following line foregrounds the physical nature of this relationship ("every atom belonging to me as good belongs to you"), the preceding line emphasizes its verbal or linguistic nature ("I celebrate myself, I sing myself"). Thus the form of the first stanza reflects the polarity of language and body, a polarity perfectly balanced and reconciled by the "assumption" that takes place—also balancing and reconciling poet and reader—in the middle line.

What does Whitman suggest in these lines about the nature of the sociolect and its relation to his private poetic language, or idiolect? Even if we grant, with Riffaterre, that the idiolect of a particular poem must at times depart from the logic of the sociolect, my reading of Whitman would suggest that it is not necessary for the idiolect by its very existence to exclude or expel the sociolect that it seeks to replace or refine. In the case of Whitman's "Song of Myself"—and, I would argue, in all of Whitman's poems—the idiolect will in fact *use* the logic of the sociolect, comment on that logic, and enter into a dialogic relationship with it.

The original (1856) title of the poem, untitled in the 1855 edition and not given its current title until 1881, was the apparently unprepossessing "Poem of Walt Whitman, an American." Unlike "Song of Myself," with its suggestions of lyricism and the egotistical Sublime, the earlier title reflects

Whitman's purpose in the first two editions: to present the poet in a radically democratic light, demystified of all the trappings of culture and tradition. Signed more like a newspaper article than like a conventional poem, Whitman's text will introduce him simply as "an American" like all other Americans—part of the social and sociolectic fabric of the nation.[8] The first lines of the poem continue in this same vein, proposing a personal identity that reflects a corresponding national identity. In "celebrat[ing]" himself and "sing[ing]" himself, Whitman replaces the normal logic of nationalistic celebration—the Fourth of July, the national anthem—with that of personal celebration. Likewise, the "every atom" that is shared between poet and reader encodes the American (democratic) political ideal in which every part of the nation belongs to every American citizen. The American ideology of a nation based on equality and generosity—and therefore deserving to be celebrated in the popular imagination through songs and holidays—serves as the background for Whitman's idiolectic expression in the poem. Thus the Riffaterrean "ungrammaticalities"— or transpositions of normative language use— that define a poem's "literariness" by connecting it with a generic intertext, I argue, can equally well define a poem in relation to the more general symbolic context of the sociolect. If the literary tradition or canon into which an author's work is inserted by an intertextual connection is read not as entirely separate from the sociolect but as one level of the available sociolect, the choice to privilege or foreground one's relation to literary tradition through recourse to a generic intertext will inevitably situate the author at a higher level of cultural distinction. Thus when Whitman does foreground his canonical membership by signaling intertextual borrowings or revisions, he also foregrounds his distance, his linguistic and sociocultural distinction, from the overall population, from those who speak in "everyday" language. It is this simultaneous embrace of the sociolect and attempt to distinguish himself from it that defines his double logic of distinction.

Whitman's poetry provides an ideal vehicle for a contextual study of the relationship of sociocultural discourse and literary intertextuality. *Leaves of Grass* presents an extreme example of the subjective lyric voice, yet at the same time it is continually in dialogue with coded cultural forces. As has been amply demonstrated by various critics, poems like "Song of Myself," "Crossing Brooklyn Ferry," "The Sleepers," and "Song of the Exposition" are linked to specific social, cultural, and historical referents such as contemporary views of sexuality, slavery and the Civil War, immigration and the growth of cities, the women's movement, technological progress and materialism, spiritual revivalism, and various forms of popular literature, art, and performance. However, the significance of Whitman's central poems is not exhausted by such referents and their attendant discourses. I am interested in the textual moment at which the poet's voice interacts with these in the construction of a personalized symbolic register, or idiolect.

The terms of my study raise the theoretical question: to what extent can the production of a literary text be said to constitute a plane of interaction between sociohistorical forces and specifically literary or intertextual ones? To some degree, the methodology deployed by the New Historicism in English and American studies has established the ground for such a question; its reliance on the interdependent claims of the textuality of history and the historicity of text bridges the methodological and theoretical gap between traditional literary-historical practice and intertextual criticism. For the purposes of this discussion of Whitman's poetry, I find the Bloomian/Riffaterrean model, based on an exclusively literary intertextuality, less useful than a historico-cultural model that accommodates an intertextual relationship with the various discourses, both literary and nonliterary, operating at a given moment in history.

Marshall McLuhan has suggested one approach to intertextuality that can more successfully accommodate the role of sociohistorical forces in literary production. McLuhan "looks for the key to intertextual facts not in the history of the creative individual but in the evolution of the media."[9] At certain pivotal moments, including the Renaissance and early twentieth-century Modernism, McLuhan argues, "texts appear which seem to break with the monolithism of meaning and of language imbued with the cultural weight of preceding works" (35). These periods of intellectual crisis typically produce experimentally intertextual works, such as those of Cervantes and Rabelais, which enact "the mixing of genres on a colossal scale." McLuhan identifies a historical linkage between new forms of media and a new readership, which in turn necessitates a change in generic convention. Whitman's mid-nineteenth-century America was similarly a time of technological changes in the printing industry, which led to changing patterns of publication, distribution, and readership. The creation of new stereotyping procedures in the 1820s and 1830s and the invention of the automatic steam press in 1835 led to mass production in what had been a relatively small industry. It was a period that witnessed the appearance of a penny press that produced sensationalist newspapers as well as a mass-produced popular literature of pamphlet and dime novels. By 1842, when Whitman took over the *New York Aurora*, he would claim that it was "almost impossible to calculate" the number of papers printed in the city of New York, a number that may have been as high as twenty-five at the time; a decade or two later, the quantity and circulation of newspapers were still growing. Whitman's entry into the field of American cultural production at midcentury represented the importation of the self-consciously unarty newspaper (a kind of publication that had no pretentions to cultural distinction) into a world that had been dominated by the monthlies, with their middle-class aspirations to literary knowledge and taste. Whitman's cultural perspective as a "hack" journalist differs markedly from that of both the Transcendentalists and the fireside group; it is in large measure this different cultural orientation that enables a poetic performance disruptive of the circulation of symbolic cultural goods.

Whitman was well aware of these interrelated changes in the cultural marketplace. In his 1856 open letter to Emerson, which would serve as the afterword to the second edition of *Leaves of Grass,* Whitman called attention to the "current nourishments" to the creation of a significant national literature:

> Of authors and editors I do not know how many there are in The States, but there are thousands, each one building his or her step to the stairs by which giants shall mount. Of the twenty-four modern mammoth two-double, three-double, and four-double cylinder presses now in the world, twenty-one of them are in These States. The twelve thousand large and small shops for dispensing books and newspapers—the same number of public libraries, any one of which has all the reading wanted to equip a man or woman for American reading—the three thousand different newspapers, the nutriment of the imperfect ones coming in just as usefully as any—the story papers, various, full of strong-flavored romances, widely circulated—the one-cent and two-cent journals—the political ones, no matter what side—the weeklies in the country—the sporting and pictorial papers—the monthly magazines, with plentiful imported feed—the sentimental novels, numberless copies of them—the low-priced flaring tales, adventures, biographies—all are prophetic; all waft rapidly on. (*LG,* 733)

Whitman does not shun or deride such popular literature. Unlike the intellectual elite, who sensed a growing chasm between high literary culture and low forms of mass-produced reading matter, he embraces the "active ephemeral myriads of books" as a necessary component of American culture as a whole, as less polished forerunners of distinctively American literary forms:

"What a progress popular reading and writing has made in fifty years! What a progress fifty years hence! The time is at hand when inherent literature will be a main part of These States, as general and real as steam-power, iron, corn, beef, fish." Whitman's passionate defense of a hitherto unimagined range of popular forms is a powerful statement of a democratic cultural agenda. In his own poetic production, he would engage changing notions of cultural taste in a way that would both comment on and enter into the field of cultural production.[10]

Recent books by David S. Reynolds, Betsy Erkkila, and Kenneth Price have explored Whitman's relationship to, respectively, popular culture, sociopolitical environment, and the literary canon. My project seeks not only to trace Whitman's relation to historical and cultural sources but to understand the process by which Whitman negotiated, distinguished, or chose between discourses in terms of what I have called his double logic of distinction. In seeking to map an opposition between idiolect and sociolect, between literary intertext and sociohistorical context, I shall ask to what extent the poems in *Leaves of Grass* are involved with a sociocultural matrix and, to the degree that they resist or support such a matrix by their participation in a high cultural literary genre or tradition, what kind of intertextual sources they contain or develop.

In his study of nineteenth-century American literature and popular culture, *Beneath the American Renaissance,* David Reynolds describes as "reconstructive criticism" that method which seeks to interpret the text in light of its cultural and historical references. Reynolds presumably takes his cue from Fredric Jameson, who called for a turn to historical analysis that would involve "the hypothetical *reconstruction* of the materials—content, narrative paradigms, stylistic and linguistic practices—which had to have been given in advance in order for that partial text to be produced in its unique historical specificity."[11] Reynolds's book represents an impressive scholarly attempt to "reconstruct" the source of nineteenth-century cultural references, but it falls short of engaging in the kind of analysis Jameson calls for: one which seeks to discover how cultural discourses impose aspects of their code upon the linguistic and formal structure of the poem. In exploring the interplay of various codes or levels of discourse within the text, my work seeks to formulate a theoretical distinction between Whitman's use of nonliterary sources and his use of literary models. Such a distinction appears crucial in the case of a poet like Whitman, who himself expressed ambivalence about the value of a literary canon conceived as an elitist system of verbal or aesthetic references. Yet at the same time the distinction is not always clear, or even desirable, as both Jameson and New Historicists such as Stephen Greenblatt have pointed out. Both Greenblatt and Jameson challenge the assumption (held by New Critics as well as traditional literary historians) of an absolute and secure distinction between literary foreground and political background or, more generally, between artistic production and other kinds of social production.

This said, such distinctions continue to be made, implicitly if not explicitly, in most contemporary criticism, despite the claims of at least some New Historicists that all sources must be treated on an equal playing field, that all historical documents and discursive codes should be equally considered as "texts." My theoretical premise is that while there is often no clear demarcation between texts (literature) and nontexts (nonliterary discourse), all forms of language use are also not equally "textual," at least when viewed within the historical context of their own utterance. I do not posit a "natural" speech (one exhibiting an unproblematic relationship to nature, emotion, and history), but I do wish to suggest that nonliterary language is not coded or patterned by the same kinds of ideological, linguistic, and intertextual forces operating in a self-consciously produced literary work. Literary texts, even those purporting to imitate life or natural speech, are operating within a matrix of tradition, literary convention, and readerly expectation for which there is no parallel in nonliterary utterance. The self-conscious attempt at "literary" writing entails a crucial difference in the approach of the author. In some cases, this difference may be more one of degree than of kind: as the range of human experience is successively formed into language, organized into societal discourses, filtered at given historical moments into a more particular sociolect, and further refined into "literature" as the author moves toward an aesthetic idiolect, it also progresses toward a more highly organized, more specialized and self-consciously articulated code, one operating against the background of the lexical and grammatical rules of normative language use. Thus the sociolect, that organizational level between the language as a whole and the individual's idiosyncratic use of an element of discourse, can also serve as a middle ground between "textuality" (that which in Riffaterre's terms constitutes the "literariness of literature") and "history" (that which we take as everything outside the matrix of literary texts).[12]

Whitman's use of the sociolect most often involves a discursive decontextualization (or recontextualization) that brings the poem closer to an idiolectic register; this mode of poetic composition is a type of what the Russian formalists called "defamiliarization." Yet the semiotic process through which Whitman's poems achieve this defamiliarization is not definable in terms of the intertextual or formal closure which for a formal semiotician like Riffaterre would constitute their "textuality." Instead, Whitman's achievement can best be measured by what Richard Terdiman calls a "social semiotics."[13] For Terdiman, linguistic and semiotic difference should be measured "not simply as diversity or abstract variation but as inscribing authentic conflict and projecting authentic [social] change" (27). Thus in a work like *Leaves of Grass,* with its foregrounded social referent, it is not simply the idiolects of previous literary works but more importantly the sociolect itself—and the ideologies embedded in it—that are challenged and destabilized. Stephen Greenblatt has gone beyond Terdiman's position in arguing that in works of literature "intention and genre are as social, contingent, and ideological, as the historical situation they combine to represent."[14] This is a persuasive thesis when posed in such general terms; however, the sociohistorical analysis of "intention," in the case of a poet like Whitman, is highly problematic. As I demonstrate in my chapter on Whitman and slavery, for example, there is no single intention governing his work and displaying a consistent underlying ideology. Instead, there may be a conflicting set of *different* ideologies, both aesthetic and political, informing Whitman's poems. Rather than a purely social or ideological act, Whitman's characteristic poetic involves the response to a perceived gap in the discursive register—for example, in the discussion of slavery or of the body—which can be filled only by a constant effort at differentiation from both generic conventions and available discourses.

Whitman's *Leaves of Grass* has generally been granted a privileged status as one of the two most highly differentiated American poetic texts of the nineteenth century (the other being the collected poems of Emily Dickinson). Few readers would contest Whitman's claim to have carved out a new poetic space. My purpose here is neither to question nor to support claims of his originality and creative powers, although it will become clear in my readings of Whitman's poems that his work is in very significant respects *distinct* from that of the authors contemporary with him. I will also leave it to others to debate the relative poetic strength exhibited by Whitman in his psychotextual relation to other writers. It is, however, apparent to me that Whitman's use of the nonliterary sociolect represents a far more radical attempt than that of his American poetic contemporaries to transform or question the matrix of inherited societal and literary discourse.[15] It is Whitman's conscious desire to become a "great" poet, to transcend the work of his contemporaries, that provides the secondary meaning that can be conferred upon the term *distinction* in the title of this study. Ultimately, Whitman's poetry, like all memorable examples of literary production, cannot be reduced to either a direct reflection of political realities or a simple reworking of literary tropes. It achieves its effect by articulating a wide scope of cultural, social, and political discourses through various modes of cultural transcendence, such as rarification, sublimity, distinction, intertextuality, and stylistic appropriation.

Before concluding this theoretical discussion, I would like to make a final clarification of my approach. My use of the concept of the sociolect is concerned less with the relative dominance or marginality of a given discourse (its ideological status within a community) than with the accessibility of given discourses and verbal formulations to an individual within a given society. Further, I do not view Whitman's poetry primarily as a site of conflict between dominant and minority discourses. I will attempt to maintain a subtle but important distinction between Whitman's destabilization or decontextualization of inherited discourses and a conscious or unconscious "subversion" (in the terms of Terdiman or David Reynolds) of those discourses or of the societal structures that underlie them.

As will become clear in the course of my discussion—especially in the case of an issue like slavery but also in his responses to the city and to discourses of the body and sexuality—I do not see Whitman's writings as marked (at least on a primary level) by the kind of radical social or political agenda identified by Betsy Erkkila in *Whitman the Political Poet.* This is not to say that his poetry is apolitical; Whitman was highly aware of the tremendous disparities in social, economic, and political power that existed in his day, and of the abuses that resulted from such inequities.[16] But while Whitman is clearly interested in staking out an ideological position that is in dialogue with that of the dominant discourse, he presents his poetics less as an antagonistic alternative to established discourses than as an attempt to catalogue, question, or destabilize the abundant forms of language he finds around him. The level of Whitman's overt political beliefs is of interest to me primarily as it impinges on his poetic use of particular discourses or tropes.

What strikes us powerfully in Whitman's poetry is the number and diversity of discourses that occur and intersect. Several critics have noted the exceptionally large number of different words Whitman uses—far more than any other nineteenth-century American poet and more than virtually any other poet in the English language.[17] This indicates something significant about Whitman's practice. It is a practice of borrowing from various social, cultural, and linguistic registers; of moving, to quote Robert Creeley, "among an extraordinarily wide range of occupational terminologies and kinds of diction found in diverse social groupings"; and, in so doing, of juxtaposing "terms appropriate to markedly different social or occupational habits."[18]

In Whitman's poetry, such instances as the black whale in "The Sleepers," the ferry in "Crossing Brooklyn Ferry," or the figure of the prostitute in several poems operate in exactly this way, moving from a more general place in the discursive register to a more specific place in Whitman's symbolic code. Whitman's poetic goal was not that of displacing, annihilating, or subverting bourgeois values or of countering the discourses in which the middle class expressed those values. In most cases, in fact, he attempted to recreate the goals, values, and aspirations of the "American working man" (much as his attitudes and expression managed to offend many of his middle-class readers). Whitman envisioned his project largely as a poetic construction of the American land and people; thus "America" itself could stand, in his ideological framework, as the "class" from which he wrote. Rather than a conflict between the intellectual and artistic elite and the bourgeois mainstream, *Leaves of Grass* enacts a conception of New World aspirations placed against the ideological backdrop—the "dominant discourse" writ nationalistically— of Old World traditions. Whitman perceived no hegemonic social practice, at least within his own country, against which to frame his poetic project. If his poetry is revolutionary or subversive, it is so less in the context of a political or social movement (against a dominant system of culture or social class) than in the context of literary and cultural norms. If he shared with European contemporaries like Baudelaire and Rimbaud the vision of poetry as a "language experiment" providing "new words, new potentialities of speech," the uses to which he saw this new, revitalized language being put differed completely from theirs. For one example, the techniques of irony, satire, and parody, which nineteenth-century French intellectual writers used to distance themselves from the bourgeoisie, were not to constitute an important part of Whitman's poetic arsenal in *Leaves of Grass*. As he wrote in his notebook of 1855-56, his poetic language would be one containing "no puns, funny remarks, Double entendres, 'witty' remarks, ironies, Sarcasms—only that which is simply earnest, meant—harmless to any one's feelings" (*N*, 8).[19]

Whitman's radicalism lies not in his subversion of, or even his resistance to, normal language use but in his capacity to resist closure of form, idea, or discourse. His radical openness to verbal, social, and somatic experience is a challenge to both bourgeois status quo and oppositional intellectual, but it is at the same time an invitation to the reader to experience with him the societal and linguistic energies that shape his poems. As we shall see below, Whitman's most significant contribution to poetic practice lies in his ability to fill gaps in the previously accepted discursive register, to achieve a distinction defined not by his distance from the language and experience of the common man or woman but rather by a distance from the limitations imposed by the poetic canon and by the work of his contemporaries.

 CHAPTER ONE

Intertextuality and the Poetics of Distinction

The trouble is that writers are too literary—too damned
literary. . . . Instead of regarding literature as only a
weapon, an instrument, in the service of something larger
than itself, it looks at itself as an end—as a fact to be finally
worshipped, adored. To me that's a horrible blasphemy—
a bad smelling apostasy.
    —Walt Whitman to Horace Traubel

Every really new person, (poet or other), makes his style—
sometimes a little way removed from the previous models—
sometimes very far indeed.
    —Walt Whitman, letter to *Harper's Magazine*

Conceiving Distinction: From Journalism to the Carnivalesque

Sometime during the late 1840s Whitman began to "elaborate the plan" for
the first of the poems to be incorporated in *Leaves of Grass*, though it was not
until 1853 or 1854 that he had "the first definite conception" of what kind of
poems they would be.[1] What were the forces that led Whitman to abandon
popular or conventional poetic modes and to make a radical break toward a
strongly divergent idiolect, toward a poetic mode marked most strongly by its
distinction from that of his contemporaries? Were these forces literary or sociohistorical or a combination of the two? What were the discursive parameters defining Whitman's understanding of poetry at the time, and why did
they allow him a freedom so radically different from that of other poets? My
discussion in this chapter will share elements with previous studies that have
sought answers to these questions, but it is more directly concerned than

earlier critics have been with the role played by social class and cultural distinction in determining Whitman's relationship to the literary canon, to other fields of discourse, and to a potential audience.[2]

If we are to examine the changes in Whitman's discursive practice as it develops over the 1840s and 1850s, the most enlightening place to begin looking may be his journalistic writing from those years. When compared with an explicitly literary form of writing such as the poems in *Leaves of Grass*, which rely heavily on the reader's expectations of generic convention and intertextual reference, Whitman's journalistic writing characteristically situates itself quite differently relative to linguistic systems of sociocultural distinction. Journalism, at least as it was practiced in nineteenth-century America, involved not an effort to differentiate linguistic form and expression from everyday discourses but rather an effort to report on the existing events and conditions of the sociohistorical field in such a way as to make them accessible to a nonliterary and undifferentiated public. At the same time, however, the journalistic writing of Whitman's day represents a discursive system that, like literary writing, was guided by particular generic and rhetorical conventions—conventions which may be less immediately apparent than those of poetry but which nonetheless played an important role in the definition of journalistic discourse.

Whitman was involved with journalism throughout his early adult life. Starting as a journeyman newspaper printer in his early teens, he had by the time of the first publication of *Leaves of Grass* in 1855 been editor of four journals—the *New York Aurora*, the *Brooklyn Daily Eagle*, the *New Orleans Crescent*, and the *Brooklyn Freeman*—and had worked for at least ten other papers. The relationship of Whitman's journalistic writing to his subsequent poetic career has been explored by various commentators, including Shelley Fishkin, but none seem able or willing to speculate on exactly how his "puzzling transformation" from journalist into poet was accomplished.[3]

Fishkin's analysis relies on a belief in Whitman's own claim to value "fact" over "fiction," to work for a mimetic or journalistic portrayal of everyday life as opposed to a self-consciously artistic stance. In Fishkin's reading, Whitman becomes a successful poet when he allows the social discourses to function, relatively unchanged, within his poetic texts. Yet at the same time that she identifies a rather unproblematic insertion of a journalistic style and stance within the idiolect of Whitman's most important poems, she also points to "poetic inspiration" as the source of Whitman's greatest writing. Like Whitman, Fishkin wants to have it both ways: to evoke a writing based on a nonliterary reality, which at the same time participates in the Western poetic tradition of inspiration. It is the polarization of these two extremes—artistic inspiration on the one hand and the journalistic engagement with facts on the other—that requires closer examination in the analysis of Whitman's poetic evolution. Clearly, a great deal of Whitman's poetic writing does engage with social and political realities; nonetheless, the journalistic act of observing, transcribing, and cataloguing those realities, however sensitively it is done, does not poetry make. The challenge for any critic of Whitman is to explain the transformation of various forms of journalistic and other non-literary discourse into literature, without resorting to the kinds of mystification with which Whitman's poetry has always been surrounded, and which he in fact may have promoted.

If Whitman's *Aurora* articles of 1842 were intended to provide "pictures of life as it is," his poems of 1855 would have a far more ambitious design, as he explains in the preface to the first edition of *Leaves of Grass*. The poet must have the power "to destroy or remould" reality, and to indicate to his readers "the path between reality and their souls" (*PW*, 438–39). Poetic expression, he argues, unlike that of journalistic writing, or even "fiction or romance," is responsible to a universal or cosmic vision. Though poetry is still concerned with "facts," it is poetry's capacity to transform those facts rhetorically or aesthetically that distinguishes it from other forms of writing:

> As they emit themselves, facts are shower'd over with light—the daylight is lit with more volatile light—the deep between the setting and rising sun goes deeper many fold. Each precise object or condition or combination or process exhibits a beauty—the multiplication table its—old age its—the carpenter's trade its—the grand opera its—the huge-hull'd clean-shap'd New York clipper at sea under steam or full sail gleams with unmatched beauty—the American circles and large harmonies of government gleam with theirs—and the commonest definite actions and intentions with theirs. (*PW*, 449–50)

In Whitman's transcendental vision, poetry will have the effect of denaturing the facts of everyday existence even while presenting them. Whitman is quick to point out that the "true poet" does not seek to hide the truth through "ornamentation," "tricks," "lies," or "exaggerations." Nevertheless, Whitman's poetic theory of "showering over" the facts with light and "beauty" is just such an ornamentation, a dressing up of common reality. Even the style of the passage, with its reliance on poetic devices such as repetition and highly foregrounded syntactic patterning, reflects a desire for legitimation within the code of the literary. Whitman is less interested in presenting the world as it appears by the common light of day (through the ostensibly objective discourse of journalism) than in capturing the depth and "volatility" that can be conferred on experience by the artistic process. Thus the logic of positivist representation has been replaced by the logic of sublimation or distinction. Whitman's list of "facts" is itself revealing: the very eclecticism of his examples suggests the contents of a newspaper or popular journal, with articles on the arts, on politics and government, on trade and technology, and on education and everyday life. But if the journalistic register commonly associated with the sociolect is maintained in the examples themselves, the way they are to be treated enters the realm of the poetic, the idiolectic.

Pierre Bourdieu has theorized this same process of aesthetic sublimation, one which leads to the formation of sociocultural taste, or distinction. For Bourdieu, discourses such as that of literary writing attempt to replace those aspects of life closest to natural process with a "second nature" or "counternature"—one that expresses a mastery of both physical and social existence by systems of cultural transcendence. According to Bourdieu, this domination is achieved "by an act of artistic sublimation which is predisposed to fulfil a function of social legitimation."[4] Just as Whitman's principle of poetry legitimates the "objects," "conditions," "actions," and "intentions" of American life, so, Bourdieu argues, does all literary and artistic discourse attempt to negate "natural" forms of pleasure (those which are viewed as "inferior, coarse, vulgar, mercenary, venal, servile") in order to affirm the "sublimity of those who can be satisfied with sublimated, refined, distinguished, disinterested, gratuitous, free pleasures." It is principally the inversion or sublimation of bodily functions ("food and sex"), that makes possible what Bourdieu calls distinction, that aesthetic disposition which operates according to its own rules. Bourdieu allies the concept of distinction with high culture as it is manifested in all art forms; classical schools of dance, music, theater, art, and literature evolve within the culturally educated classes as responses to more demotic or popular forms of those same activities. Thus "taste," in all its manifestations, serves as a cultural means of distancing one's pleasures and occupations from those of the common man or woman, and of thereby creating an entirely separate aesthetic universe that reaffirms socioeconomic and spatial boundaries.

As David Reynolds suggests, nineteenth-century America was a locus of countertraditional forms of literary experimentation, of attempts to overturn what was rapidly becoming a reified system of sociocultural distinctions in American life and culture. In Reynolds's analysis, a "restless democratic culture" (always lying "beneath" the apparently genteel surface of American life and art) produced not only a carnivalization of social distinctions but also a corresponding linguistic freedom in which "multiple meanings proliferated and unambiguous language was automatically nullified."[5] Authors like Poe, Hawthorne, Melville, and Whitman were liberated by their American status and environment from the systems of language, culture, and intertext that determined British literary production.

Reynolds is correct in finding a relatively greater social and cultural mobility in American life than in its English or European counterparts, but he exaggerates the liberating effects of democratic America on its literary culture. Nineteenth-century America was not only "a kind of carnival culture, one that abolished the social distance between people and yoked together the high and low in an atmosphere of jolly relativity" (444). It was also a culture in which sharp class distinctions were often made, and in which it was possible to identify the emergence of a pseudo-aristocratic class that used its money and education to designate a self-sufficient high culture. The apparent absence of the kind of dominant discourse that had developed in more stratified European societies did not prevent the development of class-based modes of speech and behavior which, especially within the literary realm, were governed by rigid conventions. American poetry, as one instance of such cultural production, did not create itself in a sociohistorical vacuum in the way Whitman himself often suggests it might: like any postcolonial literature, it had a long-standing tradition of poetry to engage, alter, or resist.

In this context, Whitman's creation of a poetic persona as one of the "roughs" was a far more radical step than Reynolds's portrayal would suggest. Unlike virtually all his poetic contemporaries, Whitman chose to write outside the prevailing or even the acceptable literary codes of his day. He sought to create for himself a poetic identity that would resemble in significant ways Bourdieu's Rabelaisian counter-artist, the poet who rejects not only "art for art's sake" but all previously accepted forms of aesthetic discourse.

The difficulty in assigning Whitman to a particular mode—the carnivalesque, the conventional, or the subversive—lies in the fact that his own relationship to the discourses of class, culture, and aestheticism are far more complex and equivocal than he himself acknowledges. Whitman's radically democratizing intentions for his poetry were not always fulfilled. His claim to have abandoned in *Leaves of Grass* practically all of the elements of traditional lyric—conventional themes, stock ornamentation, narratives of love and war, famous people, legend, myth, romance, euphemism, and rhyme—is controverted by his poetic texts, which contain elegies (including one to the president of the nation), an entire volume of poems on war, numerous love poems, and mythic and romance elements as well as examples of euphemism, ornamentation, and even rhyme. His claim to have created absolutely nothing "for beauty's sake" seems overstated in light of poems such as "When Lilacs Last in the Dooryard Bloom'd" and "Out of the Cradle Endlessly Rocking." By their participation in a mode of traditional poetic lyricism, these poems belie Whitman's radical persona: that of a cultural iconoclast seeking to dismantle or overturn the dominant forms and values of the English and European literary traditions.

Whitman's self-styled iconoclastic relationship to a systemic canon of works and tastes, and his counterclaim to be the demotic poet of labor and everyday life, promote a vision of the poet who stands outside the institutions of literary culture (and the socioeconomic conditions that make such a culture possible). Yet despite Whitman's protestations to the contrary, he was deeply involved with a canon of previous literary texts which in themselves constitute a means of cultural and aesthetic distinction.[6] Leo Spitzer's 1949 *explication de texte* of "Out of the Cradle Endlessly Rocking" is an extreme formulation of what most other readers at least partially acknowledge: Whitman's participation in a system of literary intertexts. Spitzer reads the poem as "a powerful original synthesis of motifs which have been elaborated through a period of 1500 years of Occidental poetry."[7]

For Harold Bloom, Whitman is situated in a more localized intertext as well, that of the "Emersonian American Sublime": Whitman is the "American bard at last," one who can express poetically what Emerson can only suggest in his essays and speeches. Although Whitman denies his indebtedness to Emerson (and later denies having read Emerson at all by the time of *Leaves of Grass*), he is, according to Bloom, only repressing the centrality of Emerson's influence and thus "programmatically forget[ting] the fathering force." Bloom locates Whitman's "swerve" away from Emerson (and, presumably, from the Romantic tradition Emerson represents), in his denial of the distinction Emerson makes between the Soul and Nature. Where Emerson distanced himself from his own body, and thus from both sexuality and death, Whitman "overproclaims the body," always having "much too much to say about sex and death."[8]

Literary Culture and the Discourse of Distinction

Despite the undeniable importance of literary intertexts in Whitman's poetic works, it has been well established by recent critics that Whitman's poems and nonpoetic writings radically subvert his era's notions of cultural tradition and literary decorum on thematic, discursive, and stylistic levels.[9] Bourdieu describes in *Distinction* a similar subversion: in applying his notion of cultural distinction to literary analysis, Bourdieu takes his cue from Bakhtin's theories of textual dialogism and heteroglossia. Bourdieu theorizes the way in which a radical relativization or "carnivalization" of past literary modes and genres by the heteroglossic positioning of those older forms within the modern text can lead to the fragmentation and subversion of literary formulas, especially those involving "high [cultural] positions and symbols" (408). In Bourdieu's cultural critique, a writer like Rabelais appears as a counter-artist: a writer who will invert all forms of aesthetic conventionality in order to establish a new cultural order that flouts the very signs of distinction on which the dominant culture rests.

Whitman incarnates in the nineteenth century Bourdieu's counter-artist when he uses the poem as a means of celebrating the body, thereby establishing a classless and "natural" order in opposition to the dominant cultural regime and its associated literary canon. Like Rabelais, Whitman will at times reverse the aesthetic sublimation of popular desires by subverting "the values in which the dominant groups project and recognize their sublimity" (Bourdieu); his rhetoric of the democratic "en masse" appears to overthrow, or at least to circumvent, more conventional societal and poetic attempts at cultural distinction. Whitman's progression from journalism to poetry, a form of writing which foregrounds its intertextual and its aesthetic status in a way that traditional journalism does not, also forced him to rethink the status of literary writing, to subvert the aesthetic distinction inherent in an intertextual practice by privileging aspects of discourse and experience that such literary intertexts ignore.

Rather than evoking the carnivalesque pleasures that form the popular imagination of Rabelaisian culture, Whitman articulates his questioning of cultural values in terms of a more earnestly American argument with dominant European sociocultural structures and institutions.[10] Whitman attacks the class system on which he believes the European notion of "literature" to have been founded; he argues that the purpose of literary writing has always been "to magnify and intensify its own technism, to isolate itself from general and vulgar life, and to make a caste or order" of the highly literate.[11] For Whitman, a culturally elitist literature that rejects the "vulgarity" of everyday life implies a concommitant embrace of hierarchical, even monarchic political exclusivity. Whitman's democratic "language experiment," his destruction of the boundaries between self and other, and his designation of the physical body as a figure for inherent social dynamics all suggest a privileging of identification over difference that is consistent with Bourdieu's definition of "popular" cultural forms. Whitman's poetic is predicated on equality rather than class distinction, on participation rather than exclusion, and on biological standards rather than sociocultural ones.

Whitman's own relationship to the literary, and more particularly the poetic, canon appears to have gone through three fairly distinct phases. In the 1840s and early 1850s, he expresses approval of the Romantic canon; he promotes Wordsworth, Keats, Byron, and Burns as well as American contemporaries like Emerson, Bryant, and Longfellow. In a second phase, spanning the mid- to the late fifties, Whitman appears to reject all poetic models, including most noticeably his poetic "master," Emerson. Hints of Whitman's dissatisfaction with the literary canon can be found beginning in the early 1850s, about the time that he began to formulate what would be his distinctive poetic idiolect. In 1851 he criticized Wordsworth's poem "To My Sister" for its Romantic devotion to nature rather than to man, and he accused Bryant of the same tendency.[12] In a notebook entry from the early 1850s he chastised Keats, whom he had praised in 1846 as "one of the pleasantest of modern poets," for his overreliance on classical myth: "Of life in the nineteenth century [Keats's poetry] has none any more than the statues have" (*NUPM*, 1770). And in his self-review of the 1855 *Leaves of Grass*, he claims to have founded a "new school" of poetry that would be independent of all previous models.

Yet despite this apparent rejection of the literary, Whitman never lost interest in the canon itself or in literary history. Several of his unpublished manuscripts—dating from 1855 until the 1860s—are lists of poets and their dates. These lists reveal a desire to formulate his own sense of a canon of significant writers: they include catalogues of the historical development of English poetry, of contemporary authors (Byron, Hunt, Shelley, Coleridge, Southey, Moore, Campbell, Crabbe, Rogers, Keats, and Wordsworth), of the "New English Poets," including Alexander Smith and Matthew Arnold, and finally of poets from various countries in western Europe.[13]

After 1860, motivated both by his own commercial failure as a poet and by the traumatic onset of the Civil War, Whitman enters the final phase of his engagement with the literary canon, expressing from this point on an ever greater appreciation of the Anglo-American poetic tradition, including even a poet such as Tennyson, for whom he had previously shown relative contempt. The trajectory of Whitman's opinion of Tennyson exemplifies the more generic trend in his relationship to the literary canon, especially since he considered Tennyson to stand with Shakespeare and Sir Walter Scott as one of the three English authors best known to American readers. After dismissing Tennyson as a "jingler" before the war, Whitman begins to appreciate and even to imitate some of his "verbal melody" (*PW*, 477) in the postwar period. Whitman initiated a correspondence with Tennyson in 1871 and wrote positive comments on the British poet's work in his notebooks of 1878; in 1881 he gave Tennyson a mostly favorable, though still reserved review in the essay "Poetry To-day in America—Shakespeare—The Future," and by 1887 he had further revised his opinion in a positive direction, making the curious comment in "A Word about Tennyson" that although he still finds him undemocratic, he "like[s] him the better for it." Whitman's praise of Tennyson's work and character is full of superlatives: the English poet displays the "finest verbalism" and a "superb character." Tennyson's faults have been converted into virtues: his mannerisms are "noble and welcome" and his moral stance, conventional as it is, remains "vital and genuine" (*PW*, 570–71).

Even Whitman's later writings, however, indicate that, if he was willing to temper the harshness of his opinion of Anglo-American poetic writing, he continued to harbor doubts, especially concerning Emerson and the fireside poets. Whitman's critique of his most significant American contemporary, Emerson, reveals a desire to create a straw man against whom he could define his aspirations for American poetry in general, and more specifically reveals his desire to establish in his own work a "popular" poetic form unlike the intellectually elitist writing of Emerson and the Transcendentalists. In 1856, when Whitman still believed in the potential of *Leaves of Grass* to be a truly popular work in his own time, he predicted to Emerson sales of more than twenty thousand copies a year. Fifteen years later, Whitman would realize in "Democratic Vistas" that if his poetry could not attain anything like that readership in his day, it would ultimately prove popular in another sense: later readers would appreciate its value as a poetry of the people, of the "masses."

Though Whitman claims that he is "not insensible to [Emerson's] deepest lessons," he proceeds in his 1880 article "Emerson's Books, (The Shadows of Them)," to treat Emerson's writings in a disparaging, even dismissive fashion. Emerson "possesses a singularly dandified theory of manners" and prefers "verbal polish" and "quaint conceits" to true sublimity, and it is doubtful whether he "really knows or feels what Poetry is at its highest, as in the Bible, for instance, or Homer or Shakspere" [*sic*] (*PW*, 517). We might find the harshness of Whitman's criticism surprising, especially of a man who, as Whitman writes the following year, "stands unmistakably at the head" of American poets (*PW*, 267). However, the subtext of Whitman's comments is not Emerson but American (high) culture. Beginning his remarks with the observation that Emerson's pages are "too perfect," Whitman launches into a cultural critique both of Emerson's art and of those readers who continue to support its literary status:

> And though the author has much to say of freedom and wildness and simplicity and spontaneity, no performance was ever more based on artificial scholarships and decorums at third or fourth removes, (he calls it culture,) and built up from them. It is always a *make*, never an unconscious *growth*. It is the porcelain figure or statuette of lion, or stag, or Indian hunter—and a very choice one too—appropriate for the rosewood or marble bracket of parlor or library; never the animal itself, or the hunter himself. Indeed, who wants the real hunter? What would that do amid astral and bric-a-brac and tapestry, and ladies and gentlemen talking in subdued tones of Browning and Longfellow and art? The least suspicion of such actual bull, or Indian, or of Nature carrying out itself, would put all those people to instant terror and flight. (*PW*, 515–16)

Whitman's anti-"cultural" rhetoric is as powerful here as anywhere in his writing. Beginning with a seemingly innocuous criticism of Emerson's work, he proceeds metaphorically to pull the expensive Persian rug out from underneath the entire cultural system of which Emerson is part—a system of "ladies and gentlemen" who exemplify Bourdieu's notion of cultural distinction as a "counter-nature" in opposition to corporeal or physical reality. Moreover, the bric-a-brac, tapestries, and expensive furniture to which Whitman compares Emerson's poems place them in the context of the late nineteenth-century commodity fetishism critiqued by Marx; Emerson's works have crossed the line from art to kitsch.[14]

Such a rhetorical tour de force on Whitman's part cannot disguise his interest in the question of poetic distinction—one that is clear even from the terms in which he dismisses Emerson. For Whitman, "Poetry at its highest" is exemplified by the Bible and by the works of Homer and Shakespeare, all of which had served as models or intertexts for every Romantic poet and every English poet since Milton. (Even his capitalization of *Poetry* confers on poetic writing a distinction that separates it from other cultural forms.) Whitman, then, does not reject all forms of aesthetic production but only the particular form of culture—decorous, domesticated, artificial—that he finds exemplified in Emerson.

In a notebook entry from 1872, Whitman makes the most obvious rhetorical differentiation between two kinds of culture and their attendant literary expressions. Here, he views Emerson as emblematic of "Culture" and "Literature" (as opposed to the more democratic "culture" and "literature"). Whitman associates Emerson with American cultural theories that remain "absorbed in interests and tendencies not those of Democracy," and that have "never cordially accepted the idea of American Personalism, nor earnestly contributed toward it" (*NUPM*, 1721). He concludes with the powerful formulation that "the highest of *literature* untrammels us, frees us entirely from *Literature*" (my emphasis). Whitman's comments might usefully be read in the context of Raymond Williams's observation that the nineteenth century experienced a fundamental change in the categories defining art and the aesthetic. *Literature*, which had previously denoted the wider general field of written texts, would come to indicate a more specific field of imaginative or creative writing: "Thus the category which had appeared objective as 'all printed books' . . . now became a necessarily selective and self-defining area . . . not all 'literature' was 'Literature.'"[15] Such a change was clearly significant for Whitman: in his own recognition of an essential difference between literature and Literature, Whitman signals his reluctance to enter the narrower field of cultural production defined by an understanding of aesthetic production and reception as a means of cultural distinction.

Yet despite the strength of his statements against what he viewed as the excesses and elitism of Emersonian Culture, the expression of Whitman's cultural attitudes in his published essays of literary criticism, as well as in his prefaces to the editions of *Leaves of Grass*, is fraught with an ambiguity and ambivalence concerning his own authorial bind within the double logic of distinction: Whitman wants distinction from the culturally distinguished, yet still requires distinction from popular culture and journalistic discourse. He does make the celebratedly democratic assertion that "to have great poets, there must be great audiences too," but he is not willing to dispense with the category of poetic "greatness." In an essay on Shakespeare, Whitman cites as the most "distinctive" poems those which are "the most permanently rooted"— namely, those of the European epic traditions from Homer to the Renaissance. Elsewhere he evaluates poetry according to a hierarchical system of classes ("first class," "second class," even "third or fourth class"), claiming that truly "first-class" poems include only "a score or two, or less, of typical, primal, representative works, different from any before and embodying in themselves their own main laws and reason for being" (*PW*, 539). Unlike works of the second class, which are only "offshoots" or "more or less imitations of the first," first-class works are undeniably *distinct* from other forms of literary production: they make their own laws and are "amenable" only to those same laws. Whitman's rhetoric takes on culturally elitist overtones when he echoes the "sharp warning" of Margaret Fuller: "It does not follow that because the United States print and read more books, magazines, and newspapers than all the rest of the world, that they really have, therefore, a literature" (*PW*, 521). Whitman's admonition, printed in the 1882 *Specimen Days & Collect*, contradicts or at least interrogates his own contention that the size of the American readership alone would guarantee a fruitful poetic future.

What Whitman posits in these writings is nothing less than a theory of literary distinction. As in Bourdieu's paradigm, Whitman is torn between the impulse toward the celebration of popularity and the equally strong impulse toward the sanctification of cultural rarity. Bourdieu maintains that this "dual discourse" of cultural affiliation is present to some degree in the work of any writer: "Intellectuals and artists are thus divided between their interest in cultural proselytism . . . and concern for cultural distinction, the only objective basis of their rarity; and their relationship to everything concerned with the 'democratization of culture' is marked by a deep ambivalence which may be manifested in a dual discourse on the relations between the institutions of cultural diffusion and the public" (*Distinction*, 229). Clearly, the circumstances confronting an American poet of the mid-nineteenth century were very different from those Bourdieu envisions for the French writer.

Whitman's choice is not simply between popularity on one hand and elitism on the other; to a large extent Whitman's radicalism (and thus his cultural rarity) is defined precisely in terms of his democratization of what he perceived as culturally elitist tendencies in Romantic poetic discourse. Whitman's intended audience was nothing less than all of America (or at least his idea of all of America), and thus he would have had highly ambivalent feelings about the role of "institutions of cultural diffusion" in determining a particular stratum of the available readership for his work. Yet such objections are not sufficient to negate the validity of Bourdieu's claims. Bourdieu's notion of distinction as a polarizing force in all artistic and literary activity throws into relief a fundamental gesture in Whitman's poetics: ambivalence concerning distinction on both a sociocultural and a poetic level.

In an undated notebook entry from the 1860s or 1870s, Whitman describes the poetic function in the elitist and neo-Romantic terms that begin increasingly to punctuate the rhetoric of his later writings. The poet builds an "impregnable and lofty tower . . . overlooking all—the citadel of the primary volitions, the soul, the ever-reserved right of a deathless Individuality— and these he occupies and dwells, and thence makes observations and issues verdicts" (*NUPM*, 1575). Ironically, given his democratic rhetoric, the problem of establishing a "first-class" national poetry in America was a dominant, even obsessive preoccupation for Whitman. As late as 1891, in an essay with the provocative title "American National Literature: Is There Any Such Thing—Or Can There Ever Be?" Whitman concludes that "the United States do not so far utter poetry, first-rate literature, or any of the so-call'd arts, to any lofty admiration or advantage—are not dominated or penetrated from actual inherence or plain bent to the said poetry or arts" (*PW*, 668). When Whitman does speak about an important American literature, it is almost invariably with reference to the future.

Whitman's 1881 "tribute" to the American poets Emerson, Longfellow, Bryant, and Whittier, published in *Specimen Days,* represents the poet's defensive attempt to stave off criticism of what were seen as his own contemptuous attitudes toward his contemporaries, rather than a completely sincere comment on the quality of American poetic writing.[16] Even here, Whitman uses his words carefully. He refers to his contemporaries as a "mighty four" but never uses the epithets "great" or "first-class"; he claims them as an important "poetical beginning and initiation," not as a finished product of any lasting literary value. Whitman's rhetoric of somewhat muted praise, itself an attempt to atone for past arrogance, still leaves open the possibility of his own work being the first distinctly American poetic project, the first "autocthonic song" of the United States. Here, as throughout Whitman's writings, we find implicit the conflicting desires both to overthrow "culture," defined as refinement and prestige, and to pursue a high cultural mode; he seeks a "first-class" aesthetic project in the service of an undifferentiated populace. From the 1855 preface on, Whitman attempts to separate literary distinction from class distinction, aesthetic refinement from social elitism. But to maintain such a separation in anything other than a rhetorical sense is an untenable proposition: the cultural capital necessary to achieve one part of the equation to a large degree establishes the other.

The essay "Democratic Vistas" of 1871 defines more thoroughly the "programme of culture" he had already begun to articulate in the 1855 preface. Both Betsy Erkkila and Alan Trachtenberg have contrasted Whitman's cultural manifesto with its British counterpart, Matthew Arnold's *Culture and Anarchy* of two years earlier.[17] Whitman's alternative to Arnold's "sweetness and light" appears to be a representation of the democratic state marked by "perfect equality" (the "averaging" of the people). His vision of culture would extend to all social classes, all occupations, all geographical areas, both sexes, and, at least at times, to all racial and ethnic groups: "I should demand a programme of culture, drawn out, not for a single class, alone, or for the parlor or lecture-rooms, but with an eye to practical life, the west, the working-men, the facts of farms and jack-planes and engineers, and of the broad range of the women also of the middle and working strata" (*PW*, 396). Whitman rejects the process by which high culture is usually determined— "gather, trim, conform . . . and be genteel and proper" (*PW*, 394)—and replaces it with a process of empirical observation and restatement "in terms consistent with the institution of these states" (*PW*, 425).

By the time of Thorstein Veblen's turn-of-the-century sociological study *Theory of the Leisure Class*, a sense of economic, social, and cultural class divisions was so crystallized in the American mind as to make possible the theoretical discussion of sociocultural distinction Veblen provides, one not very different in substance from the categories of distinction more rigorously analyzed by Bourdieu. Veblen anticipates Bourdieu's critique of cultural taste by identifying in late nineteenth-century American society a "leisure-class theory of life" valuing antiquated and rarified forms of culture over practical and modern ones:

The enjoyment and the bent derived from habitual contemplation of the life, ideals, speculations, and methods of consuming time and goods, in vogue among the leisure class of classical antiquity, for instance, is felt to be "higher," "nobler," "worthier," than what results from a like familiarity with the everyday life and the knowledge and aspirations of commonplace humanity in a modern community. That learning the content of which is an unmitigated knowledge of latter-day men and things is by comparison "lower," "base," "ignoble,"—one even hears the epithet "sub-human" applied to this matter-of-fact knowledge of mankind and of everyday life.[18]

Veblen even goes so far as to theorize those "canons of taste" which are produced by a given race or tradition by "the protracted dominance of a predatory leisure-class scheme of life." Such canons of taste deprecate "matter-of-fact knowledge" and favor what Bourdieu calls "gratuitous" or "free" modes of cultural expression and production. For Veblen, the acquisition of such "disserviceable anachronisms" as ancient languages and the classics not only contributes to the perpetuated mystique of the cultivated classes but actually "acts to derange the learner's workmanlike aptitudes" and to distance members of the leisure class from the excluded masses. The reification of social class as cultural capital represented by the "useless" knowledge of the classics is analogous, for Veblen, to the conspicuous consumption of expensive or rarified material goods. Even the English language, as it is spoken by the upper classes, becomes a tool for cultural distinction; it must be marked as "classic," both in leisure-class conversation and in literary texts, by archaic and excessively elevated diction and by an avoidance of neologisms and practical modes of speech.

Veblen's analysis expresses in more theoretical terms the latent characteristics of American social and cultural life that Whitman already recognized at midcentury. In "Democratic Vistas," Whitman performs an analysis of the innate cultural distinction between the "People" on the one hand, and the "merely educated classes," which he aligns with the European aristocracy, on the other. In an evocative literary metaphor—one crucial to my own reading of *Leaves of Grass*—Whitman compares the less privileged classes to a poem that is ungrammatical and scans roughly:

Like our huge earth itself, which, to ordinary scansion, is full of vulgar contradictions and offence, man, viewed in the lump, displeases, and is a constant puzzle and affront to the merely educated classes. The rare, cosmical, artist-mind, lit with the Infinite, alone confronts his manifold and oceanic qualities—but taste, intelligence and culture (so-called), have been against the masses, and remain so. . . . But the People are un-grammatical, untidy, and their sins gaunt and ill-bred. Literature, strictly considered, has never recognized the People, and, whatever may be said, does not to-day. . . . It seems as if, so far, there were some natural repugnance between a literary and professional life, and the rude rank spirit of the democracies. (*PW,* 376)

Whitman makes two distinctions here: between the cultured classes and the "People," and between the professional world of letters (where "taste, intelli-gence, and culture" are the highly valued triumvirate) and the "artist-mind" ("rare, cosmical . . . lit with the Infinite") of the true poet, or Whitman himself.

In his "Song of the Exposition," written to commemorate the fortieth an-nual exhibition of the American Institute in 1871, Whitman provides a poetic illustration of some of Veblen's central ideas, including the commonsensical reminder at the end of *Theory of the Leisure Class* that "the ideas of to-day are most effectively expressed in the slang of to-day" (400). In his poem, Whitman calls on the muse to leave behind the works of the past and to join him in "far superber themes": "To exalt the present and the real, / To teach the average man the glory of his daily walk and trade" (*LG,* 202). At the height of his rhetorical zeal, Whitman imagines his muse in an environment so modern and devoid of poetic decorum that it strains the aesthetic forbear-ance of even sympathetic readers:

> Making directly for this rendezvous, vigorously clearing a path for
>   herself, striding through the confusion,
> By thud of machinery and shrill steam-whistle undismay'd,
> Bluff'd not a bit by drain-pipe, gasometers, artificial fertilizers,
> Smiling and pleased with palpable intent to stay,
> She's here, installed amid the kitchen ware!
>
> (55–59)

In terms that would constitute mock-epic in the hands of another poet, Whitman earnestly attempts to present a practical, industrial American land-scape as an alternative to the topoi of classical and Romantic poetry. To envi-sion his muse, borrowed from classical temples and romantic castles, happily surrounded by chemical fertilizers, kitchen equipment, drainpipes, gasometers, and thudding machinery, is to eschew all pretense of privilege or refinement as adumbrated by Veblen. Yet despite the novelty of its rhetorical message, the poem fails to provide aesthetic balance or power to match its thematic content. Here the juxtaposition of discourses Whitman bravely attempts only overwhelms the aesthetic potential of the poem. The language of religious or transcendental fervor ("exalt," "glory," "superber themes") appears almost gratuitous in the context of the other discourses Whitman privileges: that of activity and physical health ("daily walk and trade," "making directly for this rendezvous," "vigorously clearing a path for herself," "striding," "bluff'd not a bit") and that of machinery and technological progress, evoked by the hypertechnical terminology of *gasometers.*

Whitman proceeds in the next section of the poem to depict the various processes by which physical labor is converted into usable products: cotton into cloth, flour into bread, gold ore into bullion, type into printed pages. Like Veblen, he contrasts these examples of useful, active labor with the wasteful decadence of upper-class "idlers": "The unhealthy pleasures, extravagant dissipations of the few, / With perfumes, heat and wine, beneath the dazzling chandeliers" (135–36). In rejecting both the epic and the "old romance" as poetic modes of social privilege, Whitman creates for himself the persona through which he is still viewed in the popular imagination: the wild, untutored poet of antiliterary leanings.

Whitman's portrayal of a working-class muse must be read as a response as much to social conditions in his own day as to a literary canon of past works. As Larzer Ziff has indicated, class distinction often went hand in hand with literary distinction in midcentury America, where the wealthy and gentlemanly classes held the controls of both literary production and consumption. "In believing they would be the producers as well as the consumers of American literature," Ziff remarks, the upper classes "easily fell into the stuffy notion that literature was not only for the well-bred but could be produced only by the well-bred."[19] In *The Autocrat at the Breakfast Table,* published only three years after the first edition of *Leaves of Grass,* Oliver Wendell Holmes writes of the creation of an American aristocracy, "a de-facto upper stratum of being, which floats over the turbid waves of common life like the iridescent film you may have seen spreading over the water about our wharves."[20] Holmes's commentary prefigures Veblen's caustic critique of the more entrenched leisure class that would evolve by the turn of the century.

Money is the basis of this class, Holmes writes, but money is only the beginning:

> Money kept for two or three generations transforms a race,—I don't mean in manners and hereditary culture, but in blood and bone. Money buys air and sunshine, in which children grow up more kindly, of course, than in back streets; it buys country-places to give them happy and healthy summers, good nursing, good doctoring, and the best cuts of beef and mutton. . . . As the young females of each successive season come on, the finest specimens among them, other things being equal, are apt to attract those who can afford the expensive luxury of beauty. The physical character of the next generation rises in consequence. It is plain that certain families have in this way acquired an elevated type of face and figure . . . which in one or two generations more will be, I think, much more patent than just now.

Holmes presents a vision of a "chryso-aristocracy" which becomes increasingly distinct—both culturally and physically—from the common man and woman, such that any rapprochement between the two groups seems impossible. Holmes's portrait is clearly part of a discourse of class and privilege that finds its inverted form within Whitman's idiolect. In the social analysis of Holmes and Veblen on the one hand, and in the poetic vision of Whitman on the other, we find two opposing social trajectories with their attendant discourses: one of increasing privilege and exclusivity (the creation of a socioeconomic and even physiological aristocracy), and one of the democratic "averaging" of all Americans as physical and spiritual equals.[21] Yet it is significant that these apparently polarized discourses both use as their privileged figure the physical body. Whitman's own interest in the body as register of social distinction was not an isolated one but part of a larger societal preoccupation with the body as marker of cultural position.

That Whitman was not only aware of such a discourse of distinction as that represented by Holmes but deeply concerned about its effects is made clear in an unpublished two-line poem from 1860–61 ("Of My Poems"):

> All the others were singing the distinctions, and what was to be
>   preferred,
> Therefore I thought I would sing a song of inherent qualities in a
>   man, indifferent whether they are right or wrong.

"All the others" are presumably those poets writing within the mainstream discourse of cultural privilege defined by Holmes, Dana, Longfellow, Lowell, Emerson, and others of their social and educational background. Whitman's brief *ars poetica* is general enough to cover all the aspects of distinction and preference that he feels are restrictive: social, physical, racial, moral, political, national, geographical, and cultural as well as literary. The fragment is important both in its rejection of a kind of distinction or preference as a mode of literary discourse and in its explicit demarcation of Whitman's "I" from "all the others." As such, it is a clear indication of how distant—and distinct—Whitman felt from the discourse of other poets writing at midcentury; it was this inverted sense of distinction (a positive rendering of exclusion necessitated by his own lack of cultural capital) that would contribute to the development of a highly distinctive poetic style.

The American Poet? Whitman vs. Longfellow

Whitman's position vis-à-vis his national culture was unique among his poetic contemporaries. As Roy Harvey Pearce suggests, Whitman was comfortable with neither of the two extremes represented by the American poetry of his day: the elite and intellectually challenging poetry of Emerson and the Transcendentalists—in which the solitary individual is portrayed as preferable to the "en-masse"—and the popular and accessible poetry of the fireside group. If the fireside poets were "members of an elite which had to a degree foresworn its allegiance to high culture, so as to learn to identify with the audience for popular culture," and Emerson a poet who largely rejected popular forms in order to project an Adamic, private, ego-centered self, then Whitman was alone in realizing the difficulty of resolving the tension between the individual and the "en-masse," between the exigencies of high art and the more democratic posture of popular writing.[22]

If Pearce's assessment is accurate, the position Whitman held at midcentury was crucial in his development: it was in attempting to resolve this dilemma that Whitman created a new genre of American poem. The most significant poems in *Leaves of Grass* are neither the personal, Adamic lyrics of Emerson nor the public and outwardly political forms adopted by the fireside group (odes, treatises, and religious and reformist poems). Whitman's poems combine the two tendencies in presenting a publicly private poetry, a poetry that could absorb and rework current discourses without the limitations generic to more conventional forms of lyric.

In the well-known "Inscription" to the 1867 *Leaves* ("One's Self I Sing"), Whitman introduces distinctions only to collapse them. The distinctions he foregrounds in this brief poem—One's-Self/En-Masse, separate person/ Democratic, physiognomy/brain, Female/Male, laws divine/Modern Man— suggest the more general distinctions that are embodied in his work as a whole: private/public, lyric/epic, national/universal, background/poem, social/aesthetic. Each of these pairings represents an important opposition for Whitman, an opposition which he believes must be explored and then ultimately collapsed or rejected. Paradoxically, his poetic goal is to make distinctions among the vast array of available words and meanings so as to constitute or inaugurate a basic Americanness that on one level is without distinction—democratic and egalitarian—but at the same time is literarily and historically distinct from all other national cultures and from his own contemporary poetic culture. Both implicitly in his idiolect and explicitly in his social reference, Whitman takes on the impossible poetic task of presenting a core Americanness that for all its tremendous diversity is united in a common moral, historical, and aesthetic purpose.

Longfellow is the poet who in many ways can be seen as Whitman's opposite within midcentury American poetic culture. It is no accident that Longfellow becomes the privileged example of literary sociologist William Charvat's attempt to define the popular, middlebrow, professional poet, one whose "combination of technical competence and contemporaneity produces 'respectable' verse in which the poet succeeds in communicating with his generation."[23] Longfellow's success as a professional poet depended not only on the intrinsic qualities of his writing (a "vocabulary and syntax familiar to his audience in his time") but also on his ability to identify and reach the appropriate segment of his potential audience. From 1838 to 1845 Longfellow exhibited a kind of literary schizophrenia, publishing in every available format from the deluxe illustrated edition at seven dollars a copy to the twelve-cent penny paper. But by 1845, according to Charvat, he had determined his true market: "an audience that included all levels except the two extremes—the short-story readers at the very bottom and the intellectuals (the Transcendentalists) at the very top" (109).

From the mid-forties on, Longfellow never failed to be at least a reasonably successful commercial poet, earning between $1,000 and $3,000 a year ($7,400 in the bonanza year of 1856, after the publication of *Hiawatha*), and averaged $1,800 a year, roughly the same as his Harvard salary. On his retirement from the Harvard faculty in 1854, he became America's first self-supporting professional poet. Though sales of Longfellow's books could not compare with those of best-selling novels of the day, they were impressive for poetry: in 1856 alone, thirty thousand copies of *Hiawatha* were sold, along with forty thousand of his *Collected Poems*. In the same year, Whitman failed to sell even a thousand copies of his *Leaves of Grass* and almost certainly sold far fewer than that.[24]

It is not too much to say that Longfellow and Whitman represent opposite ends of the spectrum of American poets in their day. Longfellow was a popular poet because he conformed to a conventional conception of what the nineteenth-century American writer should be; he wrote about things readers wanted to hear, and packaged them in such a way as to make them more hearable (after all, his poems were heard in millions of American livingrooms and schoolhouses before they were widely read). Aside from a considerable interest in technical experimentation with verse forms, Longfellow was not a poet who would attempt to engage the sociolect in any new or controversial way, or who would push the intellectual and aesthetic capacities of his readers beyond the limits of what they had been conditioned to expect from poetry. He was, at the same time, a highly "literary" poet in a way Whitman would never be: a respected member of the intellectual elite, a professor of literature at the nation's most prominent institution of higher learning, and a successful translator of European poetry, including Dante's *Divine Comedy*. Longfellow published translations from eighteen different languages and edited the voluminous 1845 anthology *The Poets and Poetry of Europe*. The extent of his involvement in such pursuits indicates a desire to participate in an international literary community and to set standards for the formation of a universal literary canon: in short, to establish literature as an institution by and for itself. Ironically, we see no contradiction in mid-nineteenth-century America between high literary pretensions and appeal to a fairly large readership; on the contrary, it was Whitman and not the seemingly more erudite Longfellow who suffered the neglect of the common middle-class reader.[25]

Whitman's stance with respect to literary culture differs from Longfellow's in one further respect: from the beginning of his poetic career, Whitman announces himself as a strong proponent of literary nationalism—even in some cases of literary isolationism or originalism—in opposition to the Eurocentric position staked out by Longfellow, Richard Henry Dana, and other members of the Boston-based literati.[26] The controversy over America's literary independence from Europe, especially England, reached its height in the late

1840s and early 1850s; Emerson was an early spokesman for a distinctively American literature, but Whitman and others soon joined the debate.[27] When Whitman rhetorically asks, in a *Daily Eagle* editorial of 1847, whether the United States is not a "mere suburb of London," he alludes with sarcasm to a dialogue in which Longfellow would soon take the opposing side. Longfellow's Mr. Churchill, the protagonist of his 1849 novel *Kavanagh*, discusses the matter of a national literature with Mr. Hathaway, a literary editor who is a caricature of the literary nationalist. Hathaway speaks in platitudes, claiming that if our literature "is not national, it is nothing"; Churchill assumes the discourse of reasoned intellect, arguing that what is "best in the great poets of all countries is not what is national in them, but what is universal."[28] But where Churchill views American literature as a "continuation" of the English tradition, and the American people as "English under a different sky," Hathaway proposes a national poetry that corresponds strikingly with Whitman's vision: "[A] national literature commensurate with our mountains and rivers. . . . a national epic that shall correspond to the size of the country. . . . a national drama in which scope enough shall be given to our gigantic ideas, and to the unparalleled activity and progress of the people. . . . a national literature altogether shaggy and unshorn, that shall shake the earth, like a herd of buffaloes thundering over the prairies!" (113–14).

The debate between Churchill and Hathaway illustrates two opposing discourses of literary and cultural affiliation at midcentury. On the one hand, we find a more established, even reactionary stance in Churchill (Longfellow), one guided by an overruling belief in tradition, in the permanence of the literary canon, and even by a kind of cultural nostalgia: literature must evolve "slowly but surely," it must be "worthy of our forefathers," it must be the result of "culture and intellectual refinement," and it must above all reflect "universality." For Hathaway, on the other hand, a "real poet" must be "original," untainted by too much culture or imitation, and in contact with the forces of both nature and society. As Hathaway says of the young poet he is currently touting: "Nature made him with her shirt-sleeves rolled up." If we recall Matthew Arnold's admonishment of Whitman's attempt to "trade merely on his own bottom and to take no account of what the other ages and nations have acquired," we see that Arnold's rhetoric is almost identical to Longfellow's. But trading on one's own bottom (or, to use Longfellow's metaphor from *Kavanagh*, trying to make a tree grow "with its roots in the air") is what one does when one feels excluded—socially, economically, educationally, geographically—from the centers of literary power and the sources of cultural capital. Hathaway's image of Nature with her shirt-sleeves rolled up would have been as attractive to Whitman as it was unattractive to Longfellow and Arnold.

Despite his affinities with the substance of Hathaway's rhetoric, Whitman is a more subtle and convincing spokesman for American literary independence than his fictional counterpart. Rather than relying on the *reductio ad absurdum* of Hathaway's argument (that if it is not national, "it is nothing"), Whitman is careful to begin his *Daily Eagle* piece by acknowledging the greatness and continuing significance of English models—Shakespeare, Spenser, Milton, and others—and by differentiating his editorial stand from "the petty misnamed nationality . . . which sees nothing to applaud, except it be of native birth" (*GF*, 2:239). Like Longfellow, Whitman recognizes the importance of the canon—"they are the true kings of earth—the kings of the immeasurable realm of human hearts!"—but he also recognizes something that Longfellow, for whatever reason, does not see: that the world has "spread itself," that Old World values and forms no longer correspond to the "genius" of the New World, and that American writers cannot be content "to live only on the strength of that aliment [English authors] have furnished" (240). Rather than "copy with a servile imitation, the very cast-off literary fashions of London" or "wait for English critics to stamp our books and our authors, before we presume to say whether they are very good or very bad" (238), the American literary community must recognize its distinctiveness from British models and learn to trust its own cultural taste. The difference between English and American poetry that Longfellow is ready to collapse, or to view only as a continuity, represents for Whitman a crucial distinction, as his forceful editorials on the subject from as early as 1846 and 1847 suggest.[29] Whitman's relationship to the fields of literature and literary culture will always remain intimately entangled with a larger sociolect involving nationality, national culture, and national character. Whitman's uniquely strong personal identification with his nation necessitates certain cultural, canonical, and intertextual orientations; however, tensions in his poetics occur when his desires as a political thinker are not commensurate with his desires as a poet.

In comparing Whitman's relation to the high literary discourse with that of a poet like Longfellow, three factors appear crucial: the composition and size of the poet's audience; the poet's relation to literary tradition, canon, and contemporary practice (his cultural or literary capital); and, finally, the poet's orientation with respect to social and cultural structures at large—his notion of distinction and distinctiveness. The intersection of these factors raises important questions. How did Whitman's lack of audience and of commercial success shape his attitudes toward sociocultural privilege and literary tradition, both of which were on some level embodied by Longfellow and to a lesser extent by the other fireside poets and the Transcendentalists? And did the resentment brought on by Whitman's commercial failure and his sense of exclusion from the literary and publishing world of his day contribute to his embrace of future-oriented literary nationalism as an argument with and a substitute for both Romantic discourse and the larger poetic canon?

Post-Romantic Discourse and the Example of Bryant

In *Romantic Foundations of the American Renaissance*, Leon Chai pointedly excludes Whitman from his discussion, arguing that the inclusion of Poe in his study as the representative post-Romantic poet of midcentury America "makes it possible to view Thoreau and Whitman as representative of a later phase of the American Renaissance, one in which the relationship with Romanticism is mediated through the vision of Emerson."[30] However, Chai's decision to omit Whitman is not so easily justifiable given the continued force of Romanticism as a literary discourse at midcentury. Emerson and Transcendentalism were far from being the only influences on Whitman's poetry. Emerson's rhetoric certainly served as a powerful counterforce to the vitiated neo-Romantic synthesis proposed by Bryant, Longfellow, and others of the fireside group. Yet the prevailing assumption that the discovery of Emerson was the crucial factor in Whitman's transformation from the talented but uninspired journalist, hack story writer, and amateurish poet of 1846–47 to the radical poetic voice of 1855 needs to be more closely examined. As Lawrence Buell comments, "Emerson is normally seen as having begotten Whitman—a deed so portentous that in some expositions Emerson rather than Whitman becomes a key reference point."[31] Buell thinks primarily of Harold Bloom here, but other critics also persist in overstressing the uniqueness of Emerson's influence on Whitman's writing. I do not wish to imply that the influence of Emerson was not of great importance to Whitman's poetry, but I do wish to suggest that the exclusive focus on Emerson and Transcendentalism by Chai and other scholars may obscure the very significant involvement of Whitman with different poets, including both the American Bryant and the British Romantics. In fact, there exists some evidence that the characteristic poetic voice that would emerge fully in the poems of *Leaves of Grass* was already latent in Whitman before his full exposure to Emerson's ideas.[32] Although Whitman was aware of Emerson as early as 1842, he does not seem to have paid him or his ideas a great deal of attention before the 1850s. In Whitman's December 15, 1847 *Daily Eagle* review of one of Emerson's lectures, for example, there is nothing to suggest a passionate involvement on Whitman's part. He refers to Emerson's "inimitable lectures," but the passage quoted from the lecture, on beauty and memory, is an unremarkable example of Emersonian philosophy (*GF,* 2:270–71). Emerson's influence was probably of no greater importance to Whitman at this stage of his career than that of the popular post-Romantic poetry written by Bryant and other anthologized poets of the day.

For a poet beginning to write in America in the 1840s, the most readily available poetic discourse would clearly have been that of British Romanticism. The most popular poets in America in the first half of the century were the British Romantics Byron and Scott, and the most representative anthologized poems of the 1840s and 1850s were by and large watered-down versions of various English Romantics: Washington Allston's "The Sylphs of the Seasons" (Coleridge), Richard Dana's "Daybreak" (Wordsworth), Nathaniel Willis's "Spring" (Keats), and FitzGreene Halleck's "Red Jacket" (Byron). Buell defines this literary "orthodoxy" as "a conservative sort of Romanticism first espoused by the Boston literary establishment during the 1820s and 1830s" (44). These American Romantics "commended literature as a vehicle of moral advancement, approved the hopeful Romantic vision of human nature's capacity for improvement," and recommended as literary models Wordsworth and Scott. As a journalist and book reviewer, Whitman was well acquainted with the work of many of these writers, at the very least in anthologized form. He made liberal use of poems from George Cheever's anthology—*Common-Place Book of American Poetry*—as epigraphs for his 1842 temperance novel *Franklin Evans*, including poems by Bryant, Willis, Dana, Henry Pickering, Levi Frisbie, and Thomas Wells; it is difficult to believe that he could have completely avoided the influence of this contemporary poetry, which, in its ensemble, constituted a discursive standard of poetic writing. Whitman may not have been a Romantic, but his foundations were largely in Romanticism. Burns was among his favorite poets, and he was conversant with at least the major works of the other Romantics: in an 1846 article in the *Daily Eagle*, Whitman speaks of the "sweetness of majesty" of Goethe, "the fiery breath of Byron," and "the fascinating melancholy of Rousseau" (*GF,* 2:243).

With the publication of anthologies such as Bryant's *Selections from the American Poets* (1841), Cheever's *Common-Place Book of American Poetry* (first published in 1831 and reprinted many times), and Rufus Griswold's *Poets and Poetry of America* (eleven printings from 1842 to 1850), post-Romantic poetry by a large number of American writers was for the first time made accessible to the average reader. Bryant printed selections from some seventy-eight poets, the vast majority of whom were contemporary writers; Griswold included eighty-three, of whom thirty were authors not included by Bryant; Cheever anthologized still other writers. That well over a hundred American poets were anthologized in the first half of the nineteenth century is an impressive indication both of the rapidly growing popularity of poetry during Whitman's boyhood and adolescence and of the desire by many within the literary community to organize a *canon* of American poetic writing that might stand against the more established canon of British poets. Many of these poets were born between 1790 and 1810; they were, therefore, of a generation slightly older than Whitman's, and a generation to which the fireside poets—Bryant (1794), Longfellow (1807), Whittier (1808), and Holmes (1809)—belonged. It was also a generation that included a number of poets whose work is largely forgotten now, but who achieved a degree of popular success in their day: John Brainard, Nathaniel Willis, FitzGreene Halleck, Charles Sprague, John Pierpont, James Percival, Isaac McClellan, John Neal, Henry Ware, Andrews Norton, W. B. O. Peabody, and Lydia Sigourney, to name only the most commonly anthologized. These poets came of age at the height of Romanticism; their work is strongly influenced by the idioms of Romantic nature poetry and by the Sublime, sentimentalized, and religious modes of the Romantic lyric. Even more successful and more talented poets like Bryant, Whittier, Longfellow, and Emerson were clearly writing within the bounds of Romantic discourse. The popular magazines of midcentury—*Harper's*, *Graham's*, and later the *Atlantic Monthly*—reinforced these tendencies with articles on Leigh Hunt, Wordsworth, and other Romantic figures.

If Whitman's poetry in the first edition of *Leaves of Grass* represents an obvious departure from post-Romantic poetic convention, it accomplishes an even more surprising departure from his own poetic practice to this point. In "The Play-Ground," published in 1846, Whitman presents a conventionally sentimental poetic discourse reminiscent of Whittier and other popular poets of the time. The poem concludes:

Methinks white-winged angels,
    Floating unseen the while,
Hover around this village green,
    And pleasantly they smile.

O, angels! guard these children!
    Keep grief and guilt away:
From earthly harm—from evil thoughts
    O, shield them night and day!

                (*EPF*, 330)

The use of archaism ("methinks"), the weak rhymes and repeated use of apostrophe, the hackneyed phrases, and the generally maudlin content of the poem all indicate Whitman's intent to imitate the popular post-Romantic mode of his day, an intent that he would apparently abandon by the late 1840s.

Whitman's critical taste appears to be similarly conventional at this point. In his October 1846 review of Longfellow's "Poems," Whitman writes that Longfellow is "gifted by God with a special faculty of dressing beautiful thoughts in beautiful words," and praises him as a "genuine Converser with the Ideal" (*GF*, 2:297). Whitman cites a passage from a poem entitled "Spring Rain," which appears above all to be a rather mediocre imitation of Coleridgean Sublime. Among the lines quoted by Whitman are the following:

Down to the graves of the dead,
Down through the chasms and gulfs profound,
To the dreary fountain-head
Of lakes and rivers under ground;
And sees them when the rain is done,
On the bridge of colors seven
Climbing up once more to heaven,
Opposite the setting sun—

That Whitman was as impressed as he was by this passage indicates that he was at this point aesthetically satisfied by the derivative post-Romantic discourse of his contemporaries.

By the early to mid-1850s, however, Whitman's attitude changed dramatically, and he began to reject those aspects of Romantic discourse which he

saw as privileging a transcendent vision of nature, myth, or spiritual enlightenment over a sense of contemporary social reality. Whitman saw the contemporary English poet Alexander Smith's "A Life Drama," which he read in
the mid-fifties, as "imbued with the nature of Tennyson," and presumably
with that of poets like Wordsworth, Keats, and Shelley as well: "He is full
of what are called poetical images—full of conceits and likenesses—in this respect copying after Shakespeare and the majority of received poets" (*NUPM*,
1771).

Whitman's own attempt to avoid being one of the "received poets" has
been well documented. Nevertheless, Whitman did ingest Romantic principles, even unconsciously, both from the models of European poets he read
and from the Americanized version of Romanticism he found exemplified in
the poetry of the fireside group, especially Bryant. Prior to 1850 and Whitman's "discovery" of Emerson, Bryant served as the young poet's most important example of a national bard—not surprisingly, given his status as the
foremost American poet of his day. In an 1846 editorial, Whitman speaks of
Bryant in what he himself must have recognized as hyperbolic terms: Bryant
is "a poet who, to our mind, stands among the first in the world," a "beautiful
poet" whose works deserve "a rank far higher than has been accorded to
them by many accomplished men" (*GF*, 2:260–61). Whitman's desire, during
the pre-*Leaves* period, to believe that America was capable of producing
poets on a par with England's finest was fed by an exaggerated appraisal of
the work of contemporaries like Bryant and Longfellow.

Whitman's first awareness of Bryant's poetry may have come as early as
1832 or 1833, when he typeset popular poems by Bryant and others as an apprentice printer for the *Long Island Patriot*. He certainly knew Bryant's work
by 1841–42, when he published stories alongside works of the elder poet
in the *Democratic Review*, and he contributed poems and other writings to
Bryant's *Evening Post* in 1850 and 1851. Bryant also served Whitman as a
model of the successful and politically committed poet/journalist that he
himself aspired to be; Whitman's assumption of the editorship of the
Brooklyn Daily Eagle in 1846 gave him a position parallel to if less prominent
than Bryant's own at the *Evening Post*. How much of a personal relationship
existed between the two poets is not altogether clear. Whitman's account of
their frequent meetings and "long rambles" together are unsupported by anything in Bryant's writings, but in his 1888 conversations with Horace
Traubel, Whitman is fairly explicit about his relationship with Bryant, both
personal and poetic: "Bryant was very nice to me generally: he seemed to

follow my history somewhat, knew about me. . . . I liked Bryant as a man as well as a poet. He, I think, liked me as a man; at least I inferred so from the way he treated me" (*WOT*, 243–45).

I am not so much concerned here with instances of direct literary influence as I am with the way in which Whitman and his contemporaries were situated with respect to the literary intertext and to the conventional discourses evoked by literary culture. Bryant's poetics, though they may not have been known to Whitman in the specific form in which they appear in his 1825 "Lectures on Poetry," can serve as an example of typical neo-Romantic discourse as reflected in the American literary imagination: in other words, as a sociolectic standard for poetic theory and practice. The four lectures Bryant delivered at the New York Athenaeum in April 1825 are the only direct and formal presentation of his poetics. Although Whitman would obviously have been too young to attend these lectures in person, he would have gathered a general idea of Bryant's poetic stance from his conversations with the older writer, if not from his published writings. It must have become clear to the aspiring poet of *Leaves of Grass* by the time he gave serious thought to Emerson's Transcendental ideas that Bryant's limitations as an original thinker and creative writer would prove an obstacle to the further development of American poetry.

In the third lecture, "On Poetry in Its Relation to Our Age and Country," Bryant argues that while America is capable of producing good poetry, it will not be the result of any discourse particular to this continent. Bryant is in fact wary of the attempt to create a new "American" language: "If a new language were to arise among us in our present condition of society, I fear that it would derive too many of its words from the roots used to signify canals, railroads, and steamboats—things which, however well thought of at present, may perhaps a century hence be superseded by still more ingenious inventions."[33]

Bryant's argument, that a literary language based on national industry and geography is inadvisable because it will ultimately prove obsolete, is a curious one. It is also precisely contrary to the belief Whitman would himself express: that it is the spontaneous novelty of the American language, its capacity to absorb equally all aspects of the nation's historical, cultural, and even industrial development, that would constitute its aesthetic validity.

In the final lecture, "On Originality and Imitation," Bryant attempts to balance the opposing virtues of classical imitation and Romantic originality, decrying each approach as dangerous in isolation from the other. Bryant's rhetoric expresses derivative critical platitudes; he makes no grandly Romantic claims for the poet such as Shelley's "unacknowledged legislators of the world" or Emerson's "liberating gods," yet he is also not entirely convinced by neoclassical theories of imitation. Above all, he appears to favor an elegant decorum, balancing "the imagination, the passions, and the intelligence" while rejecting vulgarity or extremism of any kind. Bryant is most lively when discussing how *not* to write, but even here he adopts the discourse of moderation: he deplores the "grandiloquous nonsense of eupheuism," the "laborious wit of the metaphysical poets," and the "puling effeminacy of the cockney school" as well as the "childishness" of the Lake school, the "abruptness, extravagence, and obscurity" of Byronic poets, and similar excesses in various other styles. Bryant's literary theory is predicated on a golden mean of poetic practice in which "beautiful diction, glowing imagery, strong emotion, and fine thought are so combined as to give them their fullest effect on the mind" (*Prose,* 43). Poetry should be created with a firm knowledge of poetic tradition—in fact, such a knowledge is essential to any work "which is destined to live"; but, if relied on too heavily, such learning can weaken "the native vigor of genius."

Judging from the tone and content of Whitman's writings on literature from the 1840s, and from his friendship with and respect for Bryant, Whitman would at that time have accepted unquestioningly most of Bryant's assumptions. The fact that Whitman's published poetry shows little change between 1838 and 1848, the year he left his editorship of the *Daily Eagle* to pursue political activism and freelance writing, indicates that he gave no serious critical attention to his own poetic writing for a decade. Not only did his use of discursive conventions not progress during this period, but he continued to republish his earliest poems with only slight changes.

Bryant's "The Prairies" (1833), a poem that epitomizes the tendencies of American Romantic poetry and that would presumably have been well-known to Whitman, balances a patriotic historical vision of America with a Romantic sense of the power of nature. The poem begins with the poet/speaker observing the vast prairies of the American West, moves to a historical vision of the prairie's various forms of human habitation, and ends in a moment of subjective contemplation, "in the wilderness alone."[34] Despite the national ideal in the poem that would reconcile natural forces with human destiny, Bryant's Romantic convictions place the human speaker at a remove from the natural phenomena he attempts to incorporate into a larger synthetic vision.

In the early 1850s, before he achieved the poetic voice that would result in the more fully developed poems of *Leaves of Grass,* Whitman worked on a draft of a poem entitled "Pictures," parts of which served as early versions of material that would appear in the 1855 poems. Like Bryant's "Prairies," Whitman's poem presents a poetic panorama that serves as a paean to the New World. But whereas Bryant's poem operates on the principles of logical development and stylistic decorum, Whitman's text challenges the discursive rules promulgated by Bryant's lectures and illustrated by his poems. As if consciously avoiding Bryant's blank verse, and at the same time defiantly transgressing all the critical definitions of poetry contained in Bryant's lectures, Whitman presents long, irregular, proselike lines which have, in Bryant's terms, no "metrical harmony," which include material that is both "disgusting" and "trivial," and which "task" and "fatigue" the understanding, at least that of a typical midcentury American reader (Bryant, *Prose,* 13).

Whitman was clearly conscious of his break with Bryant and of the unbridgeable chasm that he created between them when he began *Leaves of Grass.* When asked by Traubel if Bryant ever cared for his work, Whitman replied that the older poet was "interested, but afraid." He went on to provide a rare and revealing assessment of his relationship to a poetic contemporary:

> I remember that he always expressed wonder that with what he called my powers and gifts and essential, underlying respect for beauty, I refused to accept and use the only medium which would give me complete expression. Bryant said to me, "I will admit that you have power, sometimes great power." But he would never admit that I had chosen the right vehicle of expression. . . . Bryant belonged to the classics, like the stately measures prescribed by the old formulas; he handled them marvelously well. Breaking loose is the thing to do—break loose, resenting the bonds, opening new ways. But when a fellow breaks loose, or starts to, or even only thinks he'll revolt, he should be quite sure he knows what he has undertaken. (*WOT,* 245)

Whitman's strong expression of revolt from Bryant's "classical" practices is particularly interesting because it is one of the few occasions on which Whitman so directly states the terms of his own agon. His observation that he had "often tried to think of [himself] as writing 'Leaves of Grass' in Thanatopsian verse" (245) indicates the extent of his self-consciousness about the significance of his own formal breakthrough; his realization that

"Bryant would fare as badly in 'Leaves of Grass' verse as [he] would fare in 'Thanatopsis' verse" (245) emphasizes the importance he placed on the idiolectic markers of distinction that separate the work of every poet, or at least every significant poet, from that of every other.

Whitman not only differs radically from Bryant in his use of form; he also departs strikingly from Bryant's representation of the American symbolic landscape. Bryant suggests at the beginning of his poem that he seeks to comment on the American landscape and even to adopt a new language in which to characterize it: "The unshorn fields, boundless and beautiful, / For which the speech of England has no name / The prairies." But aside from the evocation of American icons—"the red man," "the Rocky Mountains," "the beaver"—Bryant makes little attempt to invest his poem with a sense of Americanized diction or expression. His America is only comprehensible in relation to instances of European history and culture: the burial mounds of Native Americans are compared with the Parthenon of ancient Greece; the beaver's dam is compared to a "little Venice," and the bee to an "adventurous colonist." It is hardly surprising, at the end of the poem, that Bryant feels himself to be "in the wilderness alone," since his own discourse reflects an inability to absorb the American continent on its own terms.

Whitman, on the other hand, collects in his poem a gallery of "pictures," or images, that reflect the egalitarian poetics on which he will base the poems of *Leaves of Grass*. The form of the poem itself, a largely unorganized catalogue of portraits from various times and places, militates against Bryant's post-Romantic lyric, which relies on the subordination of individual figures or images to a central image-pattern or idea. In "Pictures," the "divine Christ . . . enroute to Calvary" stands opposite the "divine tongue" of Socrates, not to mention the mythical figures of Lucifer, Adam and Eve, and the personified figures of Death, Day, and Night. Whitman also evokes many of the events of Western history, including the more unattractive ones: prison-ships, guillotines, executions, slavery, grisly martyrdoms, and "corpses of lost explorers." Finally, we find an almost random assortment of the contemporaneous details of American life: slavegangs in the South, Iroquois warriors in the northern woods, farmers in the West, a truckman in Boston, the Congress in Washington, a whaler on the Pacific, trains in Chicago, and even the "celebrated rough," later to become a persona for the poet himself, in Manhattan. Whitman makes no attempt to translate his images into conventionally poetic discourse; they remain in many cases self-consciously depoeticized presentations of either the commonplace materials of everyday life—"brick, lime, timber, paint, glass, and iron (so now you can build what you like)"—or the anti-aesthetic details of human existence. Whitman portrays the "drudge in the kitchen, working, tired," the "laborer, in stained clothes, sour-smelling, sweaty," and the "quell'd revolted slave" with "the handcuffs, the hopple, and the blood-stained cowhide."

While the lines in "Pictures" are by no means traditionally poetic in the terms defined by Bryant or Longfellow (or by the British Romantics), they are a clear instance of Whitman's idiolectic appropriation of poetic devices in order to differentiate his own language from that of everyday speech. Here we find the selective use of archaism (or poeticism) in "quell'd . . . slave," the suggestive hyphenation of "sour-smelling" and "blood-stained," the alliteration and rhythmical patterning of "stained clothes, sour-smelling, sweaty" and "the handcuffs, the hopple, and the blood-stained cowhide," and the detailed and richly connotative imagery of many of these phrases. Whitman's double logic of distinction is evident here: his poetic writing clearly foregrounds its differences from everyday language, even from a journalistic mode of discourse; yet the differences in presentation and subject matter from Romantic or post-Romantic poetry signal a further distinction within literary discourse, one which allows Whitman to present himself as the democratic "poet of reality" who can cut through the encrusted history of sociocultural distinction. Whitman's use of the poetic text to arrive closer to the things represented necessitates a distinction from both literary and everyday discourse.

Bryant's vision and language in "The Prairies" differ clearly from Whitman's, both in their goal of achieving and maintaining a mode of pastoral domesticity and in their willingness to conform to an ideal of post-Romantic writing. Bryant imagines at the end of the poem a future civilization that "soon shall fill these deserts":

> From the ground
> Comes up the laugh of children, the soft voice
> Of maidens, and the sweet and solemn hymn
> Of Sabbath worshippers. The low of herds
> Blends with the rustling of the heavy grain
> Over the darkbrown furrows.

These lines demonstrate why "The Prairies" was an effective piece of nineteenth-century poetic writing: the poem exercises in an unobtrusive way the conventions of post-Romantic pastoral poetry. Though "The

Prairies" must certainly be judged a minor poem within the context of Romanticism as a whole, Bryant's poem was a highly successful attempt to postulate an American version of the British Romantic lyric.

By the early 1850s, Whitman no longer shared either Bryant's pastoral view of the American land and people or the conventionalized poetic discourse in which Bryant represents that vision. Bryant's depiction of a tamed wilderness and a society of Christian respectability can be contrasted with Whitman's radical statement of America's future, one which involves a "phallic choice" between the "finesse of cities" and "the breeding of full-sized men, or one full-sized man or woman, unconquerable and simple." The characteristic idiolect of *Leaves of Grass* is already present in its embryonic form; Whitman's attempt to gather in carnivalesque fashion various forms of social discourse within a poetic pronouncement, to report in a quasi-journalistic register the "raw facts" of social existence, expresses an astonishingly forceful rupture with the conventions of poetic discourse, especially with the American Romantic mode employed by Bryant. Rather than forming a completed poetic statement (a completion of the art gallery that would comprise his idiolect), the images of "Pictures" open spaces into which Whitman will move his ever-expanding project.

Yet Whitman's rejection of the "stately measures" and "old formulas" embodied in Bryant's "Thanatopsian verse," however much it liberated him from the "bonds" of a more conventional Romantic poetry, also posed severe problems for Whitman's poetic career, problems which he himself had not fully anticipated. Despite his contention in the 1855 preface that the true poet should "despise riches" and the belief he expressed in that same year that post-Romantic poets like Tennyson and Longfellow were "jinglers and snivellers and fops" (*IR*, 28), Whitman was clearly troubled by his own lack of commercial success. He was also impressed by the success achieved by other poetic works such as Martin Tupper's *Proverbial Philosophy*, a phenomenally popular book which ran to eighteen editions by 1854 and sold over a million copies in the United States alone: Whitman called Tupper "one of the rare men of our time" in 1847. If Whitman believed that "the proof of a poet is that his country absorbs him as affectionately as he has absorbed it" (*PW*, 459), he was sorely disillusioned by the reception of his first two editions of *Leaves of Grass*. After the disastrous response to the 1856 edition, Whitman sank into an "obstinate three year dumbness," only to emerge in 1859 with the more conventionally lyrical "Out of the Cradle Endlessly Rocking" (then entitled "A Child's Reminiscence"). He not only placed his poem in the popular *Saturday Press* but also wrote an anonymous review of the poem indicating the keenness of his desire for its popularity: "The vast, extending, and ever-widening circles, of the general supply, perusal, and discussion of such a work, have still to come. The market needs today to be supplied—the great West especially—with copious thousands of copies."[35]

Whitman's efforts notwithstanding, nothing approaching such a market for his poetry materialized, despite a gradually increasing appreciation of his work within literary circles. The mainstream magazines were slow to print his work, and the anthologies ignored him, even as late as the mid-1870s.[36] On finding himself excluded from the "great Omnibus gatherings" by Emerson, Bryant, and Whittier, Whitman wrote bitterly that it would "prove a pretty page of the history of our literature" to have put in "such as Nora Perry and Charles Gayler [while] carefully leaving Walt Whitman out."[37] The reasons for this continued exclusion presumably stemmed from a combination of factors: a prudish reaction to the explicitly sexual nature of many of his poems, an inability on the part of editors and readers to appreciate his stylistic innovations, and a preference among editors and anthologists for poets who were well-educated New Englanders of the professional classes. This last factor may be of more importance than might at first appear. The geographical concentration of anthologized poets in New England is quite overwhelming: of the fifteen most frequently anthologized poets alive in the 1850s (measured by their appearance in the Bryant, Cheever, and Griswold anthologies), all but one were New Englanders. As Buell remarks, "Except for Philip Freneau and Edgar Allen Poe, America produced no important poet before 1855 who was not of New England extraction" (105). The particularized strain of American poetic writing exemplified by the fireside poets—essentially a more conservative form of British Romanticism mediated through Bryant's early work—was also largely regional in focus. Poets like Poe and Whitman, who came from outside the New England states, appear to have had a different relationship both to American poetic culture and to the British Romantic canon.

It was largely as a result of his very different position in relation to the predominant Romantic and post-Romantic models of his age, and to the anthologized poets of midcentury America, that Whitman would increasingly adopt the role of a "solitary singer" apart from a rapidly growing choir of poetic voices. While it is possible to view at least the mature Whitman as a poet who owed more to Emersonian Transcendentalism than to Romanticism in its original manifestation, the poetic agon against which Whitman struggled in his formative years was clearly Romantic rather than

Transcendental. Just as Emerson himself began to write poetry based on the Wordsworthian and Coleridgean Sublime in the late 1820s, Whitman found himself with virtually the same poetic models in the 1840s. The aspect of Romantic lyric that first inspired Emerson—the Orphic mode of revelation and transcendence—may have differed somewhat from the more domesticated, pastoralized, and sentimentalized strain of Romanticism that influenced Bryant, Longfellow, Whittier, and the early Whitman; however, despite individual differences in idiolectic and ideological emphasis, all these poets spoke essentially the same post-Romantic poetic language, one understood and accepted not only by them and by the poetic community at large but by communities of publishers and readers as well.[38] In fact, it was in the 1830s and 1840s that the rise of the middle-class American magazines proved crucial in the development of American poetry both by introducing middlebrow readers to the Romantic canon and by providing a ready market for American poems.[39] Journals like *Graham's, Harper's,* and *Putnam's* affirmed both an audience and a set of discursive conventions for the culturally accepted poetry of midcentury, as did the anthologies that began to appear during the same period. It was against this backdrop of an increasingly hegemonic poetic discourse, a discourse based on a set of vitiated Romantic principles, that Whitman was to stage the "revolt" that rapidly led to the poems of *Leaves of Grass.*

Indebted to Literature

In his March 1847 *Daily Eagle* essay entitled "Honor to Literature!" Whitman still writes in terms more consistent with Longfellow's Churchill than with Hathaway. Whitman's reading of Disraeli's highly canonical history of English literature (a "consistent and harmonious" rendition of British literary history) inspires only laudatory comments: "How much the world is indebted to literature, and literary men! how nearly all that has advanced humanity has been advanced by them! how *they* have been the conservators of virtue which consists not in abstractions, but in realities! . . . Through the long dreary stretch of periods which the lover of his race fain would turn from, the silver rein of literature alone, and what it carries with it, sparkle like a brook athwart a barren moor" (*GF,* 2:259). Whitman's identification of Anglo-European literary culture as not only a great aesthetic achievement but an essential and positive moral force in human history (even, hyperbolically, the force that has "advanced humanity" more than any other) seems to be disputed by many of his later claims. The metaphorical image of the "silver rein of literature" seems a particularly uncharacteristic one for Whitman to choose, implying as it does both the artistic transcendence of the poem itself (even the conferral of a kind of monetary value on distinctively literary production) and the guiding or restricting hand of cultural power behind the reins. The final simile of the sparkling brook (literature) standing out against the barren moor (history) concretizes the very distinction between literary art and historical event or discourse that Whitman would later attempt to subvert. From 1847 to 1855, Whitman's rhetoric alternates from the lavish praise of literary tradition and culture to the total rejection of artistic distinction. In contrast to the 1847 reviewer, Whitman's 1855 "rough" is, like Hathaway's national poet, an originary writer: he is taught by nature alone, has no literary influences, and appeals chiefly, as Whitman writes in one of his anonymous reviews, to "young men and the illiterate."

These conflicting images of the poet and his audience represent another instance of Whitman's deeply ambivalent attitude toward the discourses of cultural production and distinction. Constantly fluctuating between the "silver rein of literature" on one hand and the "free and naive poetry" (*PW*, 477) of the democratic "en-masse" on the other, Whitman emphasizes the profoundly self-contradictory nature of his poetic enterprise. If Whitman was, as one contemporary reviewer (Charles Eliot Norton) astutely called him, "a compound of the New England Transcendentalist and New York rowdy," he was also a poet aware of those two conflicting roles and of the need to find a poetic discourse adequate to them both. Negotiating the tension between his desire to develop a distinctive style as a poet and his (seemingly contradictory) desire to merge with the American populace compelled him to embrace discourses that had previously been excluded from poetic writing. It was Whitman's response to these discourses that formed the basis for his poetic treatment of the subjects to be discussed in the chapters to follow: race and slavery, the growth of the city, and the (sexual) body.

 CHAPTER TWO

The Invisible Discourse:
Slavery and Subjectivity
in Leaves of Grass

It was the whiteness of the whale that above all appalled me.
   —Herman Melville, *Moby-Dick*

Now the vast bulk, that is the whale's bulk, seems mine.
   —Walt Whitman, "The Sleepers"

White Whale, Black Whale

In early 1851 Herman Melville completed a novel entitled *The Whale,* which saw its first American publication later that year as *Moby-Dick.* The book featured a mysterious and demonic White Whale whose confrontation with his human pursuers ends in their violent destruction. Four years later, Melville's fellow New Yorker Walt Whitman published his poem "The Sleepers," in which a huge and potentially deadly *black* whale becomes an allegorical representation for the destructive power of American slaves in revolt against white society.

As an editor and book reviewer, Whitman certainly knew of Melville's novels (he had in fact reviewed both *Omoo* and *Typee* in the *Brooklyn Daily Eagle* in 1847); however, there is no positive evidence that Whitman read *Moby-Dick* or that its ideas had any influence on his work. But whether or not Whitman's use of the whale in "The Sleepers" was suggested by Melville's novel is perhaps of less interest than the larger question posed by the juxtaposition of these two texts: what was the discursive and symbolic status of the whale within their shared sociolect? Was the whale, in fact, a site of interaction between a literary intertext and a larger cultural matrix? As V. N.

55

Volosinov pointed out in *Marxism and the Philosophy of Language* (1929), certain words and concepts are invested at points in history with a special importance, a particular semiotic accentuation that results from their central place within the socioeconomic system of the society:

> Every stage in the development of a society has its own special and restricted circle of items which alone have access to that society's attention and which are endowed with evaluative accentuation by that attention. . . . In order for any item, from whatever domain of reality it has come, to enter the social purview of the group and elicit ideological semiotic reaction, it must be associated with the vital socioeconomic perquisites of the particular group's existence; it must somehow, even if only obliquely, make contact with the bases of the group's material life.[1]

Two such "accentuated" sign systems in midcentury America were those surrounding slavery and whaling. Like Whitman's "The Sleepers," a poem to which I will return in greater detail below, Melville's novel uses the figure of the whale to interrogate both the political implications of race and the inherited western symbology of color. Since the literary order is in constant interaction with the various orders of societal discourse that comprise the sociolect, it is not surprising that in texts by two of the most significant authors of the day, the symbol of the whale should occur in highly politicized contexts. After all, the whale represented for midcentury Americans far more than an arbitrary literary symbol: it constituted what Jürgen Link has called a "collective symbol" or "interdiscourse," a word or object that stands in relation to several discourses and thus can be appropriated for different purposes in various kinds of speech or writing.[2] What is not so easily explained, however, without recourse to the idea of a literary intertext, is the intersection of the collective symbol of the whale with the discourse of slavery in two independent works by American authors of this period.

In the prefatory material published within *Moby-Dick,* Melville includes "extracts" taken from various written sources that deal with whales. From these quotations, we can derive at least four areas of discourse that inform Melville's project: biblical and literary references to the whale or Leviathan; writings in natural history and anatomy; accounts of whaling expeditions and voyages; and reference to Hobbes's "Leviathan" as a metaphor for the state or government. The symbol of the whale operates in several discursive stances: the spiritual, the aesthetic, the economic/industrial, the historical, the scientific, and the political. Melville appears to be preparing us for the whale to occupy in the novel a discursive position that reflects its discursive position within the sociolect of the larger society. In addition to foregrounding the discursive elements of whales and whaling, Melville also plays throughout the novel with the value of the whale as a form of what Link calls "elementary literature," a site of cultural sign formation. The novel is filled with clichés and jokes about whales (beginning with Hamlet's "Very like a whale," listed among the extracts), with figures of speech based on whales, ritualistic acts relating to whales, and stereotypical conceptions of the whale.

Clearly, the intertextual references to *Moby-Dick* in world literature could be counted in the hundreds, if not the thousands. The question to be asked is: was Whitman's poem one of these instances? Internal evidence would suggest that it may have been. Two of the words Whitman uses in both the poem and its prose notebook version—"bulk" and "flukes"—appear with some regularity in Melville's novel. Even if these echoes were coincidental (both words are common enough in discussions of whales and whaling), thematic echoes are persuasive. Whitman's "sleepy" and "lethargic" whale differs ostensibly from Melville's voracious and seemingly ubiquitous creature, but both are associated with the demonic (Whitman's with "Lucifer," Melville's with various mythical and deistic figures), both are unnaturally large, both will kill when driven to it by attack or injury, and both are strongly identified by the color of their skin. Melville's whale is famous for its white markings, and there is an entire chapter ("The Whiteness of the Whale") given over to discussion of the various meanings of its whiteness within the world's mythologies. The White Whale is compared among other things to the White Steed, the "most imperial and archangelical apparition of that unfallen, western world," and the white color is said to give Europeans "ideal mastership over every dusky tribe." In chapter 40, the negro Daggoo is identified as the "undeniable dark side of mankind—devilish dark at that," and the black cabin boy Pip appeals to the mercy of a "big white God aloft there somewhere in yon darkness." As Albert Boime writes, the white body of Moby Dick increasingly becomes not a source of purity or spiritual enlightenment but "a panoramic screen for the projection of the darkest fantasies of the white human imagination."[3] Melville manipulates color symbolism with the ironic intention of overthrowing or questioning racial stereotypes, but he does so "on the basis of the traditional religious cosmologies that envisioned existence as the clash between the children of light and the pagan or infidel children of darkness" (5). Beneath the seeming "dazzle" of western civilization, Boime concludes, "lies a truly 'dark' barbarism that it has projected onto peoples of color to justify their pacification" (13).

Whitman would certainly have seized upon the discursive potential of the whale as symbol, even without recourse to Melville's novel. Like Melville, Whitman would have placed the issue of slavery and the symbol of the whale in many different discursive contexts, including those of science, economics, and politics. My treatment of Whitman and Melville is meant to be suggestive rather than exhaustive: to provide an instance of a possible case of literary intertextuality that implies a far deeper sociocultural intertext. Like slavery, whaling was one of the major economic systems of the nineteenth century— it would be only mildly hyperbolic to say that whaling was to the coastal New England economy what slavery was to the southern states. Further, Melville's use of the *Pequod* to represent the ship of state threatened by its own policies, including slavery, would have appealed to Whitman, who in his own poem satirizes the naive "sportsmen" who float overconfidently above the slumbering whale.[4]

In fact, the connection of whales and slavery is not as far-fetched as it might at first appear. Michael Rogin has observed that Melville's own linking of the two might have been suggested by an 1851 article in the *New York Herald* on "Anti-Slavery Agitators," which compared the "mighty republic" to a "mighty whale struggling . . . in the terrible current of the boundless sea."[5] But in Melville's book, rather than the abolitionist fanatics drowning the whale, as in this article, the whale finally sinks the fanatic and his ill-fated ship, thus saving the Union from the monomaniacal proslavery forces that threatened to destroy it. Such a reading is supported by Melville's comparison of the whale's power to sink ships with the plagues' power to free the Jews from slavery. Whether or not Rogin's reading is an accurate one, it demonstrates the way in which the whale had become a potent symbol within contemporary political debate.

What does this discussion of intertexts and interdiscourses signify for a critical examination of Whitman and slavery? Whitman's relationship to the literary intertexts and the social discourses of his time is a highly complex matter, often involving simultaneous reference to both intertextual and extratextual matrices. In the discussion that follows, I explore in a more systematic way the various discursive, personal, and intertextual factors that interact in Whitman's literary attempt to comprehend race and slavery. My argument leads me back to a consideration of Whitman's poem "The Sleepers" and in particular to its later excised passage concerning Lucifer and the black whale.

Slavery and the Sociolect

Whitman's relation to the historical and political fact of slavery has been a source of critical controversy throughout the past half-century. In 1933, Charles Glicksburg set off the debate with his assessment that Whitman's position on slavery displayed a "striking consistency" in its refusal "to be carried away by the passions of the hour": "The tragic vicissitudes of war did not shake Whitman's central conviction about slavery and his attitude toward the South. . . . Slavery, it is true, was a noxious evil, and he wished, no man more so, to see it destroyed. But slavery was not the only evil in the world. . . . The main thing, after all, was the preservation of the Union."[6] Glicksburg's commentary not only defends Whitman against the charge of being too mild in his denunciation of slavery ("he wished, no man more so, to see it destroyed"), but it also assumes that the reader will agree with Whitman's fundamental (and, for Glicksburg, self-evidently logical) stance. Phrases like "it is true" and "after all" lead the reader to the conclusion that Whitman was justified in valuing the preservation of the Union over the abolitionist cause, and that he did so not with a sense of doubt or inner conflict but with a consistent and self-righteous confidence in his own convictions.

Forty years later, however, Ken Peeples would maintain in the black studies journal *Phylon* that exactly the contrary was the case. Whitman's writings were not unshakable in their convictions about slavery but instead were "often ambiguous and inconsistent"; at times, Whitman even appears to have been "an ardent defender of the rights of slaveholders," and his "most singular flaw" was that of subordinating "his poetic ideals [of universal equality and freedom] to the pragmatism of provincial politics." Peeples concludes: "Whitman was a product of his times who was not able to transcend the rampant anti-black sentiment of American society."[7]

Most commentators on Whitman's writing have attempted to situate their own readings of Whitman's relationship to race and slavery between these two extremes. As in these examples, they attempt to define an ideological stance and then to defend or attack Whitman on the basis of it. My principal purpose here is not that of adding to the biographical or ideological polemic surrounding Whitman and slavery. My interest is twofold: to examine the interaction between discourses of race, slavery, and abolition within Whitman's poetry, and to use the evidence this examination supplies in analyzing the semiotic and aesthetic results of the historical forces influencing Whitman's poetic composition. The opposing claims of Glicksburg and Peeples have already posed some of the questions that must be answered, not just about Whitman but about the work of any poet who engages political or social issues: What is the relationship between poetic expression and nonpoetic discourse? Does the writer's decision to be "poetic" necessitate a degree of ambiguity and inconsistency in his or her political positions? Are "poetic ideals" in conflict with pragmatism or politics? Does being a poet require a capacity, or even a desire, to "transcend" the component discourses of a given society?

My examination of Whitman's poetic passages dealing with slavery will highlight the relationship between, on the one hand, political discourses and the beliefs and rhetorical strategies they incorporate, and on the other hand, the process of poetic creation, a process that, while in dialogue with political forces and discourses, must also remain to some degree separate from them. Unlike the poems of contemporaries Whittier, Lowell, and Longfellow—which overtly criticize the institution of slavery while celebrating emancipationist discourse—Whitman's slavery passages are not examples of "occasional" poetry. Rather than representing the local and explicit combination of politics and poetry (abolitionist literature), they embody the organic integration of a more comprehensive political vision—Whitman's democratic ideal of America—into the poetic text. And yet, paradoxically, the relationship between poetic stance and extrapoetic political beliefs remains highly problematic in Whitman's work.

In *Whitman the Political Poet,* Betsy Erkkila moves beyond the analysis of previous critics in asserting that slavery can be read in the mid-nineteenth century as a text "inscribed with the contradictions of an entire culture," the "original text of America." But while Erkkila suggests that it is this complex and contradictory "text" that provides the background for many of Whitman's poetic experiments, she remains within the dialectic represented by Whitman's own commitment to a political agenda or set of agendas. In reading slavery as the most central social issue of Whitman's time, but not as a part of a sociolect that can enter his poetic text in ways other than those determined by his stated political views, she fails to problematize the relationship of his poems to the discourses of slavery in America. As Erkkila suggests, it was in large part Whitman's personal and political response to the discourses of slavery that enabled him to evolve from "party journalist to political poet" in the late 1840s and early 1850s. However, as regards the nature of racial difference, Whitman's poetic texts display a degree of ambivalence that at times undercuts the poet's stated convictions.

Whitman's interaction with the sociocultural discourses of his day involves a participation in the flux of everyday existence to an extent that none of his poetic contemporaries even approached. Yet his poetry did operate as part of an elite system of literary texts; despite his stated desire to write a democratic poetry that would be of relevance to every reader, his work was inaccessible during his own lifetime to all but a fairly small, elite readership. Whitman's desire, however, was to create a poetic language that would reject the high or sublime mode formulated in terms of class-based distinction, but without simply relying on a naive or unformed presentation of social and cultural discourses, without merely reiterating a sociolect or system of "elementary literature" as it was made available to him. In other words, he sought to create a new form of distinction, one that would include both himself and the "en-masse." Whitman's poetic would neither aspire to high cultural modes of aesthetic distinction nor accept the available alternative of popular, stereotyped forms. Instead, his project would involve a radical decontextualization of inherited discourse, such that while demotic language and popular discourses were integrated into the poem, their context or cultural parameters would be modified or transformed. Rather than the circumvention or euphemistic treatment of social and historical discourses that is characteristic of most literary writing (and that was particularly true of the vast majority of American poetic writing in the mid-nineteenth century), Whitman's poems juxtapose in destabilizing ways elements of discourse that can be used to serve as a basis for a new poetic language, one differentiated both from European (Romantic) models and from the poetic writing of his American contemporaries. Whitman's cultural program, at once a linguistic one, would be to create poems that could mediate between various registers of discourse in the process of incorporating both personal (lyric, sublime) and national (historical, sociocultural) experience. Whitman's dialogic method would involve a process of distinction whereby the components of the sociolectic matrix, the various interdiscursive codes generated by forms of "elementary literature" and exemplified by forms of popular and canonical literature in his own day, would be selected, sifted, refined, recombined, crystallized, juxtaposed, and foregrounded.

Mikhail Bakhtin's master trope of heteroglossia already accounts for a kind of social semiotics, one in which the creation and transmission of meanings is always affected by the social context producing the set of discourses from which a given utterance is taken.[8] Bakhtin's model of the text as a pluralistic space (in dialogue with itself) mirrors the larger discursive space I have designated the sociolect, although it does so in a way that stresses intramural (intratextual) relations rather than intertextual ones. While Bakhtin's work provides important theoretical concepts for my own, it is insufficient as a model for the intertextual workings of the poems in *Leaves of Grass*. First, Bakhtin's idea of the heteroglossic or dialogic mode is developed in "Discourse in the Novel," an essay specifically concerned with the novelistic genre, not with poetry. Second, because of the specific generic characteristics of conventional lyric poetry—the absence of speaking characters and narrative layering, the shorter length, and the greater emphasis on formal and linguistic foregrounding—the kind of social and ideological analysis Bakhtin performs on the novelistic text is carried out quite differently from that for the lyric. Where novels can be differentiated from each other on the basis of the way in which they mix and manipulate style, speech, and voice (the way in which they present the reader with "heterogeneous stylistic unities" [*Dialogic Imagination*, 261]), the lyric, at least as traditionally conceived, depends upon an inner unity of diction, style, and form.[9] Thus studies of the lyric poem cannot rely as heavily on the inner activity or "turbulence" of the text to indicate its relationship to a historical or sociocultural context; they must depend more heavily on those intertextual methods that explore a poem's relationship to a literary canon, to "tradition," to generic convention, to contemporary modes or schools, and to the poet's other works.

Despite the apparent limitations of Bakhtinian concepts of heteroglossia and textual dialogism for the study of poetry, however, I find Bakhtin's schema useful for a reading of Whitman's poems, especially those in which the relationship of poetic text to political agenda is foregrounded. Unlike the lyric poems of the fireside poets, Whitman's texts are hybrids that partake of elements of the novelistic genre. The longer poems of *Leaves of Grass* in particular contain both narrative structures and speaking characters in the guise of poetic personae. The formal and generic ambiguity of Whitman's poems reflects a larger ambiguity about the purposes to which the poems are to be put: they are ultimately not reducible to any particular agenda or discursive convention, such as the "antislavery" poem or more generally the poem of political protest.

In relation to the issue of slavery, Whitman faced an additional problem. Even where he sought an integration of poetic form and sociopolitical discourse that would allow him to incorporate a discussion of race and slavery within the larger vision encompassed by his idiolect, he discovered the lack of a suitable discourse for the kind of democratic poetic he sought to articulate. He was forced to create in response to the available sociolect a new form of discourse that could fill the gap left by the absence of an interior and unmediated discourse of slavery: that of the slave's own voice. Thus the passages in Whitman's poems concerning slavery can be read not as a reflection of particular sociopolitical positions but rather as a creative response to lacunas in the discursive conventions of his day, including those already within the symbolic code as forms of literary or protoliterary discourse. Despite the popularity of slave narratives, there existed in the popular white imagination no culturally unmediated voice of the slave's subjectivity from which Whitman could draw in constituting his view of the interiority of black experience. Whitman's attempt to reconstitute the invisible discourse of the slave was only partially successful. In fact, as we shall see below, his early project of formulating a discourse based on black American dialect and speech patterns was ultimately abandoned. Despite the boldness of his attempt to deal with African-American consciousness more directly than did his poetic contemporaries, Whitman's avoidance in his poems of the very black speech he investigates in his notebooks may represent an inability to incorporate fully the slave's subjectivity within the bounds of his own idiolect.

Whitman's poetic treatment of slavery is not synonymous, or in many cases even harmonious, with his outwardly stated (political) goal of a universally embracing democracy.[10] The textual dialogism exhibited in Whitman's poems is a formal embodiment of his highly complex relationship to the matrix of social discourses concerning slavery. His engagement with the discourses of slavery was not static; it evolved over time and reflected the changes brought about by specific laws and events, such as the Wilmot Proviso of 1846, the Buffalo Free-Soil Convention of 1848 and the European revolutions of the same year, the Fugitive Slave Law of 1850, the Dred Scott decision of 1857, the insurrection and execution of John Brown in 1859, the outbreak and painful struggle of the Civil War, the Emancipation Proclamation of 1862, and the death of Lincoln in 1865. But while his discourse on slavery evolved, he remained consistent in one respect: throughout his career Whitman displayed a reluctance to adopt the politically radical abolitionist stance of contemporary poets like Emerson, Whittier, Lowell, Bryant, and even that bastion of cultural respectability, Longfellow.

In large part, the differences between the overt attitudes expressed by Longfellow, Lowell, and Whittier, on the one hand, and Whitman on the other, were regional rather than temperamental. Abolitionism was a more powerful movement in New England than in New York, where southern Democrats remained an important force and where anti-abolitionist sentiment ran high throughout this period. The radical cachet of abolitionism in the literary circles of Boston was a far more influential phenomenon than it was in New York, and even a reluctant political spokesman like Longfellow would have had more incentive than would a New Yorker like Whitman to publish antislavery poems. These regional differences were exacerbated, in Whitman's case, by class and occupational differences. Anti-abolitionism was a particularly strong force among New York's working men. Racial tensions ran high in the 1830s, as the laboring class to which Whitman belonged— journeymen and small masters—expressed resentment over both the incursions of blacks into the work force and the attempts of middle- and upper-class abolitionists to interfere with states' rights. According to Sean Wilentz, the racial attitudes of white workers in New York ranged from "distrust of the small, unskilled black community" to "outright racism" and a fear that blacks would "take over white neighborhoods and 'mullatoize' them." At times these feelings even erupted into violence, as in July 1834 when crowds of angry white working men stormed abolitionist meeting halls, sacked the stores and houses of abolitionist reformers, and pillaged black homes and churches.[11]

Such racist sentiments appear not to have changed by 1850, when the labor movement as a whole "could not have cared less" about the issue of the Fugitive Slave bill (Wilentz, 382). Given the prevalence of such strong racist and anti-abolitionist attitudes among Whitman's fellow "roughs," and among the culturally nationalist or nativist groups with which he was at times associated, it would have been extraordinary for him to embrace, at least outwardly, an abolitionist platform. That he went as far as he did in denouncing slavery can itself be seen as testimony to the strength of his democratic vision. Nevertheless, Whitman's political views concerning race and slavery were often in conflict with an ideal of democratic poetry, which demanded that he inhabit the subjectivity of each human being in the United States, including the slave.

Ultimately, Whitman was to prove radically innovative in his poetic use of slavery, far more so than those who took unequivocally abolitionist positions. Whitman's virtual creation of a new poetic language for dealing with the inherent contradictions posed by slavery was necessitated by the failure of both literary and social discourses to provide an adequate means of achieving interiority, of "entering into" the experience and discourse of the American slave.

Although highly visible as an economic and social icon, the southern slave was largely invisible to white society. Not only did white authors fail to express in more than a conventionally literary fashion the subjectivities of blacks, but the discourse of liberated blacks themselves, such as the ex-slave Frederick Douglass, was largely co-opted by the genteel expression of white abolitionism. As Houston Baker has indicated, Douglass's texts adopt the rhetoric of the dominant culture of white abolitionism—especially its Christian morals and sentimental psychology—and thereby leave out the "otherness" of black culture; the fact that no "separate written black language is available" to Douglass leaves him no alternative but to cast his narrative in terms of white discursive conventions.[12] Clearly, a more radical discourse of black nationalism and even of rebellion did exist in the antebellum period, as evidenced by the openly expressed anger and calls for violence against white society in the published discourses of David Walker and Henry Highland Garnet. Walker's *Appeal . . . to the Coloured Citizens of the World* (1830) and Garnet's *Address to the Slaves* (rejected by the Buffalo Convention but published in 1848) provide evidence that a form of black antislavery discourse not in line with the language of Douglass or white abolitionists would have been available to at least some readers; however, the extent to which such language permeated the consciousness of white America (or, indeed, of Whitman himself) is unclear. Walker's rhetoric, and especially his extraordinary admission to white readers that "we hate you" and his direct warning to white society ("wo, wo, will be to you if we have to obtain our freedom by fighting"), do appear to anticipate the words Whitman gives to the black speaker in "The Sleepers." Nevertheless, my notion of an invisible discourse of black subjectivity remains a valid if somewhat ironic one, given the position of Whitman's (almost completely white) contemporary readership.[13] Whites were seldom if ever privy to an untranslated utterance of black pain, anger, and desire, and as David Van Leer points out, Douglass and other former slaves like him were susceptible to an "anxiety of ethnicity" that made it impossible for them to know or express "the self as Other without opening an epistemological chasm between the knowing subject and the known self":

Douglass's characterization of his own epistemological dilemma, when applied to his readers, leaves them no means to understand slavery. On the one hand, to know black culture as difference, as Douglass himself does, seems racist in a white audience. . . . On the other hand, knowing black culture as essentially the same as white inevitably collapses into knowing it *as* white. . . . The white belief that slavery is "knowable," then, reduces a problem of epistemological difference to one of insufficient data. Douglass's insistence on his own inability to "read" difference relocates the philosophical question of unknowability at the heart of a genre that its white sponsors intended merely as a means of gathering and disseminating facts.[14]

Whitman's attempt to overcome these same practical and epistemological limitations in a way that did not assume either the essential difference or the essential sameness of black experience was vastly more daring and more imaginatively resonant than that of his poetic contemporaries. It may in fact have been Whitman's distance from contemporary abolitionist rhetoric that enabled him to formulate such a distinctive language for depicting slavery.

The Slave's Body Electric

In a series of notebook entries from the early 1850s, Whitman carries on an inner argument concerning the questions of liberty, race, and slavery. Having decided to leave aside the practical reasons for opposing slavery ("Will it pay?"), he introduces what he considers the deeper argument at stake—the philosophical question of racial and social inferiority:"The learned think the unlearned an inferior race. The merchant thinks his bookkeepers and clerks and sundry degrees below him; they in turn think the porter and carmen common; and they the laborer that brings in coal, and the stevedores that haul the great burdens with them" (*DN,* 762). Whitman identifies an essential principle of human society: there exists a discourse of inferiority and prejudice that extends beyond the borders of race. According to his democratic principles, such a hierarchy of privilege and oppression is untenable, and he must attempt to reconcile his racial beliefs with his larger sense of equality:"But this is an inferior race. Well who shall be the judge of inferior and superior races. The class of dainty gentlemen think that all servants and laboring people are inferior. In all lands, the select few who live and dress richly, make a mean estimate of the body of the people."

Despite Whitman's lingering belief in racial disparity ("But this is an inferior race"), he attempts to convince himself that such distinctions may be more the result of social differences than of innate racial characteristics. The two sets of oppositions Whitman establishes—"dainty gentlemen" versus "servants and laboring people," and the well-dressed few versus the "body of the people"—demonstrate the superficiality on which such distinctions rest. The metonymic equations of class privilege with dress and of labor with the (naked) body make clear where Whitman's sympathies lie and introduce one of the central rhetorical formulations of *Leaves of Grass*.

How exactly Whitman intended to use the discourses of slavery and race in *Leaves of Grass* is not clear; it is significant, however, that three of the first five poems he wrote for the 1855 edition—"Song of Myself," "The Sleepers," and "I Sing the Body Electric"—contain important passages dealing with different aspects of slavery. That Whitman was intending to include slavery and race as integral components of his democratic vision in *Leaves of Grass* is further supported by entries in his "Primer of Words," written during the years immediately following 1855. In the "Primer," which, though never published during his lifetime, was an important corollary to Whitman's poetic language experiment, both slavery and black dialect are suggested as possible discourses for poetry. "Slavery" is listed along with other historical, geographical, and economic categories under the rubric "Words of These States." In another entry, Whitman argues that the dialect of blacks has provided an entirely new vocabulary ("hundreds of outré words, many of them adopted into the common speech of the mass of people"), and a new method of pronunciation ("wide open pronunciations as *yallah* for yellow—*massah* for master"), while at the same time suggesting "the further theory of the modification of all the words of the English language, for musical purposes, for a native grand opera in America" (*DN*, 730). None of these ideas appears to have had a direct impact on the poems of *Leaves of Grass;* there is no directly quoted black speech in Whitman's poems.[15] Perhaps some of the "outré words" Whitman mentions do enter the language of his poems—which on one level are an attempt to capture the range of common speech practiced by the American people—but it is difficult to determine what words these are, since he does not list them. We can only speculate about the ways in which the sense of a "wide open pronunciation" and of a "native grand opera" may have influenced Whitman's overall project.

However, the larger significance of these passages in the "Primer" is that they point to Whitman's continuing thought about black speech, and by extension about black life. In a notebook fragment, Whitman proposes to write a "Poem of the black person," in which he would "infuse the sentiment of a sweeping, shielding protection of the blacks—their passiveness—their character of sudden fits—." What is revealed here is a desire to understand, promote, and protect the "black person," whom he cannot construe in other than the stereotypical conceptions of black character. Nonetheless, the very attempt to conceive of a poem as a vehicle for conveying a sense of black subjectivity, instead of as a means of promoting general abolitionist sentiment, can be seen as a radical one; it is certainly the point of departure for slavery passages in "Song of Myself" and "The Sleepers."

It is difficult to imagine poetic contemporaries such as Whittier or Longfellow engaging in such speculations. Whittier's antislavery poems, in which the physical or linguistic presence of actual slaves is minimal to begin with, tend to de-emphasize any defining racial characteristics or to recast them in highly euphemistic terms. In "The Slaves of Martinique," the woman is described as "Dark, but comely, like the maiden in the / ancient Jewish song" and her lover as "the strong one and the manly, with / the vassal's garb and hue."[16] Their speech is similarly removed from any naturalistic register and reflects the same tendency to archaism and inverted syntax as the rest of Whittier's writing. Both the rarity with which Whittier's protagonists are allowed to speak for themselves in his poems and the avoidance of any effort to render that speech mimetically when it does occur indicate the lack of a poetic space for the interiority of the slave's experience. Part of Whitman's poetic project would be to fill the gap left by this invisible interior discourse: in the three poems in which he deals most powerfully with slavery, he would find various alternatives to the exteriorizing and conventionalizing poetic discourse of Whittier and Longfellow. His alternative strategies for "entering into" the slave include the ironic reformulation of conventional discourses of slavery, a personal identification with the slave through the use of the first person pronoun, the breakdown of metrical form in order to approximate the slave's mental or physical state, and the creation of visual images corresponding to the psychic reality of the repressed slave.

The most striking example of his appropriation and reformulation of the discourses comprising the mid-nineteenth-century sociolect of slavery is in "I Sing the Body Electric," where Whitman replaces the voice of the slave auctioneer with his own. Not satisfied to utter poetic commonplaces about the goodness or nobility of slaves, or about the evils and horrors of slavery, Whitman takes upon himself the task of "selling" the slave's body: not to a slaveholder, for whom it represents merely a unit of production, but to the reader, who must learn to value fully the intrinsic beauty of an "other." In taking this imaginative and discursive leap, Whitman transforms one of the central institutions of the slave society, the auction of human bodies, into a highly original appropriation of a cultural intertext.[17]

In the 1855 version of the poem, Whitman introduces the scene with a sudden and unadorned image: "A slave at auction!" Only the exclamation point hints at the drama that is to come. Whitman offers to "help" the auctioneer, a "sloven" who "does not half know his business," but in reality the poet will be taking his job away from him, and with it the right to degrade and humiliate the slave being sold. Thus far in the poem, Whitman represents a scene well-known to midcentury Americans, one encountered in the books of Douglass, Stowe, and others, if not in actual experience. On one level, the auction scene is presented in highly realistic terms: the slovenly auctioneer is a highly visible icon of the slave trade. But on another level, Whitman presents a deeply ironic commentary: to consider men's and women's bodies as a part of a "business" is an absurd perversion of language, given Whitman's contention in the previous section: "The man's body is sacred and the woman's body is sacred . . . it is no matter who."

In contrast to Whitman's poem, Whittier's "The Panorama," published the following year, provides a more stereotypical portrayal of the auctioneer as the "shrewd-eyed salesman, garrulous and loud" who combines "the negro-driving bully's rant" with "pious phrase and democratic cant" (*Complete Poetical Works*, 177). Where Whitman withholds moral judgment of the auctioneer, reserving his explicit blame for the institution of the auction defined in larger sociopolitical terms, Whittier portrays the salesman himself as an agent of evil, symbolically identified with the horrors of slavery itself. Whittier's need to cast aspersions on the auctioneer's character as well as his professional role indicates an adherence to the sentimental conventions of Stowe and others, who represent all aspects of slavery, including the auction, in melodramatic terms. The players in this tragedy are not realized human individuals (as they are for Whitman) but moral exemplars either of Christian virtues ("wedlock, home, and kin") or the absence of those virtues (the hypocritical and self-serving auctioneer with his "filthy jest").

Whitman's most significant rhetorical move in the poem, that of taking over the auctioneer's speech, allows him to move from the sociolectic presentation of the first lines to an idiolectic expression of wonder and praise at the body of the slave he is "selling":

Gentlemen look on this curious creature,
Whatever the bids of the bidders they cannot be high enough for him.
For him the globe lay preparing quintillions of years without one
    animal or plant,
For him the revolving cycles truly and steadily rolled.

(CP1855, 123)

Suddenly we are transported from the familiar discourse of buying and selling slaves to the unexpected discourse of science and evolution. In later versions of the poem, Whitman would change the personal pronoun *him* to the
impersonal *it*, thus objectifying the "body electric" still further at the cost of
de-emphasizing the human individual. Betsy Erkkila reads the passage as a
"defense of black personhood" in which Whitman delivers "an oration on
the glories of black humanity" (126). The passage is in fact more complex
and problematic than Erkkila suggests: it reflects much of the same ambiguity
and ambivalence found in Whitman's other writings on racial issues. Even
in its original version, the passage raises certain important questions. If
Whitman wanted to extol the virtues of an evolutionary process that had presumably resulted in all humankind, why choose a negro slave as his example?
Why does Whitman refer to him as a "curious creature," one with an "all-
baffling brain"? Does the slave's value rest solely on his physical attributes, or
does he have a personal and social identity as well?

On one level, the poem is clearly a democratic celebration of physical
human life: Whitman supplements or replaces the auctioneer's limited view-
point with a sense of cosmic wonder. His exploration of the slave's body is
scientifically, even anatomically detailed, yet he remains baffled by the unknown possibilities he discovers:

Exquisite senses, lifelit eyes, pluck, volition,
Flakes of breastmuscle, pliant backbone and neck, flesh not flabby,
    goodsized arms and legs,
And wonders within there yet.

The slave becomes the progenitor of "populous states and rich republi-
csm . . . countless immortal lives with countless embodiments and enjoy-
ments." Whitman implies that even the separation of the races may not be
absolute, that at some distant point in history our genetic ancestry can no
longer be traced:

How do you know who shall come from the offspring of his offspring
   through the centuries?
Who might you find you have come from yourself if you could trace
   back through the centuries?

This passage could be read as implying an even deeper irony: the slave at
auction could be anyone—any of the "gentlemen" bidding for him, or indeed
the reader. In this radically decentering scenario, the "limbs, red black or
white" that Whitman "strips" for surgical examination represent the complete union of the races, a kind of nineteenth-century "rainbow coalition."

Such an unequivocal reading is undercut, however, by suggestions in the
passage that Whitman may still subscribe to certain hierarchical notions of
racial superiority. The placement of the slave (or the slave's *body* in post-1855
versions) at the pinnacle of the evolutionary process and yet subject to observation and dissection by white readers would imply that, if anything, the
white race is even further developed. The slave is, after all, described as a
"curious creature": the fascination he holds for the onlooker and reader is at-
tributable to his status as the link between contemporary American society
and the primordial "globe" from which we came. The attributes given
the slave are either physical ones—("cunning" nerves and tendons, "exquisite" senses, "lifelit" eyes, "good-sized" arms and legs, and "red-running"
blood)—or ones that will serve his descendents in futurity: reproductive potential ("the father of those who shall be fathers") and good genetic makeup
("the makings of the attributes of heroes"). Even the personal or emotional
qualities Whitman assigns him are more in the realm of potentiality than of
actuality: volition, passions, desires, reachings, aspirations. The comparison
of the slave with the "dull-faced immigrant" in the previous section suggests
that such attributes as intelligence, skill, or wisdom are not to be found or
even sought on the auction block. Further, the slave is not brought into the
fold of the American democratic experiment; instead, he embodies "the start
of populous states and rich republics." This may represent an optimistic
view of the future of the black race, but it also suggests that the slave's descendents will have no role to play in a racially integrated America. Finally,
Whitman tells us that the man is not even to be seen as an individual but as
part of a larger process ("This is not only one man, this is the father of those
who shall be fathers in their turns"). The slave is indeed a fine *specimen* of
his race, even of humankind, but in presenting him as such, how much is

Whitman departing from the rhetoric of the auctioneer he ostensibly wishes to replace?

The second and more negative of my two readings of "I Sing the Body Electric" casts Whitman's racial beliefs in a more questionable light, but it does not completely undermine the first reading. It is from the interaction of these two contradictory movements that the passage derives its strange power. It is a passage combining the contemporary social discourses of medical anatomy, crude evolutionary biology, genealogical narrative, and social commentary—all interacting dialogically within the framing chronotope of a slave auction. Most importantly, the slave is still *observed*, seen from the outside as a silent spectacle needing to be filled with an interiority unavailable to Whitman. In this poem, Whitman does not enter into the slave's experience in any way. The speaker of the poem is a somewhat distanced observer, one whose overall attitude hinges to some degree on Whitman's relation to the absented but still vaguely present auctioneer. Whitman refers to him as a "sloven," an epithet that, while mildly derogatory, represents no strong denunciation; but in the lines that ended the 1855 edition of the poem he appears to denounce the "slave-mart" in more absolute terms:

> Who degrades or defiles the living human body is cursed,
> Who degrades or defiles the body of the dead is not more cursed.
> (*CP1855*, 124)

As an answer to the second of the rhetorical questions with which Whitman begins the poem—"And if those who defile the living are as bad as they who defile the dead?"—these lines may be only tangentially related to slavery or the slave auction. If we assume, however, that for Whitman the selling of slaves represents a significant degradation of the body, then the "curse" of slavery must come back to haunt all those who participate in it, including the auctioneer and the slaveholder. It is in "The Sleepers," the poem Whitman wrote concurrently with "I Sing the Body Electric" and which I shall discuss toward the end of this chapter, that the curse appears with tremendous power in another subsequently deleted passage: the passage from section 6 concerning Lucifer, the embodiment of black anger and oppression.

Whitman and the Discourse of Abolitionism

In an article intended to place Whitman's attitude toward slavery in its historical context, Thomas Andrews divides Whitman's prose writings, and the attitudes they convey, into four distinct periods.[18] While I would concur in essence with the division Andrews makes, I would place less emphasis on the periodization of Whitman's life and more on his gradual development of a view of race and slavery coherent enough to be expressed in poetic terms. What is striking in any adumbration of Whitman's nonpoetic attitudes is that at no point is the central issue that of slavery itself, or what Whitman calls "a respect for the rights of blacks." While Whitman does make denunciatory statements about slavery in the abstract, the primary force of his argument is at every point more practical than moral. He views the problem alternatively in terms of its legal, constitutional, social, and economic consequences (all for whites), and in terms of arguably secondary issues such as states' rights and the greed of slaveholders. Thus the discourses to which he is responding are those of political debate and not those framed by the religious, moral, and emotional appeals of radical abolitionism.

Yet despite Whitman's reluctance to take on the moral issue of slavery directly in the manner favored by the abolitionists, the late 1840s and early 1850s were the time of his greatest concern with both the socioeconomic and the philosophical dimensions of the slavery system. The issue of slavery appears to have triggered in Whitman a number of conflicting attitudes and feelings during these years. These were also exactly the years of his beginnings as a poet; in fact, his poetic response to slavery would culminate in some of the most important poems in the 1855 first edition of *Leaves of Grass.*

Whitman displayed little outward interest in abolitionists such William Lloyd Garrison and William Ellery Channing, and little patience for an "ultra-abolitionist" rhetoric, which he saw as both overzealous in its emphasis on a single issue and dangerous to the integrity of the Union. As Daniel Aaron has noted, Whitman felt threatened equally by those abolitionists who sought to tamper with slavery in the South and those expansionists who sought to erect the institution of slavery in the new territories; he saw both groups as "fanatics" who lacked the "ordinary judgment" to see what horrors a civil war or the dissolution of the Union would bring.[19] Still, Whitman's own rhetorical stance remains in most respects much closer to that of the primarily northern abolitionists than to that of the southern proslavery forces. After all, Whitman's writings, and especially his poetry, are formulated in large part within the broader context of reformist discourse. Whitman expressed great respect for feminist reformers such as Margaret Fuller, Frances Wright, and George Sand, and his own early attempts at fiction were addressed to social problems such as child abuse, alcoholism, and capital punishment.

Why, then, was Whitman so strongly opposed to abolitionist discourse? His most sustained comment on what he considers the ultra-abolitionist position comes in an article he wrote for the *Brooklyn Daily Eagle* in December 1846. After witnessing the behavior of certain "zealous persons" of abolitionist sentiment, Whitman concludes that "ultra-Abolitionism . . . has pretty well spent its fury—and, by and by, has done far more harm than good to the very cause it professed to aid" (*GF*, 1:192). He goes on to argue that slavery is an evil which "good and far-sighted men" in both the North and South already recognize as such, without the help of extremist rhetoric. But the deeply held belief in "liberty" among "American Democrats" like himself does not imply the desire to put aside "all discretion, the settled laws of the land, the guaranteed power of citizens, and so on." Whitman's basic argument emphasizes noninterference and "free action." We may devoutly wish the end of slavery, he argues, just as we wish the end of serfdom in Russia, but we cannot "violate" either the laws of the southern states or the "free thought" of their citizens by forcibly doing away with slavery: "It is to the discoveries and suggestions of free thought, of 'public opinion,' of liberal sentiments, that we must at this age of the world look for quite all desirable reforms, in government and any thing else."

Whitman's language here is cautious rather than revolutionary, relying on mundane statements of democratic principle—"liberal sentiments," "desirable reforms"—rather than deploying any rhetorical strategy that could be seen as inflammatory. Partly, this reticence can be explained by the fact that he was writing not in his own name but as part of a newspaper, one in which he would continue to editorialize *against* slavery. Whitman's need for circumspection becomes clear when we realize that the publisher of the *Daily Eagle,* Isaac Van Anden, differed strongly with him on the issue of the Wilmot Proviso and the extension of slavery into the territories; it was in fact this very issue that led to Whitman's dismissal from the paper the following year.

Whitman allies himself in the *Eagle* editorial with the "moderate" position adopted in the Massachusetts legislature, a position that would constitute an intermediary discourse that can be distinguished from either ultra-abolitionist or proslavery discourses. It was to be characterized as a discourse of "compromise," or more euphemistically in Whitman's own terms as "liberal" and "democratic." Where the extreme abolitionists believed that slavery was the single greatest evil facing American democracy, an evil that must be eradicated at all costs including the dissolution of the Union, these "moderate" forces took a more limited position. Slavery was a "great evil" and a "direct, practical denial of the essential truths of Democracy," but it was not an institution that could be changed by the actions of Congress or other national political bodies. In other words, citizens of the northern states had the right, even the obligation, to speak out against the practice of slavery, but they had little or no recourse to change it. Northerners could only offer "the bold and honest but courteous and friendly expression of opinion," and must respect "all constitutional rights, as well our neighbors' as our own" (*GF,* 1:196). The irony of this position, an irony that seems to have been more apparent to Whitman in his poetic texts than in his prose writings, is that it necessarily considers slaves as less than "Americans" or "citizens." Underlying this apparently moderate discourse, one reflecting not only the prevailing sentiment but also the legal system of prewar America, is a refusal to recognize the black person as a human being.

In his editorials for the *Eagle,* and later for the *Brooklyn Daily Times,* Whitman continued to write against slavery and especially against the expansion of slavery into the western territories. But his arguments rarely entered the province of abolitionist discourse: they seldom address the issue in terms of the moral or physical condition of slaves themselves. On some occasions, his rhetoric moves in the opposite direction, even intersecting with the arguments of the proslavery faction: the treatment of southern slaves is no worse than that of Russian serfs, Austrian peasants, or the English poor; no non-southerner has "the least shadow of a right to interfere" with southern slavery (*GF,* 1:200); there may be greater need for social reforms in the northern states than there is in the South; and, most puzzling of all from a professedly antislavery journalist, "the institution of slavery is not at all without its redeeming points" (*IS,* 87–88).

Increasingly, too, Whitman abandons the historical and patriotic argument against slavery: that Jefferson and other signers of the Declaration of Independence "anxiously and avowedly . . . sought the extinction of slavery" and saw it as "inconsistent with the other institutions of the land" (*GF,* 1:201). Instead, he makes the practical argument that the practice of negro slavery is incompatible with the interests of "White Workingmen." While this may have been to some extent true on purely economic grounds (an unpaid slave population makes the hiring of paid white workers unprofitable and thus unnecessary), Whitman's contention appears to be racially and culturally as well as economically based. In a *Daily Eagle* editorial entitled "American

Workingmen, versus Slavery" (September 1847), Whitman claims that a "stalwart mass of respectable workingmen cannot exist, much less flourish, in a thorough slave State" and that, if such men were obliged to work in a state that permitted slavery, the "sturdy independence and family happiness" of northern workmen would become something like the "miserable, ignorant, and shifty" nature of poor southern whites. For Whitman, the very fact of being put "on a par with the negro slave" would degrade the "Northern American freeman" by bringing the "dignity of labor down to the level of slavery" (*GF*, 1:209). Whitman's rhetoric here appears to be neither pro- nor antislavery: although he suggests that slavery is a degradation of human life, he takes the institution as a historical given.

Whitman's fundamental discourse in his nonpoetic writings is one that would soon evolve into the keynote of his poetic writing: the celebration of the American (white) working man in all his manifestations. Whitman elaborates his argument in terms that go far beyond the issue itself:

> Let them utter forth, then, in tones as massive as becomes their stupendous cause, that their calling shall *not* be sunk to the miserable level of what is little above brutishness—sunk to be like owned goods, and driven cattle! We call upon every mechanic of the North, East, and West—upon the carpenter, in his rolled up sleeves, the mason with his trowel, the stonecutter with his brawny chest, the blacksmith with his sooty face, the brown fisted ship-builder, whose clicking strokes rattle so merrily in our dock yards—upon shoemakers, and cartmen, and drivers, and paviers . . . upon the honest sawyer and mortar-mixer too, whose sinews are their own—and every hard-working man—to speak in a voice whose great reverberations shall tell to all quarters that the *workingmen* of the free United States, and their business, are not willing to be put on the level of negro slaves, in territory which, if got at all, must be got by taxes sifted eventually through upon them, and by their hard work and blood. (*GF*, 1:210–11)

This curiously bombastic outburst in the midst of an article arguing against the value of slavery in the territories signals an intersection of discourses in which Whitman's antislavery feelings are subordinated to his stronger commitment to the white working class. This intersection is indicated stylistically in the heteroglossic mixing of two registers: the pragmatic level of discourse suggested by the ostensible (political) topic of discussion—jobs, taxes, economic relations—and the poeticized level suggested by the hyperbolic expression and the highly descriptive and exhaustive cataloguing of the various orders of white working men (even more striking in the original text than in my abbreviated version). What is entirely ignored by this breathless rush of language (and the proud parade of white workers it represents) is the possibility of *free* blacks working alongside their white counterparts at the same trades.

A decade later, Whitman rejected the thought of free blacks *ever* achieving racial equality with whites or of entering the free market with them on equal terms. When the new state of Oregon elected in 1858 to prohibit blacks of any kind from entering its borders, Whitman wrote in defense of such a policy: "Who believes that the Whites and Blacks can ever amalgamate in America? Or who wishes it to happen? Nature has set an impassable seal against it. Besides, is not America for Whites? And is it not better so? As long as the Blacks remain here how can they become anything like an independent and heroic race? There is no chance of it" (*IS*, 90).

Only in another part of the world (unnamed by Whitman but presumably somewhere in the African continent), did he believe blacks could attain any degree of stature or self-reliance. Thus the "moderate" antislavery discourse of Whitman's earlier editorials is replaced, in the late 1850s, by the rhetoric of repatriation and racial separation. In this respect, Whitman's attitudes very much reflect the tendencies of his time. The discourse of colonizationism or deportationism, which had been prevalent in the northern states since the 1820s, experienced a significant revival in the 1850s. George Fredrickson attributes this increase in colonizationist sentiment to several causes: the growing romantic vision of black character and the accompanying belief in the ideal of a purely black state; the frustration of abolitionists, especially in light of the Fugitive Slave Law of 1850; and the growth of the free-soil movement and racial nationalism.[20] The rhetoric of the colonization societies that existed from the 1820s to the 1850s stressed noninterference with the rights of southerners to own slaves and expressed the hope that their methods would encourage the "voluntary and gradual" manumission of slaves. Like Whitman in many of his editorials, members of these societies believed that African Americans were subject to inevitable prejudices as long as they remained in the United States, and that they were fundamentally incapable of rising above their present station. In his summary of the colonizationist position, Fredrickson claims that the colonizationists saw "slavery as a social and economic evil that had taken such deep root in national life that it could be eradicated only by a cautious, indirect, and gradual approach," and that they condemned slavery not on the religious or moral grounds of the abolitionists but on the "calculating and prudential" grounds that the institution was "a threat to the prosperity and safety of society" (33). In some respects, Whitman may even have gone beyond mainstream colonizationists in expressing his concern that the degraded state of blacks in slave states would corrupt the status of white working men.

Betsy Erkkila, in her desire to preserve a notion of Whitman's commitment to a universally applied democratic ideal, understates both Whitman's ambivalence and the extent to which the discourses of abolitionist, centrist, and even proslavery forces intersect in his writings. Most other critics have likewise tended to steer away from these difficult questions. In fact, Whitman displays some of the same ambivalence in his relationship to the discourses of slavery that we observed earlier in his relationship to the democratization of literary culture. He fluctuates between a desire for a total and personal identification with black culture and a need to enforce "distinctions" between the sociocultural worlds of blacks and whites. It seems clear that when compared with the views of other antislavery poets of his age—Emerson, Whittier, and Lowell, for example—Whitman's stated opinions increasingly diverge from what he viewed as their excessively abolitionist sentiments.

Emerson provides an interesting case in point. While not an abolitionist in the most extreme sense, he was a writer whose rhetoric was clearly linked to the most generalized elements of abolitionist discourse. On the issue of the Fugitive Slave Law of 1850, Emerson and Whitman are largely in agreement; while there are minor points of divergence between their positions, they both make the essential argument that the law is at once unconstitutional and immoral. But by the end of the 1850s we detect in Whitman a movement away from Emerson's strong antislavery stance. Where Emerson made speeches in honor of John Brown both preceding and following his execution, Whitman, by his own admission, "never enthused greatly over John Brown," and while he respected Brown's courage and devotion, he did not find Brown's martyrdom troubling enough "to spoil my supper" (*WWC*, 2:186).[21] Such statements—offhand as they may be—are in marked contrast to the historical and spiritual importance Emerson attaches to the case of Brown. The end of Emerson's speech in Salem on January 6, 1860, can be read as the summation of Emerson's antislavery position on the eve of the Civil War:

> Nothing is more absurd than to complain of this sympathy [for Brown], or to complain of a party of men united in opposition to slavery. As well complain of gravity, or the ebb of the tide. Who makes the abolitionist?

The slave-holder. The sentiment of mercy is the natural recoil which the laws of the universe provide to protect mankind from destruction by savage passions. And our blind statesmen go up and down, with committees of vigilance and safety, hunting for the origin of this new heresy. They will need a very vigilant committee indeed to find its birthplace, and a very strong force to root it out. For the arch-abolitionist, older than Brown, and older than the Shenandoah Mountains, is Love, whose other name is Justice, which was before Alfred, before Lycurgus, before slavery, and will be after it.[22]

Nowhere in Whitman's writings do we find such a clear and eloquent denunciation of slavery and celebration of the abolitionist cause. Although Whitman had heard Emerson speak on more than one occasion and was certainly aware of his strong antislavery stance, the younger poet quotes Emerson only in defense of his own more universalizing position: "What right have I to speak of slavery? We are *all* slaves."[23]

Whitman may have been repelled by the dramatic, sometimes sensational tone that the subject of slavery could take on in the hands of abolitionists, but it was more likely that he felt threatened by the darker, even subversive implications of abolitionist discourse. Claiming that the "abominable fanaticism of the Abolitionists had . . . retarded the very consummation desired by the A[bolitionist] faction," Whitman concluded that he would put his faith instead in "the quiet progress of wholesome principles in our country."[24] Whitman was hardly alone in this feeling; as David Reynolds notes in *Beneath the American Renaissance,* the subversive elements that grew out of the antislavery movement were menacing to the belief systems of many nineteenth-century Americans: "On the deepest level, the existence of slavery brought into question the veracity of the Bible, the applicability of the American Constitution, and indeed the very existence of God. Several slave narratives and antislavery novels of the period launch a vigorous protest against the slave system, a protest that, in its ferocity, gives rise to savage indictments of the religious and social norms of mainstream America" (73).

According to Reynolds, Harriet Beecher Stowe's *Uncle Tom's Cabin,* the most popular and influential antislavery work of the period, combined both subversive and conventional discourses in its discussion of slavery—though what subversive elements there may be are presented in such a sensationalized form as to mitigate the threat to most readers. (Interestingly, Whitman showed little interest in Stowe's novel after its publication in 1852, perhaps because the book failed to achieve the reconciliation of subversive and conventional forces that would have presented a realistic vision of slavery.) Whitman himself was not incapable of slipping into sensationalist rhetoric when writing about subjects like the slave trade. In one of his articles from the series "New York Dissected," published in the popular magazine *Life Illustrated* in August 1856, he writes of the slavers that continue their illegal trade in New York and Salem, and he evokes the slaves in storage below the ship's deck: "We look about and imagine that we hear the barbarous gibberish of the miserable chattels, lamenting their savage homes, and wondering to each other whither their white captors are carrying them. Perhaps in desperation they attempt to rise upon the crew. They are quieted either by promiscuous musket volleys fired down the hatchway, or by a few pounds of tacks plentifully dispersed among them, so that the motion of a limb in the dense crowd inflicts smarting punctured wounds" (*NYD*, 114).

Such a statement of empathy for the actual situation of slaves still reveals Whitman's latent acceptance of racial stereotypes: the slaves speak in "barbarous gibberish" and wish to return to their "savage homes." Whitman seems more outraged by the fact that New York and Salem are being used as illegal ports for the slave trade than by the suffering of the slaves themselves, and his discussion of their condition, though graphic, is nonetheless distanced. His use of the passive voice calms and disperses the horrifying scene he witnesses, as does the synecdochic reference to "limbs," "punctured wounds," and the "dense crowd" rather than to the individual slaves themselves. As we shall see below, Whitman's poetic use of the motif of slavery allows him to engage in a far stronger personal identification with black slaves than did his journalistic writing. But such identification would not last for long on either a personal or a political level: when Emerson was lending his voice in support of the Emancipation Proclamation in 1862, Whitman said nothing.

Slavery and the Literary Intertext

What mattered most to Whitman during the key period of his involvement with the slavery issue—1846 to 1855—was not the political question of how to end slavery, or even of how to prevent it from spreading to the western territories, but rather the issue of how to become a poet. Ultimately, however, Whitman's achieved self-renewal would serve as a model for his vision of national renewal, as the elevation and purification of the individual body and spirit would be seen as moving outward to encompass the government and laws of the nation. If these political objectives formed the backbone of the project he undertook beginning in his 1847 notebook entries, the realization of his fully developed poetry in *Leaves of Grass* required the catalyst of other, more literary sources as well. Yet none of the literary models Whitman would have encountered by 1855 would go far toward explaining Whitman's poetic treatment of slavery.[25]

Though European poets, including William Blake, made reference to slavery in their works, the topos of slavery is a peculiarly American one, and Whitman's attempt to bring slavery into the larger pattern of *Leaves of Grass* represents an ambitious attempt to encapsulate in poetic form the uniqueness of his national and political vision. But for an American poet who wished to celebrate his nation's democratic experiment, the existence of slavery posed obvious problems. If contemporary social and political discourses provided no solution to this inherently contradictory situation, what about literary models? American poets before Whitman had already established a precedent for poems about slavery: notably Whittier's *Poems Written during the Progress of Abolition* (1838) and *Voices of Freedom* (1846), Longfellow's *Poems on Slavery* (1842), and Lowell's *Biglow Papers* (1848). All of these treatments are uncompromisingly critical of slavery and its effects on individuals and social institutions. Whitman, on the other hand, desires the integration of every human institution, including slavery, into his all-embracing vision of the national character. When Whitman writes in 1847 that he will be the "poet of slaves, and of the masters of slaves," he is beginning to formulate what Allen Grossman calls his "poetics of union," but he is also differentiating his own treatment of slavery from previous treatments like those of Whittier and Longfellow and from the antislavery rhetoric of Emerson and Thoreau. Whitman goes even further in this direction as he continues his draft:

> I go with the slaves of the earth equally with the masters
> And I will stand between the masters and the slaves,
> Entering into both, so that both will understand me alike
> 　　　　　　　　　　　　　　　　　　(*UPP*, 2:69)

Whitman's lines certainly represent an act of unification, but I would not agree with Betsy Erkkila that they also suggest a "short-circuiting" of the republic, or "the irreconcilability of an economy of masters and slaves within the figure of the republican self" (50). On the contrary, these lines stand for exactly such an economy. The movement in the passage—from "stand[ing] between" to "entering into" and finally to bringing about mutual understanding—figures the ultimate connectedness of poet, slave, and owner, without ever suggesting the need for emancipation or social rupture of any kind. Slave and master are linked as are body and soul in the lines directly preceding ("I am the poet of the body / And I am the poet of the soul"). Whitman's lines prefigure not the rupture of the Union that he feared but rather the continuity and strengthening of democratic forces for which he hoped, with poetry instead of politics as the reconciler.

The form these lines take, an early approximation of the free verse stanzas of *Leaves of Grass,* is also indicative of Whitman's purpose. Unlike Whittier and Longfellow, who place the discussion of slavery within a defined lyric space isolated from other national, political, or personal concerns, Whitman brings the fact of slavery into his own space—that of his body and soul and of the larger republic they represent. Whittier's and Longfellow's antislavery poems are collected in volumes, the titles of which clearly indicate their theme; Whitman's poetic treatments of slavery, with the exception of some of the early poems not included in *Leaves of Grass,* are part of a larger canvas of "America" and are interwoven with other discourses.

Whitman would certainly have been aware of the slavery poems of Whittier and Longfellow, and it is likely that he read at least some of them. Whittier was well known as a reformer and antislavery spokesman, besides his renown as one of America's foremost poets; Whitman had joined with him both in opposing the annexation of Texas as a slave state and in mourning the death of the liberal politician Silas Wright. Whitman also knew Longfellow's work well enough, as we have seen in the last chapter, to have viewed him as a model *against* which to formulate his own poetic project.[26]

Whittier's antislavery poems, published during the 1830s and 1840s and grouped together under the rubric "Voices of Freedom" in his collected poems, cover a wide range of subjects. Some are topical and were written either in response to or in commemoration of specific events; others are set in the voice of individuals ("The Farewell of a Virginia Slave Mother to Her Daughters Sold into Southern Bondage"); others deal with historical topics ("Toussaint L'Ouverture"); and still others are more general commentaries on slavery and the abolitionist cause. Longfellow's *Poems on Slavery,* unlike Whittier's more occasional lyrics, display some degree of narrative continuity. They begin with a slave dreaming of his African homeland, witness the chase and capture of another slave, and end with scenes of a slave ship, a quadroon girl being sold to a slave trader by her father, and a warning of the impending violence slavery will bring to "this Commonweal."

Unlike Whittier, Longfellow was not a writer who characteristically embraced radical causes like abolitionism, and these poems represent a departure from his usual political caution. Despite Longfellow's reservations about the abolitionists, his poems represent a deliberate attempt to take a controversial stand, and their dedication to William Ellery Channing indicates the unequivocal position Longfellow takes opposing slavery. In general, however, the quality of these poems cannot be compared with the important slavery passages of *Leaves of Grass*. In fact, with the exception of the most powerful poem in the series, "The Witnesses"—which evokes a "black Slave-ship" filled with "skeletons in chains"—the poems are more interesting as social documents than as examples of literary art. For the most part they are formally conventional, they rely on sentimental and often Christian imagery, and they present a sensationalized version of slavery that is constantly opposed to a romantic vision of the "natural" life of the free black. The affective fallacy is taken to its extreme in Longfellow's evocation of a benign, peaceful, and ennobling nature: the forests, the desert, and even the birds sing of "Liberty." When in "The Quadroon Girl" the planter decides whether to sell his daughter to the slaver, he must choose between morally polarized opposites: he ultimately elects the "world of crime" (the lucre made possible by the slave trade) over the "voice of nature" (poor but virtuous freedom).[27]

Longfellow's rather weak imitation of the Romantic mode in these poems is in sharp contrast to the powerfully realistic passages we will find in Whitman's poems. Not only are most of Longfellow's images borrowed from the familiar lexicon of the (abolitionist) sociolect, but Longfellow even appears to have borrowed some of his imagistic register more directly from Whittier's poem "The Slave-Ships," which relates the historically true story of a French ship whose cargo of 160 slaves had contracted a terrible disease and were thrown mercilessly "to the sharks." Whittier's poem ends with the ship, all its crew now blind from the spreading disease, having arrived in Guadaloupe. The scene of the "dark-hulled" slave-ship lying in the harbor of "sunny Guadaloupe" is almost exactly reproduced in Longfellow's "The Quadroon Girl," where the "Odors of orange-flowers, and spice, / Reached them from time to time, / Like airs that breathe from Paradise / Upon a world of crime." In Whittier's poem we find the same "blossom of the orange" and the same trope of a natural paradise, once again contrasted with the "slaver's darkened eye" and disrupted by the "blackness of his crime."

Whether Longfellow's borrowing from Whittier is a conscious or an unconscious one, the shared intertext of these two poets reveals the nature of the literary sociolect to which their works on slavery belong. It is one based on the abolitionist doctrine of the goodness of humanity—evidenced in a natural state—which is corrupted by the evils of slavery and the slave trade. These poets present an unambiguous discourse, and its relationship to larger political, social, moral, and religious discourses remains unproblematized. Both Whittier and Longfellow adopt an unabashedly Christian paradigm for the struggle against slavery: Longfellow calls Channing a "Servant of God," compares him to Luther, and proclaims that the abolitionist cause is guided by "the prophetic voice, that cried / To John in Patmos, 'Write!'" (20). Slavery itself is represented in dramatically biblical terms, as "This Day of Wrath, this Endless Wail, / This dread Apocalypse!" Whittier, too, is bolstered by a fervent and self-righteous New England protestantism, as he writes in "The Christian Slave" of "that vile South Sodom first and best" (50). Speaking to the hypocrisy of those who would raise slaves as "good Christians" without teaching them the true meaning of Christ's message, Whittier concludes that Christianity's "rites will only swell his market price, / and rivet on his chain."

Despite the spiritual and political importance of their message, these poets do not take on the poetically difficult task that Whitman does—that of "standing between the masters and the slaves"—for to do so would require an attempt to understand fully the respective positions, and the respective discourses, of both parties. If Whittier and Longfellow are not willing to enter into the consciousness of the slaveholder, neither are they able to portray slaves themselves in fully realized terms. In Longfellow's poems, the slaver and slave owner are portrayed only in the act of buying, hunting, or whipping their property; the slave is viewed only in such iconographic representations as a former tribal king ("The Slave's Dream"), a saintly maiden ("The Quadroon Girl"), or a hunted animal ("The Slave in the Dismal Swamp").

Although Whitman's slavery passages cannot avoid sharing certain elements with the poems of Longfellow and Whittier, it is clear that his poetic treatment of slavery is altogether different from theirs. In attempting to avoid the conventional discourses they adopt—sensationalized abolitionism, sentimental Christianity, and hackneyed Romanticism—Whitman poses himself an extremely difficult challenge. By the time of *Leaves of Grass,* Whitman was dealing with slavery in terms that reflected the larger thrust of his language experiment: he would rely on no apparent literary intertext and would conform to no easily identifiable sociolect.

"The Hounded Slave"

Between March and June 1850 Whitman wrote four poems—"Song for Certain Congressmen," "Blood-Money," "The House of Friends," and "Resurgemus"—each of which comments either directly or obliquely on the slavery issue.[28] A brief reading of these poems will help establish the radical transformation of Whitman's poetic discourse concerning slavery as he began to formulate the project of *Leaves of Grass.*

In "Song for Certain Congressmen," Whitman takes the satiric form adopted two years earlier in Lowell's *Biglow Papers* to castigate the "doughfaces," those weak northern politicians who give in to the demands of "dashing southern lords." Here the colloquial style and ironic tone almost seem to be in imitation of the speaker of Lowell's poems, but Whitman's message is his own, and it appears to be in contrast to his usual calls for compromise and moderation. His speaker, a satirically portrayed spokesman for the moderate anti-abolitionist position that Whitman had himself adopted some three years earlier, expresses the shortsighted attitude that "moving and bartering nigger slaves" is a mere "trifle" compared with the interests of the Union and "the two great parties."

Whitman's subsequent poems depart both from the rhymed and metered verse of "Song for Certain Congressmen" and from its blatant satirical and topical intent. In "Blood-Money" he departs from the tradition of political satire and turns to the mode of biblical allegory already exploited by Whittier and Longfellow. Webster is now represented as a modern-day Judas figure who will sell slaves rather than Christ for pieces of silver. The analogy is made clear at the end of the poem, when Christ is called the "brother of slaves." In "The House of Friends," Whitman continues his attack on northern politicians—"Doughfaces, Crawlers, Lice of Humanity"—who are themselves slaves to the almighty "dollar," and who are a greater blight on the North than the institution of slavery is on the southern states. Finally, "Resurgemus" is a revolutionary poem comparing the uprisings in Europe to an awakening from a "stale and drowsy lair, / the lair of slaves." Staged as a battle between the oppressive forces of monarchy and its pawns on one side ("Hangman, priest, and tax-gatherer, / Soldier, lawyer, sycophant") and the enslaved peoples on the other, the poem ends with an affirmation of the powers of freedom, metaphorically portrayed as the "seed, / Which the winds shall carry afar and resow, / And rain nourish."

As he begins to organize the ideas that will form the first poems of *Leaves of Grass,* Whitman's attention turns from the institution of slavery and its economic and political repercussions to the larger question of race in all its biological and cultural implications. In the notebooks he used to draft his ideas for poems, Whitman questions the belief—held by society at large and often by himself as well—in the innate superiority of the white race over blacks and other racial groups.[29] It is in a draft for a poem that was sketched out but never completed, "Poem of Remorse," that Whitman most directly addresses his own racist beliefs:

> I now look back to the
> times when I thought
> others—slaves—the ignorant
> —so much inferior to myself
> To have so much less right.
>
> (*DN,* 791)

Whitman—in the guise of his poetic persona—places his own racism in the past, distancing himself from what he now sees as unfortunate beliefs.

What these beliefs were, and how he felt he had come to change them, is not altogether clear. While growing up on Long Island, Whitman had encountered free blacks, many of whom were members of an unemployed class he described as "degraded, shiftless, and intemperate" (*UPP,* 2:316–17). But the most blatant example of Whitman's negative racial attitudes occurs in his 1842 temperence novel *Franklin Evans.* Whitman's portrayal of the slave woman Margaret, a beautiful "creole" associated with sexual "charms" and with calculating and jealous behavior whom Evans marries in a fit of drunken passion, appears to accept unquestioningly the racial stereotypes of his day. After Evans is deceived into marrying her—both by her designs and by his own inebriated state—he realizes that he has made a costly mistake. Spurned by her new husband, Margaret evolves into a veritable monster of jealousy and vindictiveness, finally murdering the white woman who has become a "more legitimate" rival for Franklin's affections.

Whitman's appropriation of the "mulatto wench" figure may tell us more about popular racial stereotyping of the time than it does about Whitman's personal beliefs. *Franklin Evans* was, after all, conceived and written within the conventions of a popular genre and was, arguably, not to be confused with Whitman's more serious literary endeavors. Anecdotal evidence does suggest, however, that Whitman had no personal fondness for blacks, and that he may indeed have shared the feeling of most white northerners at the time, composed of a benevolent desire to liberate and protect slaves on the one hand and a deep-seated distrust and even revulsion on the other.

If Whitman had manifested these sentiments prior to the 1855 notebooks and poems, the record provides little evidence that his personal relations with blacks had changed in the way "Poem of Remorse" suggests; in fact, he continued throughout the 1850s to express racist beliefs. One entry from his notebooks argues for the superiority of the Anglo-Saxon race and culture, which are "fast absorbing or displacing all the sluggish or barbarous tribes of men that have occupied the continents of America, Africa, Asia, and the islands of the ocean" (*DN*, 667–68). Even when Whitman speaks most strongly against slavery as an institution, as in the unpublished essay "As of the Orator," he cannot bring himself to embrace the individual slave along with the larger cause of antislavery. In writing of the hypothetical escaped slave it would be his duty to protect from arrest, he adds the apology that "he may be coarse, fanatical, and a nigger," and that he "may have shown bad judgement" in attempting to escape (*NUPM*, 2194).

Yet in "Song of Myself," when Whitman attempts to address the same issues poetically, the result is remarkably different. In fact, it is precisely the appearance of the "runaway slave" at two separate points in the poem that gives voice to Whitman's deeper engagement with the reality of slavery. Like the slave auction depicted in "I Sing the Body Electric," the escape to freedom was a central image in the nation's consciousness of slavery, one that had been graphically presented in the most popular literary text of its day, Stowe's *Uncle Tom's Cabin*. For Whitman, the escape motif had a more local significance as well, as it pointed to a source of friction between northern antislavery forces and the federal government, which since 1850 had attempted to impose the Fugitive Slave Law by sending in officers to recapture and extradite escapees.[30]

Whitman's first poetic encounter with the "runaway," in section 10 of "Song of Myself," does not celebrate either the slave or his own actions. Instead, it imagines his caring and generosity toward a fellow human being:

The runaway slave came to my house and stopt outside,
I heard his motions crackling the twigs of the woodpile,
Though he swung the half-door of the kitchen I saw him limpsy
    and weak,
And went where he sat on a log, and led him in and assured
    him.
And brought water and fill'd a tub for his sweated body and
    bruis'd feet,
And gave him a room that enter'd from my own, and gave him
    some coarse clean clothes,
And remember perfectly well his revolving eyes and his
    awkwardness,
And remember putting plasters on the galls of his neck and
    ankles,
He staid with me a week before he was recuperated and pass'd
    north,
I had him sit next me at table, my fire-lock lean'd in the corner.

(189–98)

Only in the last line does Whitman reveal the deeper significance of his anec-
dote: he will not only share his food, clothing, and house with the needy slave
but will both defend his freedom ("my firelock leaned in the corner") and invite him to participate in the communal ritual of mealtime ("I had him sit
next me at table").[31] At the same time, the poet takes a great deal of bodily
pleasure in imagining the scene, which is filled with images of sensory awareness, especially of a tactile nature. The tub of water the speaker provides for
the slave's "sweated body and bruis'd feet," the "coarse clean clothes" he
gives him to wear, and the plasters he puts on "the galls of his neck and
ankles" all suggest the sense of physical intimacy informing Whitman's
imaginative involvement with the slave's body. Unlike the passage in "I Sing
the Body Electric," where the body is observed from an external and distanced perspective, here Whitman makes physical as well as emotional and
spiritual contact with the slave.

In section 33 of the poem Whitman presents the opposite scenario: a
"hounded slave" who is recaptured before successfully escaping to the
North. In order to understand more fully the suffering of the slave, Whitman
moves from the position of onlooker and helper to a total identification
with his plight:

I am the hounded slave, I wince at the bite of the dogs,
Hell and despair are upon me, crack and again crack the
    marksmen,
I clutch the rails of the fence, my gore dribs, thinn'd with the
    ooze of my skin,
I fall on the weeds and stones,
The riders spur their unwilling horses, haul close,
Taunt my dizzy ears and beat me violently over the head with
    their whip-stocks.

(838–43)

Here we move from the natural world of Whitman as healer and caregiver in section 10 to the de-naturalized and hellish scene of a brutal capture. The unnamed "riders" with their "whip-stocks," who must force even their "unwilling" horses to participate in this perverse act, are nightmarish apparitions. The slave's wounds, so carefully healed in the earlier passage, are now reopened by "murderous buckshot" and violent whipping, so that the "gore dribs thinn'd with the ooze of my skin." If Whitman has not yet found a discourse of interiority for the slave's suffering, he has at least begun to enter into the identity of the slave in a direct and physical way: through the perforations in his skin. Whitman includes the slave here in a series of martyrs: the wife whose husband has drowned, the survivors of a shipwreck, the woman burned as a witch, the fireman killed in a collapsed building, and the old artillerist during the bombardment of his fort. Thus the slave's plight is viewed not as an isolated incident but as part of the cycle of violence, suffering, and heroism in which the "I" of Whitman's poem must participate: "I am the man, I suffer'd, I was there" (832).

Whitman's evocation of the "hounded slave" is powerful enough that its antislavery message is often assumed; however, its placement within the poem raises important questions about Whitman's overall use of the discourse of slavery. As Edwin Havilland Miller observes, there is a continuity of images in this sequence that links the slave's dripping "gore" with the fireman's "red shirt," and finally with the "ambulanza ... trailing its red drip" after the battle for the fort.[32] Though the persecution of the slave is, like the Salem witch hunts, a desecration of human decency and a disturbingly violent episode in American history, it is also presented as part of the historical process of fires, battles, shipwrecks, and other tragic events, all of which Whitman must both accept and experience: "All this I swallow, it tastes good, I like it well, it becomes mine." In attempting to enter fully into the physical and discursive space of historical process, including slavery, Whitman circumvents the more canonical treatment of slavery represented by the texts of Whittier and Longfellow. Whitman's radical departure from the sociolect can be most clearly seen when contrasted with the more conventionally poetic rendering of a hunted slave in Longfellow's "The Slave in the Dismal Swamp." Here the "hunted Negro" is presented in a highly symbolic landscape—the "dark fens of the Dismal Swamp." In a landscape of moral and spiritual darkness—a combination of fallen Eden and Slough of Despond—the "poor old slave, infirm and lame" serves as a figure for the "shame" and "disgrace" of slavery as a whole. Outside, or more symbolically, "above" the swamp, lies the world of freedom to which this slave will never escape, a world that is "bright," "fair," "glad," "free," and filled with the songs of birds who sing of "Liberty." Longfellow's slave, on the other hand, is destroyed by his particular "curse" of bondage:

> On him alone was the doom of pain,
> From the morning of his birth;
> On him alone the curse of Cain
> Fell, like a flail on the garnered grain,
> And struck him to the earth!
>
> (21)

The image of being "struck to the earth" by the "flail"—the only direct violence portrayed in Longfellow's poem—is still rendered in symbolic terms. In fact, the entire stanza is in sharp contrast to Whitman's treatment of the "hounded slave" in "Song of Myself"—one which takes place in a realistic landscape, which evokes violence in unambiguous and chillingly concrete terms, and which takes on the added immediacy of the poet's physical identification with the slave. Longfellow gives us only a distanced and ceremonialized version of the same incident. The slave feels both the "doom of pain" and the "curse of Cain"; but if the "flail" is meant to suggest the whip with which he is beaten down, both the agent of the violent act and the graphic details of its execution are left to our imagination. Longfellow's poem is effective in its manipulation of the reader's sympathy, but his portrayal works to seal off both poet and reader from the reality of slavery and from the less mediated discourse through which Whitman's presents it through the persona of the hounded slave.

"Now Lucifer Was Not Dead"

Whitman was not always able to reconcile the discourse of slavery with his vision of American democratic life as he does in "Song of Myself." The idea of a curse brought upon those who practice the buying, selling, and ill-treatment of slaves—"Who degrades or defiles the living human body is cursed"—reappears in various forms in Whitman's writings of the period. At times, he expresses the desire for a dramatic event, a turbulent social upheaval that would disturb the cursed state, the "ossification of the spirit" he believed the American acceptance of slavery had caused.[33]

It was in writing the notebook pages that served as the source for "The Sleepers" that Whitman began to formulate more clearly what guise such a turbulence might take. Immediately following the pages on which he critiques the logic of racial inferiority, Whitman writes—and then crosses out—a frightening racial allegory: "Beware the flukes of the whale. He is slow and sleepy—but when he moves, his lightest touch is death. I think he already feels the lance, for he moves a little restlessly. You are great sportsmen, no doubt. What! That black and huge lethargic mass, my sportsmen, dull and sleepy as it seems, holds the lightning and the taps of thunder. He is slow—O, long and long and slow and slow—but when he does move, his lightest touch is death" (*DN,* 763).

Here Whitman's sense of impending social upheval is materialized in the huge but still lethargic body of a whale. Already, in its notebook form, the whale serves as a powerful metaphor for the deep and deceptively "sleepy" anger of the repressed slave. The portrayal of white men as the "sportsmen" who move confidently on the surface, unaware of the whale's destructive potential, is equally chilling in its dark sarcasm. Lastly, the poet himself is present as the all-observing subject, whose sensitivity to the latent possibilities of the whale will allow him both to warn and to ironize the ignorant white populace.

When Whitman rewrites the notebook entry as the end of section 6 of "The Sleepers," he grafts it onto another fragment in which the speaker passes into the thoughts and words of a black slave:

> I am a curse: a negro thinks me;
> You cannot speak for yourself, negro;
> I lend him my own tongue;
> I dart like a snake from your mouth.

My eyes are bloodshot, they look down the river,
A steamboat paddles away my woman and children.

In the first stanza of this trial poem, Whitman moves from his own sense of guilt—"I am a curse"—to the mind of the voiceless negro who can only "think" his anger and his conception of the white man. Whitman's acknowledgment that the slave (and, by extension, the black American) has no status within the sociolect—"You cannot speak for yourself, negro"—is crucial to the vision of a nameless slave (given the "hell-name" of Black Lucifer in another draft of the poem), who will find expression only through the mute figures of a snake and a whale. The remarkable image that we find here but which is not included in the finished poem was that of his own tongue entering the mouth of the black slave, only to be converted metaphorically to a snake leaving its burrow. The poet Whitman will supply the silenced slave with a voice, but it will allow him to speak only in snakelike, darting language, the potentially violent language of the oppressed. The second stanza contains the core of what will be the Lucifer passage in "The Sleepers": a slave watches his woman and children being sold down the river.

In the version published in the 1855 *Leaves of Grass,* Whitman expands the voice of the slave to include an outburst that seems to be projected in snakelike darts of rage:

> Now Lucifer was not dead. . . . or if he was I am his sorrowful
>   terrible heir;
> I have been wronged. . . . I am oppressed. . . . I hate him that
>   oppresses me,
> I will either destroy him, or he shall release me.
>
> Damn him! how he does defile me,
> How he informs against my brother and sister, and takes pay for
>   their blood,
> How he laughs when I look down the bend, after the steamboat
>   that carries away my woman.
>
> Now the vast bulk that is the whale's bulk. . . . it seems mine,
> Warily, sportsman! though I lie so sleepy and sluggish, my tap is
>   death.
>
> (CP1855, 113)

The whale's body passes from the natural order ("the vast bulk that is the whale's bulk") to the imagination of the speaker-slave ("it seems mine") and finally to the literal embodiment of his anger and his desire for liberation and revenge. We also find in capsule form the story of slavery that necessitates the dual transformation of that anger into both the whale and Lucifer. Another manuscript fragment indicates the slave's determination to fight for his freedom: "Iron necklace and red sores of shoulders I do not mind / Hopple at the ankle will not detain me." The slave feels wronged, oppressed, and defiled by an unnamed but strongly evoked white owner who has sold away his entire family and engaged in other acts of humiliation and degradation. Like the white men in "Song of Myself" who "taunt" the "dizzy ears" of the hounded slave, this man laughs even at the plight of the slave whose wife or lover is taken away from him. Whether the Lucifer invoked here as the ancestor of this slave (Black Lucifer in an earlier version) is related to the snake of Whitman's fragment is not clear; the linkage of slavery to lapsarian images appears to have been a common trope of abolitionist rhetoric.[34] What is most significant in the passage is Whitman's creation of enabling figures for the slave's self-expression; Lucifer and the black whale, along with the snake in the earlier fragment, represent at once the slave's inability to speak within the system of dominant white discourses and Whitman's poetic attempt to give a voice to the slave. Slavery's invisible discourse is made visible through an imagined form of actual speech; this speech in turn is made accessible to the reader through the framing allegory of the whale, a figure borrowed from his contemporary interdiscourse.

Whitman may have been influenced by contemporary discursive and artistic representations in his equation of slavery with Lucifer.[35] Nevertheless, the sudden and dramatic appearance of the figure here—"Now Lucifer was not dead"—is one of the most striking moments in all of Whitman's poetry. The rebellious slave plotting his revolt—or in abolitionist discourse the oppressed slave deciding to break his chains—was certainly a well-known trope of midcentury American thought. But Whitman's adoption of this narrative as a subtext for his poem is also an example of a poetic interaction with historical discourse, a moment in which the sociolect is transformed into a uniquely Whitmanic expression. Whitman's passage is at once a phantasmagoric projection of the inner self and a realistic rendering of historical particulars. Of all the passages in Whitman's poems, this is the most powerful and unambiguous both in its denunciation of slavery and in its attempt to enter the consciousness of the slave himself. If "I Sing the Body Electric" was the exterior celebration of the slave's body, this passage in "The Sleepers" takes the extraordinary step of going beyond the consciousness of Whitman's "I" to relate fully with the dark side of human experience—to enter into the pain of the slave. This is not a cry of physical pain to be classed with those of other heroes and martyrs but a unique cry of anguish that can only be contained in such extreme formulations as the dark, sluggish, and murderous whale; the "terrible sorrowful heir" of Lucifer; the expletive ("Damn him!"); or the repetition of emotional outburst—"I have been wronged—I am oppressed—I hate him that oppresses me!"

Whitman's poem dramatizes in startlingly original poetic terms the event foreseen more conventionally in the last poem of Longfellow's antislavery sequence, "The Warning":

> There is a poor, blind, Samson in this land,
> Shorn of his strength and bound in bonds of steel,
> Who may, in some grim revel, raise his hand,
> And shake the pillars of this Commonweal,
> Till the vast Temple of our liberties
> A shapeless mass of wreck and rubbish lies.
>
> (23)

The comparison of Whitman's discourse of spontaneous subjectivity with Longfellow's classically iconographic rendering of the same event only serves to emphasize the uniqueness of Whitman's poetic vision in the passage, one which has no literary predecessors. On one level, Whitman's use of the Lucifer figure and Longfellow's representation of slavery through the biblical and literary archetype of Samson in the temple are analogous. But while Longfellow remains within the bounds of his metaphorical construction— one distancing the physical, racial, and social realities of the slave's existence—Whitman breaks through the discursive conventions of American political poetry. The closest parallel for the language and force Whitman achieves in the passage is in Blake's prophetic books, but these were unknown to Whitman until at least the late 1860s.

The passage also engages topical social discourse on two levels which comment on each other: it reflects simultaneously the discourse of white fears of insurrection by a largely unknown and therefore threatening black race, and the imagined discourse of black desperation and desire for revolt.[36] As in the case of Frederick Douglass, who could express neither difference from nor identity with his white audience, Whitman's poem indicates the inevitable epistemological chasm that exists between white and black cultures, even in the radical poetic attempt to inhabit the subject-position of a persona who is a black slave. The constant repetition of an unspecified "he" in the passage emphasizes the distance between the black speaker, who is identified only as the "heir" of Lucifer, and his similarly nameless master, who represents the entire patriarchal system. This "false" patriarchy inherent in a master/slave economy is contrasted with the "true" patriarchy represented by the egalitarian vision of Washington with his soldiers, and it is also contrasted with the healthy interracial connection represented by the maternal: the mother with the squaw in the preceding passage. At the same time, the sexual exploitation represented by the laughter of the slave owner, a wordless means of defiling or degrading the human body, is yet another instance of the linguistic separation of racial groups.

Two important questions remain for the reader and critic: what purpose did the passage serve in the poem, and why was it removed from *Leaves of Grass* in the 1881 edition? Critics have suggested various structural and thematic reasons for the passage's inclusion, but few have argued any rationale for its later deletion. In their *Comprehensive Reader's Edition,* Harold Blodgett and Sculley Bradley refer only in general terms to the "withdrawal of difficult but interesting passages from the poem" and suggest that such a withdrawal was made "not so much for aesthetic as for discretionary reasons" (*LG,* 424). Granted, the passage could have been shocking to readers in its realism and message, but would this account for Whitman's removal of it?

James Warren supplies two reasons for cutting the passage, a deletion he claims "adds coherence to the movement of the poem": first, that unlike those portrayed in other scenes, Lucifer is a figure of loss without a compensating joy; and second, that the slave passage is more topical than the rest of Whitman's vision of private and public worlds.[37] But arguments for keeping the passage are far more convincing: it completes the downward spiral of eros and death in the poem's dream vision and leads to the upward movement of the final sections; and it serves as a powerful representation of Whitman's longing for a slave revolt that will act as a purgation of both national guilt and the repressed personal guilt of the dreamer.[38]

However, if such a purgation is to take place, it appears not yet to have been completed. Unlike other figures of death in the poem, each of which is followed by a spiritual regathering, Lucifer is "not dead," and his progeny live on to attest to the communal guilt of the past embodied in the present state. The presentness of this moment is emphasized temporally by the deictic ("Now") beginning the passage and by the progression from historical past (Washington) to personal past (the squaw), to the present "sorrowful terrible heir," and finally to the vision of the future in section 7—"I . . . will go gallivant with the light and air myself." Section 7 marks a change in tone, in time, and in overall movement from the Lucifer passage: it embodies the return home of all people, including the "exile," the "fugitive," and the "immigrant." The "fugitive," presumably referring among others to a fugitive slave, "returns unharm'd" as the seasonal cycle resumes, abundance returns to the farms, and the universe is put "duly in order." All people are "averaged" by the poet: "one is no better than the other, / The night and sleep have liken'd them and restored them."

But in this process of averaging and restoring, where is the place for the unresolved anger of Lucifer and the black whale? Why must the fugitive return, even unharmed, to his former master in order for Whitman's spiritual reconciliation to take place? And, finally, why will Whitman write no more significant poems dealing with slavery or racial issues after 1855? It is these questions that may help explain the removal of the passage in "The Sleepers." As Whitman's interest in slavery waned in the period after the mid-1850s, and as his wish for turbulence was replaced by other concerns, his desire to emphasize the discourse of rebellion in his own poems declined. Whitman had gone as far as he conceivably could in these 1855 poems—especially "The Sleepers"—in entering into black experience; now he would gradually return to a greater concern for political expediency, even at the cost of a corresponding loss in the originality of his poetic vision. The very force that he attempts to communicate, figured brilliantly through the use of the whale as cultural intertext, is also the force that he ultimately needs to repress in his poem. On the referential level, the emerging force of the slave's anger will lead to a crisis in the contemporary social organization. On the semiotic level, the threat posed to the organization of the poetic text by the attempt to present the slave's unmediated discourse will lead, Whitman fears, to the dissolution of the idealized American poem that he feels "The Sleepers" must become. The very metaphor that could best capture society's attention in the 1850s—that linking the symbolic and discursive power of the whale (its status as a form of "elementary literature") with the latent but still untapped sociohistorical power of the oppressed slave—was more potent than Whitman's later poetic vision could contain.

By 1876, Whitman presumably felt that such a passage no longer served the purposes of his revised historico-poetic vision of America. At the time of his 1882 essay on the "Death of Longfellow," Whitman praised Longfellow's slavery poems for lacking exactly the qualities of immediacy and aggressivity that he himself had exploited in "Song of Myself" and the original version of "The Sleepers": "[Longfellow] is not revolutionary, brings nothing offensive or new, does not deal hard blows. On the contrary, his songs soothe and heal, or if they excite, it is a healthy and agreeable excitement. His anger is very gentle, is at second hand" (*PW*, 285).

"The Slavery Contest Is Settled"

In the period during and immediately following the war, Whitman wrote the poems in *Drum-Taps* (1865) and "Sequel" (1866), including the famous elegy to President Lincoln, "When Lilacs Last in the Dooryard Bloom'd." These poems contain almost no mention of slavery; its absence becomes in Erkkila's words a "potent ellipsis." In one of the first poems composed for *Drum-Taps,* the 1861 "Song of the Banner at Daybreak," Whitman presents a catalogue of places and people he hears and sees around him in both northern and southern states. Unlike the structurally similar catalogue of "Song of Myself," this one contains no mention of slaves, even during an imagined visit to a southern plantation. Whitman's "sweeping" view admits only "the countless profit, the busy gatherings, earn'd wages . . . the Identity formed out of thirty-eight spacious and haughty States" (lines 74–75). As in his discussions of white working men from a decade earlier, Whitman emphasizes the "earn'd wages" of busy and productive workers, thus occluding the slave labor which continued to run the southern half of the country. He does hear the voice of "Liberty," but even that liberty is left unspecific.

Whitman's reticence in talking about slavery and about the position of the black race in the United States is represented not only by a lack of antislavery passages such as those found in the 1855 poems; symbolically, Whitman turns increasingly to a vision of "reconciliation" that would unite the white "brothers" of North and South while obliterating the black race entirely. He ends the 1865 poem "Reconciliation" with the lines:

For my enemy is dead, a man divine as myself is dead,
I look where he lies white-faced and still in the coffin—I draw near,
Bend down and touch lightly with my lips the white face in the coffin.

(4–6)

Here, the rhetoric of "white faces" appears to have replaced his concern for the black race: Lucifer may not be dead, but he is *forgotten* in a postwar vision of reconciliation. Whitman's prose comments of the postwar period indicate a feeling that the black person was not to be part of a productive and unified white America. Indeed, by 1867 Whitman was beginning to question the desirability of the influx of southern blacks into northern cities; in one letter to his mother he writes of the "darkies" who "swarm in all directions": "I am not sure but the North is like the man that won the elephant in a raffle" (*Corr.* 1:323). In a letter from the following year concerning a procession in the streets of Washington by several thousand blacks, his deprecatory attitude is even clearer. The men, according to Whitman, were "yelling and gesticulating like madmen—it was quite comical, yet very disgusting and alarming in some respects—They were very insolent, and altogether it was a very strange sight—they looked like so many wild beasts set loose" (*Corr.* 2:35). If the inclusive, egalitarian discourse of "I Sing the Body Electric" seems to have disappeared in the period during and after the war, Whitman's sense of the physical beauty of blacks has diminished as well. In a diary entry from 1863, he observes a black regiment being paid: "Occasionally, but not often, there are some thoroughly African physiognomies, very black in color, large, protruding lips, low forehead, etc. But I have to say that I do not see one utterly revolting face" (*PW,* 588). The same discourses of racial inferiority that Whitman had worked so hard to eliminate from his writings of the mid-fifties have reappeared only a decade later; attributes of violence, ugliness, and bestiality are now assigned to the same people whose beauty of form and unlimited potential he had once celebrated.

Whitman's 1867 poem "Ethiopia Saluting the Colors" portrays the "ancient" black woman in South Carolina as completely separate from the American experience. She stands and greets the colors of the invading northern army, but she herself is associated with her African origins rather than with any future of her race in this country. Ethiopia is twice referred to as "hardly human" (a strange inversion of Whitman's own formulation of the sacred human body in "I Sing the Body Electric"), and she is presented as a kind of caricature of the elderly black woman: wagging her "woolly-white" head, rolling her "darkling" eye, curtseying to the regiment, and speaking in an awkwardly rendered approximation of black dialect. The woman is both "fateful" and "blear"—epithets drawn from the conventional poetic register and without the personal identification present in Whitman's earlier poems about race and slavery.

In his lecture on the death of Abraham Lincoln, first delivered in 1879, Whitman links the event of Lincoln's death with the "absolute extirpation and erasure of slavery from the States." If Lincoln's assassination was the one historical event "incisive enough to mark with deepest cut, and mnemonize, this turbulent Nineteenth century of ours, (not only these States, but all over the political and social world)," then the parallel extinction of slavery that Lincoln helped bring about was "by far the greatest revolutionary step in the history of the United States" (*PW*, 509). Yet in his poem on the same subject, "When Lilacs Last in the Dooryard Bloom'd," Whitman addresses neither the issue of slavery nor Lincoln's accomplishment in ridding the nation of that institution. For another of Lincoln's elegists, William Cullen Bryant, the connection was clear:

> Thy task is done; the bond are free:
> We bear thee to an honored grave,
> Whose proudest monument shall be
> The broken fetters of the slave.[39]

But for Whitman, despite his awareness of the social and historical reality of Lincoln's legacy, the poetic experience of Lincoln's death was not so easily equated with its historical context. Only section 15 of the poem, with its vision of battles and corpses, reflects the precise historical moment shared by president and poet.

One result of Whitman's firsthand experience of a terribly costly war appears to have been a change in his conception of his own poetic project, and perhaps in his more general conception of the poet's task. The poet was no longer responsible for expressing the ills and angers of his society; he was responsible only for finding a lyric voice adequate to the commemoration of significant moments—moments in which he attempted to join his idiolectic vision with the prevailing discourse of the society at large, rather than find a way of transposing unheard, unacknowledged, or unknown discourses into an autonomous and destabilizing poetic voice. The original epigraph he attached to *Drum-Taps,* later included in the poem "The Wound-Dresser," expresses a change in his attitude toward the war, and at the same time toward his own poetry:

(Arous'd and angry, I'd thought to beat the alarum, and urge
   relentless war,
But soon my fingers fail'd me, my face droop'd and I resign'd
   myself,
To sit by the wounded and soothe them, or silently watch the
   dead;)

(4–6)

Whitman's response to the tragedy of Lincoln's death is not one of silence but of eloquent and rapturous singing. It is not entirely one of resignation either, but one of joy, love, and praise "for the sure-enwinding arms of cool-enfolding death." Whitman turns away not only from the painful vision of slavery and its complex aftermath but from the very discourse of direct personal and political engagement in which he had earlier expressed it. Here, it is as if he winds himself in the protective and "enfolding" arms of poetic tropes and language, rather than facing the raw discourse of his prewar poems. Whitman's entire vision becomes more deeply implicated in the transcendent rhetoric of western poetic expression. It is not the dead who suffer, Whitman suggests, but the living who remain to inherit both the sadness of loss and the problems left over when the dust of war has settled. Whitman did not forget slavery and the battle against its spread that had been such an important part of his prewar consciousness, but now his treatment of the subject would be confined to prose writings. A decade after his poem for Lincoln, he writes of the joint legacies of slavery and the war in "Origins of Attempted Succession" (1875–76): "The slavery contest is settled—and the war is long over—yet do not those putrid conditions, too many of them, still exist? still result in diseases, fevers, wounds—not of war and army hospitals—but the wounds and diseases of peace?" (*PW*, 430). Though we cannot be sure exactly what "wounds and diseases" Whitman is addressing, it is likely that he refers at least in part to the racial strife that continued to plague the Reconstruction South.[40] But while he still blames the "extreme-slaveholders, the Calhounites" for the start of the war, he is more interested in celebrating the ability of the United States to survive the war with its fundamental social, political, and constitutional structure intact.[41]

That Whitman *could* have written a poem like "I Sing the Body Electric" or passages like those in "Song of Myself" and "The Sleepers" after the war is doubtful; that he had no desire to write such poems or passages is clear. He would continue to champion "the cause of Liberty and Equality everywhere," but his principal idea would be to safeguard and encourage the growth and development of the republic, to soothe the tragedy of its wounds and not to point out its flaws. The attempt to include discourses of slavery, racial injustice, and even racial understanding in his evolving poetic project was a short-lived but extremely powerful experiment, one that helped form the core of his early success as the poet of *Leaves of Grass.* The representation of slavery in these poems was not part of a political program, not synonymous with any unified social or historical discourse. Whitman's attempt to enter into the subjectivity of the slave, and to find a means of representing poetically the unassimilable, unapproachable, and virtually invisible discourse of this subjectivity, is one of his central contributions to nineteenth-century literature and culture in America.

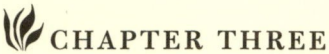 CHAPTER THREE

The Aesthetics of "Indifference": Whitman and the American City

You know it is a never-ending amusement and study and recreation for
me to ride a couple of hours on a pleasant afternoon on a Broadway
stage in this way. You see everything as you pass, a sort of living, endless
panorama . . . the thick crowd of carriages, stages, carts, hotel and
private coaches, and in fact all sorts of vehicles and many first-class
teams, mile after mile, and the splendor of such a great street and so
many tall, ornamental, noble buildings many of them of white marble,
and the gayety and motion on every side: you will not wonder how much
attraction all this is on a fine day, to a great loafer like me, who enjoys
so much seeing the busy world move by him, and exhibiting itself for his
amusement, while he takes it easy and just looks on and observes.
—Walt Whitman, letter to a conductor

Walt Whitman is the only major nineteenth-century American poet whose life and work are commonly associated with the city. Unlike the discourses surrounding slavery and abolitionism, which were absorbed to varying degrees by all of Whitman's contemporaries, the rapid growth and change of America's cities was a subject of surprisingly little interest to other poets. Edgar Allen Poe was certainly an urban writer—one who frequented the same New York as the young Whitman—but his poems are far removed from the contemporary urban environment in which he lived. Emerson and the other poets of the Boston circles expressed little interest in, and even less appreciation for, the modern city: the Transcendentalists looked to the higher spiritual ground of Nature for inspiration, and the fireside poets avoided urban subjects and settings with an almost pathological zeal, insisting upon the pastoral as the only appropriate mode for poetry.

This hostility toward anything connected with the city was not confined to poets and other literary writers but was generally symptomatic of nineteenth-century American intellectuals. In *The Intellectual versus the City*, Morton and Lucia White document the "spirit of America's reaction to the city," a reaction that was overwhelmingly negative.[1] According to the Whites, Whitman was one of the few dissenters against the "anti-urban roar produced in the national literary pantheon by Jefferson, Emerson, Thoreau, Hawthorne, Melville, Poe, Henry Adams, Henry James, and William Dean Howells," not to mention such later figures as Frank Norris, Theodore Dreiser, John Dewey, Jane Addams, Louis Sullivan, Frank Lloyd Wright, and Robert Park. America's attitude toward the city—one that ranged from nervousness, fear, and distrust to outright hostility—"might have been different if Whitman's magnanimity had predominated" (202).

For the most part, American poets of Whitman's time did not even bother to criticize the city; they simply ignored its existence. Such avoidance of urban themes and topoi represents more than an aesthetic choice: it is a defiant stand against and avoidance of contemporary social reality. The urban population increased more than one hundred fold between 1790 and 1890, with most of that increase occurring by 1860. During this entire period, the countryside was rapidly losing its populace as the city, the American metropolis, began to evolve into its present form (White and White, 212). Yet Griswold's influential anthology *Poets and Poetry of America* contained *no* poems concerned with the city, and Emerson's 1875 anthology *Parnassus* was hardly more evolved in this respect thirty years later. The division of Emerson's anthology into subjects including "Nature" and "Human Life" might suggest a place for a category of city poems, but the subheadings of "Human Life" avoid not only such sensitive urban topics as prostitution, poverty, and overcrowding but any mention of the city whatever. Domesticated themes such as "Home," "Love," "Manners," and "Holidays" hardly support the radical claims Emerson makes for poetry in his lectures and essays, claims which Whitman's poems had by that time already been fulfilling for two decades.[2]

Whitman's relationship to the city may have been an ambivalent one, but at least he was willing to engage the growing reality of urban existence, and the corresponding discourse of urbanization, in a way that other American poets were not. Let us begin by examining Whitman's relationship to the literary convention represented by the vast majority of nineteenth-century

American poetry—that of the pastoral—before engaging in a more thorough analysis of his response to its traditional opposite, the city itself.

The Open Road as New Urban Chronotope

As conventionally understood, the nostalgic pastoral mode of lyric poetry is antithetical to the social and ideological milieu of the city. In his reading of Whitman's *Drum-Taps* poem "Give Me the Splendid Silent Sun," Timothy Sweet demonstrates that although Whitman is well aware of such a convention, he insists on radically problematizing it. Whitman begins his poem with the Wordsworthian ideology of a soothing Nature apart from the city but then inverts that ideology in the second half. As Sweet comments: "The 'spontaneous songs' that the poet sings 'aside from the noise of the world' give way in the second half of the poem to an 'endless and noisy chorus'; the lyric voice is silenced by the wartime ideology of the 'world' represented by Manhattan."[3]

Such oppositions as lyric voice/active world and spontaneous songs/ noisy chorus are typical manifestations of the traditional split between the idiolectic mode of the pastoral lyric and the sociolectic mode associated with the city and historical events: in this case the exigencies of wartime. In his radical reversal of poetic allegiance, Whitman challenges the aesthetic distinction between the two discursive modes, forcefully denying any preference for one over the other. Where the poem begins with a Romantic desire to escape the city, it ends with the paradoxical gesture of embracing the very city that "hold[s] me enchain'd." "Keep your splendid silent sun"— Whitman now declares—"Give me faces and streets—give me the phantoms incessant and endless along the trottoirs!" (lines 20–24). In his enthusiastic evocation of Parisian cosmopolitanism—through the borrowing of the French word *trottoirs*—Whitman indicates a desire for the very aspects of the city that are shunned by a traditionally pastoral Romantic like Wordsworth. Whitman continues his celebration of the city in this same apostrophic mode:

> O such for me! O an intense life, full to repletion and varied!
> The life of the theatre, bar-room, huge hotel, for me!
> The saloon of the steamer! the crowded excursion for me! the torchlight
>   procession!
>
> (32–34)

Whitman celebrates the intensity, the variety of the crowd, the "trivial" differences that had confused and alienated Wordsworth in *The Prelude*. Whitman's city is that of Broadway, of the shows, and of those public places that function either as sites for the carnivalesque inversion of social distinctions ("the life of the theatre" or the "torchlight procession"), as democratic social spaces (the "bar-room" or the "saloon of the steamer"), or as spaces for the meeting and free interchange of the "en-masse" (the "huge hotel" or the "crowded excursion"). In contrast to the traditional sites of lyric poetry that Whitman evokes in the first half of the poem—orchard, open field, grape arbor, garden, woods—these urban locations seem to anticipate the fictional locales of realist novels by James, Howells, and Dreiser more than they imitate the rhetoric of the English Romantics and American fireside poets.

In "Forms of Time and Chronotope in the Novel," Bakhtin does not include a specific chronotope of the city, or of urban fiction, presumably because the city is too ubiquitous a setting in the European novel to be considered as a generic chronotope. However, he does discuss the closely related chronotope of "the road." As a site of encounter between people of varying national, religious, and socioeconomic backgrounds, the road is a chronotope in which to portray the collapse of "social distances": "People who are normally kept separate by social and spatial difference can accidentally meet; any contrast may crop up, the most various fates may collide and interweave with one another."[4] In one of Whitman's most clearly chronotopic poems, "Song of the Open Road" (1856), the poet depicts the road as a socially democratic and personally liberating space, one decidedly in opposition to the sterile and regulated confinement he attributes to life in the city. As opposed to "Song of Myself," where Whitman uses the openness of the catalogue form to undermine any distinction between city and country, "Song of the Open Road" maintains the opposition, at least on the surface. The poet is free to travel "wherever I choose," and he is free also from the various petty problems of everyday urban life. No longer forced to "ask" for his means of subsistence, the persona has suddenly become self-sufficient and self-reliant:

> Henceforth I ask not good-fortune, I myself am good-fortune,
> Henceforth I whimper no more, postpone no more, need nothing,
> Done with indoor complaints, librairies, querulous criticisms,
> Strong and content I travel the open road.

> (4–7)

In its denial both of the temporal pressures of city life (the speaker "post-pone[s] no more") and of the spatial restrictions the urban environment imposes ("loos'd of limits and imaginary lines"), the poem reflects another aspect of Bakhtin's chronotope—that of the fusion of time and space that the "open road" allows: "Time, as it were, fuses with space and flows in it (forming the road); this is the source of the rich metaphorical expansion on the image of the road as a course: 'the course of life,' 'to set out on a new course,' 'the course of history' and so on; varied and multi-leveled are the ways in which road is turned into a metaphor, but its fundamental pivot is the flow of time" (*Dialogic Imagination,* 244).

In Whitman's poem, as in Bakhtin's analysis of the novel, the road contains the "traces and signs of time's passage" and the "markers of the [writer's] era" (*Dialogic Imagination,* 244). In the second section of the poem, Whitman begins a search for such traces and markers: "You road I enter upon and look around, I believe you are not all that is here / I believe that much unseen is also here." Like Don Quixote in Cervantes's novel (one of Whitman's favorite books and one he considered a model of "priceless value" for American culture), the poet uses the road to discover the sociocultural heterogeneity of his country, including what Bakhtin calls the "social exotic," or the "dregs" of society. For Whitman, the lesson of the road is "the profound lesson of reception." He will learn to receive all people into his company, and into his poem's textual space, without distinguishing them by either "preference" or "denial":

> The black with his woolly head, the felon, the diseas'd, the
>   illiterate person, are not denied;
> The birth, the hasting after the physician, the beggar's tramp,
>   the drunkard's stagger, the laughing party of the mechanics,
> The escaped youth, the rich person's carriage, the fop, the
>   eloping couple,
> The early market-man, the hearse, the moving of furniture into
>   the town, the return back from the town,
> They pass, I also pass, any thing passes, none can be interdicted,
> None but are accepted, none but shall be dear to me.
>
> (19–24)

Whitman's radical contention that everything that passes or has passed him on the road is not only "accepted," but "dear to me," is a central aspect of his poetic stance in the first three editions of *Leaves of Grass.* In these early editions, as in "Give Me the Splendid Silent Sun," Whitman refuses to make the conventional distinctions upon which post-Romantic poetic discourse has come to rest. Whitman's catalogue of social outcasts engages the various discourses of distinction: racial ("the black"), legal ("the felon"), medical ("the diseas'd"), educational ("the illiterate person"), economic ("the beggar"), and behavioral ("the drunkard"). They are presented in a democratic mix along with the "rich person's carriage" and the "laughing party of the mechanics." The poet's embrace of this entire class of misfits, and his refusal to judge them either through moral "interdiction" or through aesthetic hierarchization, is consistent with his claim in the 1855–56 notebooks for universal "eligibility": "I, you, any one [is] eligible to the conditions or attributes or advantages of any being, no matter who" (*N*, 8).

Importantly, Whitman's vision of the open road does not participate in the pastoral impulse of literary escapism, although it does end up creating a kind of utopian social space. Whitman's road remains a powerfully social chronotope and not merely a pastoral site where the personal idiolect of the poet can be developed. The poem places Whitman in the curiously liminal space generally reserved for the fictional genre: the "open road" is a topos neither of the city nor of the pastoral world that serves as its conventional alternative. Rather than a regressive turn to the traditional dichotomies—city and country, urban and pastoral, prosaic and poetic, public and personal, sociolectic and idiolectic—the open road represents a new opposition in poetic discourse, one not merely between two types of environments and the linguistic structures needed to represent them, but between two opposing modes of sociopolitical experience.

Whitman appears to realize that the stakes of such an opposition—traditionally associated with the novel rather than with a lyric poetry based on the pastoral metaphor—must be explained to the reader, Whitman's "Camerado." With the repeated interjection of the encouraging cry "Allons!" Whitman alternately tempts, warns, lectures, and cajoles the reader to join him in his quest for a more fulfilling life, as if the forces of inertia and tradition could be overcome simply by the energy of his plea. He invites only the young, healthy, and sober to come with him on the road; unlike a panacean escape from all the ills of urban society, this voyage will require a "trial" of courage and endurance.

In part, Whitman's poem calls for the kind of disengagement from the dominant systems of urban culture that Leo Marx links to the pastoral impulse in the works of American authors like Thoreau and Melville.[5] Marx's essay is primarily concerned with the oppositional relationship in nineteenth-century American literature between the use of the pastoral mode and structures of social (urban) power. Marx's analysis of the pastoral suggests that the opposition between urban and pastoral in American literature can be understood in terms of those structures of power associated with social and cultural hegemony. Marx views the pastoral mode as an expression of the kind of cultural ambivalence that characterizes artists in world capitals, especially at moments when political and economic regimes are reaching the height of their power:

> One common feature of these historical situations has been the presence of artists, writers, and intellectuals with an inherently ambiguous relationship to the system of power and wealth represented by the capital. They are likely to be affiliated with, and in some measure beholden to, those in power, yet at the same time they also are prone to a feeling of estrangement from the system—a feeling of moral disquiet or disapproval arising from the discrepancy between their principles and the prevailing mode of domination or, at any rate, and for whatever conscious or unconscious reasons, an ambivalence issuing in fantasies or (less often) acts of disengagement. (62)

Whether or not we can locate Whitman's anxieties in "Song of the Open Road" in the systems of power and wealth that midcentury New York represented, it is clear that the poem is based on just such fantasies of disengagement as Marx describes. Certainly Whitman was well aware of the glaring discrepancies that marred his city: discrepancies, for example, between the wealthy and fashionable downtown areas and the deteriorating urban environment of the masses. Although he at times celebrated the glories of Broadway, he also felt a twinge of ambivalence about the luxury and privilege of the few at the expense of so many. Ten years earlier he had written in the *Daily Eagle* (September 1846) of the "world famed" shops along Broadway, their windows containing "all kinds of dazzling and expensive knick-knacks—bracelets, whose worth is equivalent to a comfortable house and lot—necklaces that balance an editor's ten years' salary—cameos on which the genius of art has taken pride in substantializing gorgeous thoughts—finger rings of rare worth and brilliancy." But "alas!" he adds in a later editorial (November 1846), "what a prodigious amount of means and time might be much better . . . employed than as they are here!" Whitman's vision of the open road is one that implicitly rejects the capitalist system of urban economic reality, a system that involves "balancing" the value of a diamond necklace against the modest pay of a newspaper editor, or the even lower pay of a manual laborer or a seamstress in a factory. Rather than "heap[ing] up what is call'd riches," the traveler along Whitman's road will "scatter with lavish hand" whatever he can "earn or achieve"; the "old smooth prizes" of economic privilege will be replaced by the "rough new prizes" that are awarded regardless of social position or economic accomplishment. In Bourdieu's terms, Whitman's poem flouts the various forms of social, economic, and cultural distinction: all mental and spiritual trappings of the culture are rejected (arts, government, philosophies, religions, "formules," and the literary triumvirate of "arguments, similes, rhymes"), as are the material possessions that culture makes possible—"laid-up stores," convenient homes, and even loving friends and families. Whitman's new order of the road functions as an ironic catalogue through which he can critique the traditional economic order of labor and capital, as becomes clear in section 13:

> To see no possession but you may possess it, enjoying all without
>   labor or purchase, abstracting the feast yet not abstracting one
>   particle of it,
> To take the best of the farmer's farm and the rich man's elegant
>   villa, and the chaste blessings of the well-married couple, and
>   the fruits of orchards and flowers of gardens,
> To take to your use out of the compact cities as you pass through,
> To carry buildings and streets with you afterward wherever you go,
> To gather the minds of men out of their brains as you encounter
>   them, to gather the love out of their hearts . . .
>
> (174–77)

The new social order represented by the road goes beyond the rejection of capitalist economics to constitute a critique of all social, economic, geographic, or personal exclusivity—in short, all forms of distinction. The traveler is invited to partake not only of the wealth created by successful farmers and industrialists but also of the natural bounty of fruit and flowers, of the love generated by a married couple, of the buildings and streets of a city, and even of the thoughts and emotions of individuals. Whitman's most radical gesture in the poem is that of a total erasure of the line between public and private spheres.

To what extent does Whitman's poem and its chronotope of the open road mediate between pastoral and urban modes? Certainly the road is associated with a kind of idiolectic expression: it allows for the composition of "free poems," it expresses the poet's inner nature "better than I can express myself," and it provides room for the "great personal deed." But like so many of Whitman's poems, "Song of the Open Road" appears simultaneously to reject the notion of the solitary or private individual, the "simple separate person." Nor is the poem the site of a pastoral logic to be read in opposition to an urban logic, at least in any conventional sense. In the catalogue of the "great Companions" that makes up section 12, elements normally associated with pastoral discourse are interwoven with those of urban or social reality:

> Trusters of men and women, observers of cities, solitary toilers,
> Pausers and contemplators of tufts, blossoms, shells on the shore,
> Dancers at wedding-dances, kissers of brides, tender helpers of
>   children, bearers of children,
> Soldiers of revolts, standers by gaping graves, lowerers-down of
>   coffins . . .

(154–57)

Whitman moves quickly here from one register to another, as he does throughout the poem: a line evoking the social world of cities and work is followed by a personal, lyrical line of natural description (even employing the alliterative effect of "shells" and "shore"), which in turn moves to a pairing of life (social, active, procreative) and death (solitary, static, and always, for Whitman, charged with lyrical intensity).

Thus it is difficult to situate Whitman's poem or its mode of address within any given genre. At times it reads like a manifesto or call to arms (suggested by the repeated exclamations of "Allons!" and "Listen!"), at other times like a philosophical lyric (sections 6–8), or a poem of social criticism (section 13); at still other moments we find the structure of the conversation poem (section 4), and, at the end, of the love poem. The poem's setting is generically ambiguous as well. Much as Whitman appears to favor the natural elements of earth, sky, clouds, trees, and ocean over the interior settings of houses, libraries, schools, courts, and lecture halls, it is not the physical reality of the city that he finds oppressive (as with Blake's "charter'd street" or Wordsworth's "Babel din") but the way in which physical spaces are used to restrict personal or cultural expression.

In lines 193–205, the poet provides trenchant commentary on the kind of hypocrisy the urban lifestyle represents in midcentury America, a hypocrisy that he is determined to "expose":

Behold through you as bad as the rest,
Through the laughter, dancing, dining, supping, of people,
Inside of dresses and ornaments, inside of those wash'd and
    trimm'd faces,
Behold a secret loathing and despair.

No husband, no wife, no friend, trusted to hear the confession.
Another self, a duplicate of every one, skulking and hiding it
    goes,
Formless and wordless through the streets of the cities, polite
    and bland in the parlors,
In the cars of railroads, in steamboats, in the public assembly,
Home to the houses of men and women, at the table, in the bed-
    room, everywhere,
Smartly attired, countenance smiling, form upright, death
    under the breast-bones, hell under the skull-bones,
Under the broadcloth and gloves, under the ribbons and artifi-
    cial flowers,
Keeping fair with the customs, speaking not a syllable of itself,
Speaking of any thing else but never of itself.

Here the city acts as the first link in a synecdochic chain of enclosed spaces, all associated in terms of their capacity to hide the truth. The city's streets enclose individual houses, which in turn enclose dining rooms and bed-rooms, themselves the enclosures for human bodies and the trappings (clothes, jewelry, and makeup) that isolate them still more deeply, and that emphasize their distinctions from one another. Even the face itself, the skin and skull-bone, must be peeled away to reach the underlying malaise of the city dweller.

This scene, along with the poem "Faces" of a year earlier, is as close as Whitman comes to depicting the "Gemorrah" he sometimes felt New York to be.[6] Although his critique of the false distinctions of bourgeois urban life is far less focused than that Veblen would articulate in the later part of the century, Whitman does appear to anticipate what Theodor Adorno refers to as Veblen's analysis of the "pseudo-individuality" of material life. The parlors, ornaments, and "trimm'd faces" of Whitman's city dwellers are an early version of what Veblen would find: the "sham uniqueness" of objects, "the contradiction between their form and their function."[7]

Along with this ambivalence concerning the city, "Song of the Open Road" expresses a deep-seated cultural ambivalence. The remainder of this chapter will explore these interrelated forms of ambivalence in Whitman's writing, and it will attempt to account for his relationship both to the emergent social and literary discourses surrounding the new American city and to his own experience of the city as the primary background for his poems.

Urban Poetry and Urban Distinctions: Whitman and Wordsworth

As we have seen in previous chapters, the process of reconciling opposites and of denying both social and aesthetic distinctions had emerged by 1855 as a central part of Whitman's poetic. The same process is even more particularly relevant to his poems dealing with the city. The city provides the most extreme example of heteroglossic discourses; it allows any poet willing to confront it "face to face," as Whitman is, to break down many of the traditional distinctions by which social and poetic discourses have been defined. In what James Machor calls Whitman's "urban pastoralism," the poet achieves a destabilization of traditional dichotomies on several levels: moral (goodness versus wickedness), social (individual versus community) and literary-aesthetic (pastoral versus urban). Not content with Bryant's discourse of lyric pastoralism—a discourse Bryant cannot abandon even in addressing the city—Whitman searches throughout *Leaves of Grass* for an expression of the urban-pastoral ideal, a synthesis that would allow him to bypass the traditional bipolar city/country opposition central to the aesthetic and ideological conception of his literary contemporaries. In doing so, Whitman achieves a new space (at least in American literature) for his urban persona. According to Machor, he will be neither progressive prophet nor social planner but a poetic artist transcendent of those contingent realities: "Overleaping sociopolitical interests, Whitman announces organic cities that exist by virtue of linguistic manipulation and so inhere in language alone."[8]

I am interested in examining Machor's assumptions in light of my own interest in Whitman's dialogue with the sociolect.[9] One apparent parallel to the urban/pastoral dichotomy, suggested by Machor's equation of linguistic manipulation with urban transfiguration, is the relationship between the sociolect—as represented by the language of the masses—and the idiolect, as represented by the poet's physical and linguistic escape from urban reality. Various commentators have pointed to the conflict in American literature between a belief in nature as the topos of the Romantic idiolect and the anti-pastoral urban scene as the site of everyday life, material progress, and social problems. I would like to address more specifically the role of the city as the site of the sociolect, and the city street as the physical representation of a sociolectic crossing where the language of society can enter the poetic text as the poet encounters the masses and as he combines different linguistic registers. In this respect, I differ somewhat with Machor's reading: rather than "overleaping sociopolitical interests" in an attempt to find a poetic discourse that inheres in language alone, Whitman harnesses sociopolitical forces. He encounters the city both as a site of sociohistorical and sociolinguistic reality and as a possible site of private, idiolectic, or self-consciously literary reflection.

Whitman's city also functions importantly as the space in which all forms of distinction—including that between the poet and the masses who inhabit the city—can be swept away by the poet's active involvement in the continual flow of urban life, a flux of social, personal, and physical existence given its most potent metaphorical treatment in the "flood-tide" of "Crossing Brooklyn Ferry." Whitman's approach to the city—at least that most characteristic of his city poems and passages—can easily be contrasted with that of a poet like Wordsworth, for whom the experience of the city is one fraught with the "danger of the crowd." Wordsworth makes little attempt to identify with the inhabitants of the city—the "weary throng" or "endless stream of men" which makes its "Babel din"; for him, the city streets are precisely the place in which cultural and interpersonal distinctions are most apparent. In book 7 of the 1805 *Prelude*, where Wordsworth describes his "Residence in London," he finds himself overwhelmed by the sights, sounds, and faces he encounters. His reaction foregrounds a discomfort with his own feeling of difference from the members of the crowd and with his inability to understand the human soul that lies behind the faces he sees. Wordsworth emphasizes his sense of fear and isolation in characterizing the city both as a "prison" from which he must be set free in order to write poetry (book 1) and as an "enemy" that can only be escaped by leaving the crowded street for a "sequestered nook, / still as a sheltered place when winds blow loud" (book 7). With each successive urban encounter in the poem, Wordsworth feels himself increasingly alienated from those around him. In the climactic passage that ends book 7, he is "oppressed" by the fact that "the face of every one that passes me is a mystery," and he can find no solace in the Babel-like carnivalesque of the city:

All moveables of wonder from all parts
Are here, albinos, painted Indians, dwarfs,
The horse of knowledge, and the learned pig,
The stone-eater, the man that swallows fire,
Giants, ventriloquists, the invisible girl,
The bust that speaks and moves its goggling eyes,
The waxwork, clockwork, all the marvellous craft
Of modern Merlins, wild beasts, puppet-shows,
All out-o-th'-way, far-fetched, perverted things,
All freaks of Nature, all Promethean thoughts
Of man—his dulness, madness, and their feats,
All jumbled up together to make up
This parliament of monsters. Tents and booths
Meanwhile—as if the whole were one vast mill—
Are vomiting, receiving, on all sides,
Men, women, three-years' children, babes in arms.[10]

In a catalogue that also includes a "silver-collared negro with his timbrel," as well as "buffoons" and street performers of various kinds, Wordsworth demonstrates his repulsion from the sheer complexity of differences that he encounters. Read against the backdrop of a poem like Whitman's "I Sing the Body Electric," Wordsworth's response is one that privileges a certain kind of decorum and socially ordained sanity over the democratic and decentering "jumble" represented by the racially, physically, and socially marginal. Blacks and Indians, dwarfs and giants are put in the same category as pigs, horses, wax figures, and puppet shows: all are members of a "parliament of monsters," perversions not of nature but of Nature—that principle of harmony and of orderly distinction embraced by Romantic ideology.

Wordsworth concludes that the city is made a kind of Hell by the multitude of "trivial" differences that it contains, differences that "have no law, no meaning, and no end," and that are ultimately responsible for a world "undistinguishable . . . to men." Unable to accept the tremendous variety of human types and of social layers that constitutes the city—to embrace, as Whitman does, the "whole swarm of its inhabitants"—Wordsworth falls back on God and the "spirit of Nature" to guide him, to give "order and relation" to the chaos he finds.

Wordsworth's description of London in *The Prelude*—one that emphasizes distinctions, particularly between the "sensitive" poet himself and the chaotic urban scene—(or, to place it in a socioeconomic context, between the educated man of means and the carnivalesque participants in lower-class life)—is far more typical a literary response to the city than is Whitman's. As Raymond Williams documents in *The Country and the City,* the confusion and ambivalence Wordsworth expresses about the city are intensified in the reaction of later writers like Carlyle and Thomas Hardy, who find in the experience of urban life a central paradox: "that in the great city itself, the very place and agency—or so it would seem, of collective consciousness, it is an absence of common feeling, an excessive subjectivity, that seems to be characteristic."[11] If we read "collective consciousness" as something like the sociolect—a shared language of the street—the modern city seems increasingly to be atomized by its growing size and industrialization. Rather than resulting in a greater homogeneity of type, language, or purpose, says Williams, the increased density and complexity of urban relationships causes "a social dissolution in the very process of aggregation" (*Country and City,* 216). Engels would describe in 1844 the "hundreds of thousands of all classes and all ranks crowding past each other" in "unfeeling isolation," and Carlyle commented in 1831 on the extreme separateness of people "in their little cells, divided by partitions of brick or board." Unlike smaller urban units such as the village or town, the large city is "a huge aggregate of little systems, each of which is again a small anarchy, the members of which do not work together, but scramble against each other" (*Country and City,* 215). Thus, as Wordsworth demonstrates, the city and the multiplicity of its component discourses cannot be contained within the poem, at least not as conventionally conceived. Whitman's poetic contemporaries like Arnold, Clough, and Tennyson shared Wordsworth's prevailing view of the city as inhospitable to the poetic sensibility and useful only as a negative pole in the poetic process. The fictional form of novels like those of Dickens and Victor Hugo was more successful in addressing the heteroglossia of urban life than lyric poetry had been, but novelists could not hope any more than poets to read all the various complex relationships within even a small subsection of the city.

The urban metropolis, an archetype in Western literary culture since Gilgamesh, a site of social and historical dynamics, is also inscribed within a textual dimension that is at once spatial (topographic, toponymic) and verbal (intertextual) in nature. As Priscilla Ferguson remarks, a "reading" of the modern city "requires the reader to decipher the palimpsest of urban space and to integrate the many layers of physical, social, historical, and symbolic associations that determine identity within the city."[12] Urban poetry responds to the same stimuli as its fictional counterpart: changing frames of reference and an unruly density of both cultural and linguistic material. France had Paris, England had London, and Italy had Rome, all with their long and complex intertextual histories, but Whitman's America lacked a city with the same kind of historical or symbolic complexities. Cities of any significant size were a recent phenomenon in North America; at midcentury only New York, with its total metropolitan population of about a million (and the city itself with half a million), was a large and cosmopolitan city in the European sense of the word. This difference is reflected in Whitman's literary inheritance. Where Whitman was the first significant city poet in America (and the only one until the generation of W. C. Williams, T. S. Eliot, and Hart Crane half a century later), poets had been writing about their Old World capitals for centuries: we need only think of the Rome of Propertius and Catullus, the London of Donne, Dryden, Pope, Johnson, Blake, and Wordsworth, or the Paris of Villon, Baudelaire, and Rimbaud. Whitman's own century produced a greater number of European urban poets than any previous period, a development that was hardly surprising given the demographic changes in countries like England, France, and Germany. Raymond Williams identifies the crucial point at the middle of the century when "the urban population of England exceeded the rural population: the first time in human history that this had ever been so, anywhere" (*Country and City*, 217). Compared to New York, explosively bustling as it seemed to Bryant, Poe, and Whitman, the greatest European cities were still larger: London was five to six times the size of Manhattan in 1850 (nearly three million), and even the London of Blake and Wordsworth was far larger than Whitman's city. Baudelaire's midcentury Paris, with a million inhabitants, was not only more populous but also more physically concentrated than New York. As a result of the increased importance of urban life in European national cultures, more and more of the important poets were turning to the city: in addition to Blake, Wordsworth, and Baudelaire, we find poets like Holderlin, Hugo, and Rimbaud on the European continent and Tennyson, Arnold, and Clough in England.

Yet the American city, and especially New York, with its increasingly important commerce and its rapidly growing immigrant population, also provided an intensely stimulating and as yet unexplored environment for a poet who, like Whitman, could fully appreciate the variety of its physical and discursive texture. One important fact distinguishes New York from its European counterparts. As opposed to the more ethnically and linguistically homogeneous cities of Europe, New York offered a richer density of languages and cultures. In a notebook entry from the late 1850s, Whitman mentions a lecture of "peculiar local interest" concerning "the great number of languages spoken daily in the city of New York, the classification amounting to no less *than eighty different languages* (not dialects), in constant use in the city" (*DN*, 676). He goes on to note that "no city in the world can furnish a parallel to this number of spoken languages." Later in the same notebook, Whitman emphasizes the "plentiful contributions of foreign words" (*DN*, 679) to American language; he notes that as many as half the words in current use may be of foreign origin. Though it is impossible to know with any certainty where Whitman's unusually diverse poetic vocabulary originates, it is certain that his proximity to the many foreign populations of New York during his formative years as a writer enriched his use of language. The interest in foreign words evinced in his notebooks and his liberal use of foreign borrowings in his poems are the most obvious manifestations of such cultural diversity; I would also venture the more hypothetical claim that Whitman's urban "text" provided his poems with a wider range of discursive possibilities on all levels—theme, vocabulary, and syntax—than did the pastoral or semiurban landscapes of his New England contemporaries. Whitman's poetic orientation would be dialogic or heteroglossic rather than univocal, stable, and monologic.

But if Whitman's American city contained a linguistic density greater than that of European capitals, his literary inheritance hardly provided him with a model for writing a city poem. Because Whitman would not discover Blake's work until the late 1860s, or Baudelaire's until 1875, and his exposure to Tennyson and the other Victorians came primarily after the first editions of *Leaves*, Whitman's nineteenth-century literary intertext for a literature of the city—with the possible exception of Wordsworth—would have been exclusively that provided by novels. Michael Cowan may be correct in his assertion that Emerson preceded Whitman in attempting "to assimilate meaningfully the idea of the city into his total poetic vision"; but Emerson's version of the American city, or "City of the West," was more metaphorical than real.[13] While Emerson, like Bryant, spent much of his life in cities, he also shared Bryant's antipathy for the urban experience (and especially for New York). Despite his claim that the poet should visit "without fear the factory, the railroad, and the wharf," Emerson produced even less than Bryant in the way of urban poetry.[14]

The Urban Intertext: City Poems and City Fiction

Of all the fireside poets, only Bryant spent a significant part of his life living and working in New York City. From 1825, when he accepted a job as assistant editor of the *New York Review and Atheneum Magazine*, until his death in 1878, Bryant passed at least half the year in his town house in Manhattan. Unlike Whitman, however, Bryant was not an urban poet; in fact, the poetic responses of Bryant and Whitman to the city could not have been more different. Where the city served Whitman as a central source of subject matter and even as a model for poetic composition, it seems to have held little interest for Bryant as a literary topos. Whitman would view his *Leaves of Grass* as the literary embodiment of the city itself (comparing his poems to a "great city"); he would conceive of the book of poems as "arising out of my life in Brooklyn and New York from 1838 to 1853, absorbing a million people . . . with an intimacy, an eagerness, an abandon, probably never equalled" (*WOT,* 43). Whitman's catalogues are themselves a formal embodiment of the radically diverse and constantly changing urban environment. Bryant's *Poetical Works*, on the other hand, contains only two poems that deal directly with the city or with urban life: "Hymn of the City" (1830) and "The Crowded Street" (1843). Even these two poems, rare as they are in their day, are still far from anticipating the identification with and celebration of the American metropolis that can be found in Whitman's city poems.

"Hymn of the City," despite its title, is less a paean to urban life or to the cosmopolitan glories of American civilization than an affirmation of God's presence in nature and city alike. In the poem, written as a companion piece to the better known "Forest Hymn," Bryant beholds the steps of the "Almighty"—"here, amidst the crowd / Through the great city rolled." Despite the superficial trappings of a city poem, however, the primary discursive mode establishes no break from that of Romantic nature poetry:

> Thy golden sunshine comes
> From the round heavens, and on their dwellings lies
>   And lights their inner homes;
> For them thou fill'st with air the unbounded skies,
>   And givest them the stores
> Of ocean, and the harvests of its shores.[15]

The poem ends with an extended simile comparing the "numberless throng" of the city to other natural images: the "resounding sea" as it strikes the shore and the "rainy tempest" which incessantly speaks God's name.

In "The Crowded Street," a somewhat more complex poem, Bryant adopts the stance of social commentator, witnessing in the faces of the city's "flitting figures" various urban histories: children in their "happy homes"; the youth with "dreams of greatness"; the "eager" yet dishonest tradesman; the sick, dying, and "famine-struck"; and those profligates who "hide in dens of shame." Such an urban catalogue would seem almost worthy of Whitman, but Bryant's conclusions fall far short of Whitman's optimistic social vision. Bryant can only synthesize the various images of urban life through the evocation of a higher power; only divine grace can ultimately counteract the random forces at work in the crowded street of the city:

> Each, where his tasks or pleasures call,
> They pass, and heed each other not.
> There is who heeds, and holds them all,
> In His large love and boundless thought.
>
> These struggling tides of life that seem
> In wayward, aimless course to tend,
> Are eddies of the mighty stream
> That rolls to its appointed end.
> (*Poetical Works*, 208)

Bryant's poem reflects two widely held assumptions about the American urban experience. The first is that the city is best understood as the site of two opposing tendencies—what urban historian Edward Spann calls the "progressive" (happy homes, dreams of greatness, eager workers) and the "wicked" ("dens of shame"). The second—a corollary of the first—is that human society, and the very rationalism that made possible the planning, construction, and material progress of the city, are helpless in controlling the dark forces unleashed within a large metropolis. The "struggling tides of life" that appear to Bryant to move with "wayward, aimless course" include disease, dishonesty, hunger, isolation, and various forms of physical and spiritual deprivation, all of which lead either to death or to sinful and decadent behavior.

Bryant's attitude toward the city is a perfect reflection of the contemporary sociolect; it mirrors the hegemonic view of midcentury New York. "As the metropolis grew," writes Spann, "so also grew the feeling that it had become two disturbingly different cities": a "dynamic commercial center of progressive civilization" and a "darker self . . . inhabited by the desperate and the deprived—by idlers, drunks, thieves, whores, and other clogs on the wheels of progress."[16] It was this latter version of the city that most often found its way into the popular and sentimental literature, which by and large portrayed New York as a city "dominated by the institutions of vice and dissipation, especially by the omnipresent drinking places—the liquor groceries, porter houses, taverns, and fancy saloons—with their attendant hordes of disreputable loungers, drunks, and fashionable sots" (249). Such sensationalizing accounts of urban vice indicated the most obvious manifestations of New York's problems, but they also hinted at the serious underlying social issues—overcrowding, poverty, violence, and lack of adequate educational and health care facilities. At the same time that New York was the largest and most economically vital city in America, it was also the city with the fastest growing population (much of its growth coming through immigration) and the highest mortality rate, twice the national average. Between 1840 and 1860, the population of New York's metropolitan area grew to 1.6 million, more than twice the size of its closest competitor, Philadelphia.[17] No wonder that the city's growth, and its problems, seemed out of control (or at least out of human control) to many onlookers. Both of Bryant's city poems rely on forceful, even violent imagery to convey the surging and yet cramped feeling of the urban masses: struggling tides, the resounding sea, the rainy tempest, the "choking" streets, the "sweeping" and "restless" crowd.

Bryant's appeal to divine order at the end of his poem parallels the turn among city leaders to various types of Christian reforms. The Children's Aid Society, New York Juvenile Asylum, Association for Improving the Condition of the Poor (AICP), New York Sunday School Union, and the Five Points Mission all appeared in the city at around midcentury and were joined in their local efforts by such national organizations as the Bible Society, Home Missionary Society, and Temperance Union. Yet despite all these efforts, the Protestant crusade to reform the wicked elements of New York life was inevitably a losing battle, for reasons that were demographic as much as moral or spiritual. As Spann concludes: "Probably the wisest and strongest effort would not have conquered the subterranean city, if only because commercial New York attracted a vast rootless, floating population, much of which had already been apprenticed to the wicked life. The continued deluge of European immigrants after 1845 likewise assured the persistence of poverty and slums" (276).

Other poets, on the rare occasions when cities appeared in their poems, appear to have shared Bryant's socially pessimistic view of the city as an essentially corrupting force. In "The Cities of the Plain," Whittier comments on the contemporary urban situation only obliquely, through the allegory of Sodom and Gemorrah. Without even Bryant's relatively superficial understanding of the dynamics of contemporary city life, Whittier can only speak in symbolic terms, as he evokes the "proud ones of Sodom" feasting in their banquet hall after they have been warned to join the "righteous" in leaving the city:

> Where the shrines of foul idols were lighted on high,
> And wantonness tempted the lust of the eye;
> Midst rights of obsceneness, strange, loathsome, abhorred,
> The blasphemer scoffed at the name of the Lord.[18]

In the poem's final scene, "palace and bower" are destroyed by flames, as the "red ruin" of the burned city falls on those proud sinners below.

Whether or not Whittier's poem is a conscious commentary on the dangers of contemporary urban existence—among them the unchecked growth of "vast rootless" populations as documented by Spann—it is an indication of the way in which the city becomes a symbolic site for the various moral ills that appear to plague midcentury American society. In other poems, like "Moloch in State Street" and "The Prisoners of Naples," Whittier continues to associate the urban landscape with vice and suffering. In the latter poem, he complains of the treatment of the city's prisoners, who are "Shut from the light, the greenness and the sky, / From the cool waters and the pleasant breeze, / The smell of flowers and the shade of summer trees" (*Complete Poetical Works*, 159). Implicit in the rhetoric of Whittier's poems of social reform—and typical of mid-nineteenth-century American poetry—is the opposition of a discourse of nature to a discourse of the city. The pastoral discourse of nature is presented as a universally positive or redemptive force, which in itself can right the injustices done by man in his social, urban environment. The pastoral is the site of the poet's personal and solitary communion with the beauties of the world and ultimately with God. When Whittier compares his own situation to that of the prisoners, it is the language of nature that he finds most important to his own sense of well-being:

To me the pine-woods whisper; and for me
You river, winding through its vales of calm,
By greenest banks, with asters purple-starred,
And gentian bloom and golden-rod made gay,
Flows down in silent gladness to the sea,
Like a pure spirit to its great reward!

In Whitman's early poem "Young Grimes," published in the *Long Island Democrat* in 1840, he appears to have accepted the discursive stance of Bryant, Whittier, and their contemporaries. Whitman warns of the dangers of urban life and proposes the ideal of a rural environment in which to lead a "tranquil life / Unvexed by guilt or pain." The poem's title character has rejected all the temptations of the city, including its fashions, and has chiefly avoided its nether regions:

He does not spend more than he earns
    In dissipation's round;
But shuns with care those dangerous rooms
    Where sin and vice abound.

(*EPF*, 4)

If the young Whitman is sincere in his depiction of the contented rural life of Grimes and in his admonition to the reader to "Leave the wide city's noisy din / The busy haunts of men," then his attitude toward the city must undergo a sea change before he can write the great city poems of *Leaves of Grass*. Though an argument can be made that "Young Grimes" is intended as an ironic parody of popular reform literature, its message and tone are consistent with those of some of his editorials in the *New York Aurora* of two years later and with the depiction in his early fiction of the city as a place of corruption. Emory Holloway has remarked a "gentle irony" in the poem's negative portrayal of a type resembling Whitman himself at the time: "He sports no cane—no whiskers wears, / Nor lounges o'er the town" (*EPF*, 4). But it is difficult to know whether the irony here is directed at the poet himself or at the overly prudish standards of decorum encouraged by contemporary reformers. The fact that the poem was a direct imitation of the very popular "Old Grimes," by Albert Gorton Greene, would add credence to an ironic reading, as would certain stanzas in the poem that are hard to read as entirely serious (especially stanzas 3–5). Thomas Brasher reads the poem as "humorously genial" (*EPF*, 3), but a more broadly comic or even parodic reading would be more consistent with Whitman's later attitudes toward excessive moralism and behavioral constraint. Since we know relatively little about the Whitman of 1840, it is difficult to determine the precise intentions of his early poems; however, this poem's use of the prevailing sociolect (whether serious or parodistic) is clearly in marked contrast to his invention of a new mode of city poetry in *Leaves of Grass*.

If America had failed to produce a poet of the city by midcentury, it had produced plenty of urban fiction. In the decade before the publication of *Leaves of Grass,* the quantity and popularity of urban novels, especially about New York, were remarkable. In the bibliography to her study of American city fiction, *Sodoms in Eden*, Janis Stout lists no less than forty popular and sensational novels about New York, Philadelphia, New Orleans, Boston, Lowell, and San Francisco that appeared in the decade of 1844 to 1854. Adrienne Siegel counts a total of 340 urban novels published in the United States between 1840 and 1860 (a rate of nearly twenty a year), as compared to only thirty-eight in the sixty-five-year period 1774–1839. In fact, it is fair to assume that the city novel was the most popular fictional genre of the period, far outstripping the frontier novel of westward expansion and exploration.[19] Published by such popular writers as John S. Adams, Osgood Bradbury, George Foster, Henri Foster, Joseph Ingraham, Sylvester Judd, E. Z. C. Judson (Ned Buntline), Cornelius Matthews, Peter Myers, Solon Robinson, Elizabeth Smith, George Thompson, Mary Torrey, and Metter Victor as well as by more literary authors like Lydia Child, Maria Cummins, George Lippard, Catherine Sedgwick, and William Gilmore Simms (not to mention a host of anonymous scribblers), these books carried titles like *Sam Squab, the Boston Boy, Le Bonita Cigarena; or, The Beautiful Cigar-Vender! A Tale of New York, City Crimes; or, Life in New York and Boston,* and several variants on the themes of *Mysteries* and *Miseries.* Although they display a high degree of generic similarity, the novels vary somewhat in subject matter and approach. They include romances (often tinged with the gothic), cautionary tales of "real life" in the city, and sentimental stories of the poor girl or boy made good.

One of the most successful of the midcentury pulp writers was George Foster, a New York journalist who produced such works of pseudosocial commentary as *New York in Slices, by an Experienced Carver; New York by Gas-Light;* and *Fifteen Minutes around New York* as well as the novel *Celio: or New York Above-Ground and Under-Ground.* Foster capitalized both on the current mode of sentimental and sensational fiction and on the spirit of urban reform, in writing sketches of the most lurid scenes of city life: prostitution, eating and drinking houses, gambling, prisons, and slums. Foster's sensationalist rhetoric is apparent in the first pages of *New York in Slices*, where he represents "our Large City" as "the very rotting skeleton of City Civilization"; Foster claims to strip away the "cloud of appearances" in order to reveal "a vast abyss of crime and suffering" lying just beneath the surface.[20]

Until recently, little attention had been paid to the generic and social dimensions of midcentury urban fiction, but with the studies of Stout, Siegel, and Michael Denning, and with the recent reprinting of Foster's *New York by Gas-Light* with a critical and historical introduction by Stuart Blumin, these works, and particularly those of Foster, are beginning to receive the attention they deserve. Whether or not the books by Foster and others are ultimately judged to be important for their contribution to literary or social practice, they provide a sense of the sociolectic understanding of the city during Whitman's formative years as a writer. In Foster's case, a more specific connection with Whitman can be established: Foster wrote for the *New York Aurora* in the period immediately following Whitman's tenure as editor of the newspaper in early 1842.[21] How much attention Whitman would have paid to the writing staff of the paper once he had left it is not clear, but it is certain he would have known Foster's books of the late 1840s and early 1850s, especially the immensely popular *New York by Gas-Light,* which may have sold over two hundred thousand copies.[22]

The central question raised by Whitman's proximity to writers such as Foster is how much of his knowledge of the city came from direct personal experience, and how much was mediated through the literary presentation of urban novels and "sketches."[23] Whitman may have capitalized on the rising trend of sensational urban fiction with his 1842 temperance novel *Franklin Evans*—a book more commercially successful than anything else Whitman was to publish during his lifetime.[24] However, it should be recalled that Whitman's novel actually predated the vast majority of such works. For Whitman, it was Dickens who provided an early model of urban literature; Whitman wrote in 1842 of "how much I love and esteem [Dickens] for what he has taught me through his writings" (*UPP,* 1:72). Dickens visited New York in that same year, and his description of that visit in *American Notes* was widely read on both sides of the Atlantic. What Whitman may have learned from Dickens, along with a general sensitivity to the various dimensions of city life, was an ability to leave behind the avenues and major thoroughfares and to cast a more interested eye on the habitats and inhabitants of the nether world that Dickens had found so disturbing in his own visits to the city: the slums, the lunatic asylum, and the workhouse.[25]

In the early 1840s, Whitman was still ahead of the largest crowd of American urban novelists—if not exactly at the vanguard—and it is significant that after several attempts at urban fiction in 1841–42, he abandoned the overcrowded fictional genre altogether. After 1842, he concentrated on the two forms of writing he was to find most worthwhile, or at least most effective for his purposes: a journalism that could reach his readers on a regular basis and a poetry that could reach those same readers on the timeless and transcendent level of prophetic personal revelation.

In *Franklin Evans,* Whitman tells a story that seems almost prototypical in its portrayal of the urban environment. The protagonist travels from rural Long Island to New York City in order to make his fortune there. Along the way, he is warned by a fellow traveler of the dangers of the city, particularly in regard to the consumption of alcohol:

> You are taking a dangerous step, young man. The place in which you are about to fix your abode, is very wicked, and as deceitful as it is wicked. There will be a thousand vicious temptations besetting you on every side, which the simple method of your country life has led you to know nothing of. . . . [Intemperance] will assail you on every side, and . . . if you yield to it, will send you back from the city, a bloated and weak creature, to die among your country friends, and be laid at a drunkard's grave; or which will too soon end your days in some miserable street in the city itself. (*EPF,* 145–46)

This prophecy is, of course, self-fulfilling, and after a series of disappointments Evans is seduced by the bright lights and "universal whirl" of the big city into a life of drink and dissipation. After all, as Evans himself asks, how was a "mere boy" from the country to deal with the "mighty labyrinth" of New York and with the "temptations, doubts, and dangers that awaited me there" (148)?

Whitman's short fiction of the early 1840s displays mixed feelings about New York City, as do his journalistic writings. In the earliest version of the story "The Child and the Profligate," published in 1841 in the *New World,* Whitman evokes "the great city, whose spires and ceaseless clang rise up, where the Hudson pours forth its waters" (*EPF,* 69); in "Reuben's Last

Wish" (1842) he again refers to "our great new world metropolis, New York." Yet in "The Tomb Blossoms" (1842), Whitman follows the pattern established in "Young Grimes," opposing the attractive life of the "country village" with the dissolute life of "Men of Cities": "what is there in all your boasted pleasure—your fashions, parties, balls, and theatres, compared to the simplest of the delights we country folk enjoy?" (*EPF*, 88). Whitman's narrator in the story goes on to comment on "the sickly vices that taint the town . . . the fluctuations of prices, or the breaking of banks." Judging from the range of these citations, Whitman's relationship to New York was one of great ambivalence. All we can say with any certainty is that he was already acquiring a fascination with the city, a fascination fed at once by the city's unique importance, size, and energy and by its potential to produce vice and suffering among its inhabitants.

Whitman's *New York Aurora* editorials of 1842 are equally schizophrenic. On March 14, he writes in typically hyperbolic fashion that "'our city' is the great place of the western continent, the heart, the brain, the focus, the main spring, the pinnacle, the extremity, the no more beyond, of the New World."[26] Yet only a week later he describes the appalling conditions of a young acquaintance, "Lively Frank," who has fallen into poverty, and he generalizes Frank's condition in a lengthy denunciation of the city's ills (*Walt Whitman of the "New York Aurora,"* 24–25). And in an article of March 24, "The Clerk from the Country," Whitman relates how "a clique of designing sharpers" had taken advantage of a young farmer's son from western New York, stealing his money and making him "a mere catspaw to further their schemes of villainy" (29). Whitman underscores the veracity of his story, which he claims is an example "of what vicious tricks there are going on" in the city. This same fundamental story of country and city, which he had by now told in poetic, fictional, and journalistic formats, appears to have had significant symbolic importance for him at the time.

If the 1842 Whitman had found most comfortable (or at least most commercially profitable) the persona of outraged social reformer, the 1855 Whitman of "Song of Myself" was to proclaim a very different agenda:

> I am not the poet of goodness only, I do not decline to be the
>   poet of wickedness also.
>
> What blurt is this about virtue and about vice?
> Evil propels me and reform of evil propels me, I stand indifferent,

My gait is no fault-finder's or rejecter's gait,
I moisten the roots of all that has grown.

(463-67)

Whitman, now graduated from innocent country boy to one of the "roughs," does not reject the goodness/wickedness dichotomy proposed by the discourse of social reform, but he also does not accept the moral implications of that discourse. Instead, he stands "indifferent" to the very discourse (the "blurt . . . about virtue and about vice") in which he previously took an active part.

Whitman's stance of indifference appears paradigmatic of his aesthetic and ideological position in the mid-1850s. Taken at its root meaning, the word suggests precisely the lack of distinction that Whitman promotes in his poems and other writings: an "in-difference" or lack of differentiation, similar to his idea of universal "eligibility" or his claim that all people are "dear to me." Whitman's reaction to the urban world around him is not one of moral outrage, and it is certainly far removed from Bryant's call for higher spiritual ground and divine intervention. In fact, it is less a verbal reaction than a physical one. If talk *about* moral issues is only so much "blurt," he will depict his own response in terms of physical movements: he is propelled, he stands, he adopts a particular "gait" (a nonverbal manifestation of attitude through body language), and he "moisten[s] the roots" of the various forms of life that surround him. Given the sexual encounter with the sea that precedes these lines in section 22 of the poem, this last image of nurturance is suggestive of a sexual encounter, masturbation, or an animalistic ritual of urination. Rather than the "fault-finder's" stance of the dogmatic social reformer, Whitman adopts a stance of social irreverence and physical organicism.

However, the attitude of indifference Whitman claims for his poetic persona also raises unresolvable problems for the socially concerned writer that Whitman was, problems that would only grow as time went on and as Whitman lost the bold assurance and careless abandon embodied in the persona of the first editions. If the principal meaning Whitman intended for *indifferent* was that of impartiality or neutrality (what the *Oxford English Dictionary* defines as the tendency "not to prefer one person or thing to another"), the secondary meaning of unconcerned or apathetic attitude ("without interest or feeling in regard to something") also looms in the background.[27] Whitman's writings display concern for social issues and feelings for the sufferings of the less fortunate members of his society, but the extent to which he can act upon those feelings is limited by his irreverent stance of cosmic *flâneur*. Whitman does go "down below," as M. Wynn Thomas suggests, to visit "prostitutes and drunkards, seamstresses, draymen, and many other representatives of the vast, socially depressed, laboring force of New York" (138). Yet, as Thomas also indicates, the poet is ambivalent about the means for dealing with the situation of those who are for one reason or another deprived of their social and economic rights. I would not go so far as to concur with Kristiann Versluys that "agony . . . to Whitman is only a surface phenomenon" and that evil "never touches him to the core" (53); Whitman was in fact deeply touched by the darker side of the life in the city, as poems like "Faces" and "The City Dead-House" and several of his prose writings clearly show. In fact, as we shall see, Whitman found himself increasingly unable to maintain the stance of moral indifference that characterized his initial burst of poetic energy in the 1850–55 period.

At the time of his 1855 *Leaves,* Whitman was far less interested in presenting a narrowly moralistic depiction of urban vice or an ideological commentary on strategies of social reform than he was in promoting what he felt to be a more encompassing goal: the cosmic embrace of all forms of humanity— and of all forms of human discourse. In later years, however, Whitman's indifference—what Thomas calls his "all-embracing, socially undiscriminating sympathy"—evolved into something more like an anxiety over the state of his nation's social fabric and whether anything could be done about it. The continuing growth of the city, along with the events of the war and the ensuing changes in social and moral climate, made untenable Whitman's boldly indifferent stance of the early 1850s. At the same time, it eroded the poet's capacity to engage these changes in anything more than superficial or euphemistic terms.

From *Flâneur* to Urban Poet: "Faces" in the Crowd

Despite the commercial success of his own *Franklin Evans,* it is clear that neither the gothic mode of writers like Bradbury, Judson, and Lippard nor the sentimentalism of Sedgwick, Child, and Cummins held much interest for Whitman in the 1840s and 1850s. This popular city fiction was one that had neither aesthetic importance nor a great deal of redeeming social value; it failed in particular to inject any new insight into the debate over the opposition between city and country.[28]

Though Hawthorne and Melville were more subtle and more searching in their treatment of the city/country opposition, their work was still, as Stout remarks, "informed by a bipolar scheme of tension between structured civilization and . . . a pseudopastoral impulse" (121). Melville's view of urbanism is unrelentingly negative and Hawthorne's, though more equivocal, still relies on stereotypical portrayals of the differences between rural and urban life. What Whitman appears to be striving for in his poetry of the 1850s is a more radical reconciliation of the urban and the pastoral, one not possible within the novelistic form as that form was conceived in nineteenth-century America. Where antebellum fiction had been far more successful than poetry in adopting urban themes and topoi, it was ultimately the more fluid poetic text, as envisioned and produced by Whitman, that succeeded in capturing the urban heteroglossia of midcentury America. Throughout "Song of Myself," Whitman joins visions of city and country in single lines of poetry, thus collapsing the difference between them not only through "linguistic manipulation," as Machor suggests, but through the uniquely poetic unit of the *line:* in section 15, "The city sleeps and the country sleeps"; in section 26, "Sounds of the city and sounds out of the city,"; and in section 33, "By the city's quadrangular houses—in log huts, camping with lumbermen." The experience of the city and that of the country may be diametrically opposed, but they are also brought into the same syntactic and semiotic space in a manner that defamiliarizes any such opposition. In making the metonymic equivalence between the quadrangular shape of urban dwellings and the similar shape of lumbermen's huts—separated only by a dash in Whitman's line—the poet again suggests a unity transcending the traditional discursive distinction between urban and natural locations. The two kinds of dwellings, though very different in their apparent social manifestations, are alike in their function as sites for the meditation on "Space and Time" that occupies Whitman throughout this section of his poem.

Where the novelistic form of Hawthorne, Melville, and Whitman's other contemporaries is bound within more conventional notions of space and time, Whitman's poem attempts a radical destabilization of chronotopic structure. Unlike poems such as "Song of the Open Road" and "Crossing Brooklyn Ferry," which present relatively stable chronotopes, "Song of Myself" is the ultimate expression of the lyric voice that subsumes all else, collapsing any sense of a single place, time, or unified narrative. Whitman's use of the long and varied catalogues in sections 15 and 33 is particularly conducive to this kind of antichronotopic representation, as image piles on image, event suggests event in an almost freeze-frame sequence. The city is clearly present here, but it is present primarily in passing scenes or images and not as the subject for any sustained reflection. Some urban images are presented in single lines—"The groups of newly-come immigrants cover the wharf or levee" (241)—while others are combined into small urban units:

> The machinist rolls up his sleeves, the policeman travels his
>   beat, the gate-keeper marks who pass,
> The young fellow drives the express-wagon, (I love him though
>   I do not know him;)
>
>   (280–81)
>
> The opium-eater reclines with rigid head and just-open'd lips,
> The prostitute draggles her shawl, her bonnet bobs on her tipsy
>   and pimpled neck,
> The crowd laughs at her black-guard oaths, the men jeer and
>   wink to each other,
> (Miserable! I do not laugh at your oaths nor jeer you;)
>
>   (304–7)

If these brief scenes from "Song of Myself" hint at Whitman's poetic engagement with the urban landscape in other poems of the 1855 edition, it is only the lesser known "Faces" that provides a sustained glimpse of Whitman's sojourns among the modern crowd of the city. "Faces" is one of the strangest poems in the Whitman canon, and one that has not received adequate critical attention. Along with "The Sleepers," another troubled and troubling poem from the first edition, "Faces" provides an important glimpse into the development of the poet's powers in the mid-1850s. Whether the disturbing catalogue of faces Whitman presents in this poem constitute "deft phrenological portraits" (Zweig), a physiognomic dream-vision (Aspiz), or the "real darkness" of Whitman's "tortured imagination" (Thomas), it is clear that the poem reflects Whitman's attempt to transform into poetic material his personal experiences of passersby on New York's streets. Moncure Conway relates a revealing story about a walk he took with Whitman shortly after the 1855 publication of *Leaves:*

> "Look at that face!" [Whitman] exclaimed once as we paused near the office of the *Herald.* I looked and beheld a boy of perhaps fifteen years, with certainly a hideous countenance, the face one-sided, and one eye

almost hanging out of a villainous low forehead. He had a bundle under his arm. "There," said Walt, "is a New York reptile. There's poison about his fangs I think." We watched him as he looked furtively about, and presently he seemed to see that we had our eyes on him, and was skulking off. At that my companion beckoned him, and after a little succeeded in bringing him to us, when we found he was selling obscene books. (*NYD*, 127)

What is most striking about this passage is Whitman's attitude toward the deformed boy and the entire scene of which he is part. The disgust felt by Conway (conveyed in such loaded expressions as "villainous low forehead" and "skulking off") contrasts with Whitman's own apparent curiosity about the boy and his activities. It is indeed fascinating to speculate on how the scene would be retold from Whitman's own point of view: what does he mean, for example, by comparing the boy to a poisonous snake? Are his sensational metaphor and his display of prurient interest merely intended to impress or shock the New Englander Conway—his first literary visitor and an emissary of Emerson—or are they an accurate example of his standard behavior and feelings in such circumstances?[29]

In the summer of 1856, Whitman would publish as one of his "New York Dissected" pieces in the journal *Life Illustrated* a sketch entitled "Street Yarn," which gives us some idea of what might be the first stage in this process: a rendering of physical "types" as prose sketches. At first glance, Whitman's brief "yarns" about the various people he sees on the city street remind us of the "urban sketches" of Foster's *New York by Gas-Light*. Like Foster, who provides a cross section of the urban population, ranging from anonymous prostitutes and newsboys to well-known New Yorkers like Horace Greeley and Mike Walsh, Whitman gives the reader snapshots of people from all walks of life—Episcopalian deacon, third-rate artist, Wall Street broker, leading lawyer, country clergyman, harlot, and gambler—as well as the city's more illustrious professors, poets (including Whitman himself), publishers, doctors, businessmen, and members of high society. But whereas Foster divides his sketches into chapters that maintain strict geographic and social demarcation (prostitutes in one chapter, newsboys in another, gamblers in yet another), Whitman writes his article as a single catalogue in which each of the figures, from high to low, appear in a kind of urban parade—all equal before the eye of the journalist-poet, and all equally in "uniform." Rather than traveling around the city's haunts as an investigative reporter in the manner of Foster, Whitman takes the approach of the *flâneur* most commonly associated with Baudelaire. He imagines himself standing (or perhaps "leaning and loafing") in front of the fashionable restaurant Delmonico's, watching as the "crowd flows by."

Whitman's approach also differs from Foster's in the style he adopts for his sketches; departing radically from Foster's long-winded journalese, Whitman presents his yarns as punchy, epigrammatic vignettes that read more like notes for poetic descriptions than like standard newspaper fare. Compare, for example, Foster's description of prostitutes in chapter 4 of *New York by Gas-Light*, "The Golden Gate of Hell," with Whitman's treatment in "Street Yarns." Despite his claim to represent the prostitute's life as the "steep-descending ladder of infamy," Foster shows us a "fashionable" brothel—"one of the most expensive and 'aristocratic' homes of vice in the city." After a lengthy description of the ornate house and its luxurious furnishings, he gives us a glimpse of the prostitutes themselves:

> The presiding divinities to this modern temple to Aphrodite are some of them quite beautiful, and all tolerably good-looking—a decidedly ugly woman not being able even to sell herself to much advantage in this refined and fastidious age. Some are arrayed in the latest Parisian style, according to the cuts in Sartain's magazine—while others emulate, in their style or costume, the Undine lately appearing in its pages, or the young lady combing her hair on the margin of the Fountain of Vaucluse—her only garment having discovered the laws of gravity and slipped. (95)

Whitman, on the other hand, casts his glance on a streetwalker of undetermined but presumably common rank:

> Dirty finery, excessively plentiful; paint, both red and white; draggle-tailed dress, ill-fitting; coarse features, unintelligent; bold glance, questioning, shameless, perceptibly anxious; hideous croak or dry, brazen ring in voice; affected, but awkward, mincing, waggling gait. Harlot. (*NYD*, 129)

The single word *harlot* cries out from the page, embodying the material conditions of prostitution more effectively than Foster's moral disquisitions on the evils of the profession. Whitman does not allow the prostitute to tell her life story, as Foster does; he provides only an exterior portrait. Yet in a few lines Whitman captures every salient detail of her physical and psychological existence. Foster concentrates most of his description on the fashionable style of his subject's dress (and still more on the surrounding furniture). Despite his attempts to inject the human element into the scene by relating the women's "autobiographies," he falls into the reductive mode of categorizing their physical appearance according to society's hierarchical standards: "quite beautiful," "tolerably good-looking," "decidedly ugly." Foster provides no sensory description of the women themselves—their faces, bodies, or voices—viewing them only through the sanitizing screens of fashion and mythology. Whitman, on the other hand, provides details that defy easy categorization in conventional social or moral terms: the woman is at once "bold" and "unintelligent," "shameless" and "perceptibly anxious," "affected" and "awkward." Whitman renders a gripplingly believable portrait, but without resorting to the kind of clichéd sensationalism of Foster's narrative.

If his "New York Dissected" essay demonstrates Whitman's remarkable talents as an observer and transcriber of the human scene in New York City, it remains journalistic rather than poetic in one sense: Whitman's yarns remain on the sociolectic level of types rather than delving into the more deeply personal transformation of those types found in a poem like "Faces." Whitman begins his poem in a somewhat similar fashion, cataloguing the generic faces he sees while "sauntering the pavement" of crowded city streets or "crossing the ceaseless ferry": "faces and faces and faces / I see them and complain not, and am content with all." Here he seems to have identified the basic forms of human and social existence in the city—everything from the "shaved, blanch'd faces of orthodox citizens" to the "pure, extravagent, yearning, questioning, artist's face." Yet before he can fall into a state of complacency about the human life around him, Whitman challenges both himself and the reader with a series of horrifying images:

> This now is too lamentable a face for a man,
> Some abject louse asking leave to be, cringing for it,
> Some milk-nosed maggot blessing what lets it wrig to its hole.
>
> The face is a dog's snout sniffing for garbage,
> Snakes nest in that mouth, I hear the sibilant threat.
>
> (17–21)

Suddenly we are transported out of the recognizable urban scene and into a phantasmagoric projection of repressed fears about the dark side of the human condition. Not only is the face Whitman describes deprived of all social context—(it is only a face, and not a person as defined by any interpersonal or societal role)—but it is even deprived of its humanity, reduced to the physical and behavioral level of an animal. In the notebook draft of the poem, this dehumanization is even clearer, as is the sense of disgust in the speaker:

> Why what is this curious little thing you hold before us? Do you call such a wretched creature as you have pictured here a man? Man is the resident of the earth. This is no man of the earth. This is the abject louse—the milk-faced maggot. . . . that flattens itself upon the ground, and asks leave to live, not as of right of its own, but by special favor; snivelling how it were righteously condemned, being of the vermin race, and will be only too thankful if it can dodge the stick or booted heel, and escape to its hole under the dung! (*D.N*, 767)

I quote the passage here in its corrected version (respecting Whitman's own deletions); in the original version, the ironic intention is clearer, as Whitman adds the sarcastic editorial comment: "We read in the advertisements of your new edition of our race enlarged and improved." Both the poem and the draft passage are so unlike anything else Whitman ever wrote that it is difficult to evaluate them; he appears to be so appalled by the abject state and the mag-gotlike appearance of this person—incommensurate with both his own aspi-rations for the human race and the exalted claims of the popular culture at large—that he is unable to extend either his sympathy or his spirit of poetic indifference.

In the next series of images, Whitman moves through a range of dis-courses associated with various urban locations: the pharmaceutical dis-pensary, the hospital floor, the crime-ridden street, and the morgue or grave-yard.

> This is a face of bitter herbs, this an emetic, they need no label,
> And more of the drug-shelf, laudanum, caoutchouc, or hog's-lard.

> This face is an epilepsy, its wordless tongue gives out the unearthly cry,
> Its veins down the neck distend, its eyes roll till they show nothing but
> their whites,
> Its teeth grit, the palms of the hands are cut by the turn'd-in nails,
> The man falls struggling and foaming to the ground, while he speculates
> well.

This face is bitten by vermin and worms,
And this is some murderer's knife with a half-pull'd scabbard.

This face owes to the sexton his dismalest fee,
An unceasing death-bell tolls here.

(24–34)

Strange as it is, the passage has affinities with moments in other poems. M. Wynn Thomas has connected these lines with section 6 of "Crossing Brooklyn Ferry," though there is certainly nothing in that poem that is remotely as disturbing as what we find here. M. Jimmie Killingsworth identifies "Faces" as a companion piece to "I Sing the Body Electric," the poem that directly preceded it in the 1855 *Leaves of Grass,* and the passage would seem to provide a counterbalance to the glorification of bodily health portrayed there.[30] Finally, the images of the snake and the "wordless tongue" appear to link the section with the slavery passage of "The Sleepers"; that poem, written at about the same time as "Faces," comes closest to sharing its darkly surreal vision.[31]

But what is Whitman attempting to say through his awful urban catalogue? Whitman himself seems somewhat unclear about his intentions, since he removes from post-1871 editions of the poem the crucial line that ends the section: "Those are really men! . . . the bosses and tufts of the great round globe!" In deleting the line, Whitman appears to shift the emphasis of the passage from the celebration of the ugliness he finds to a simple presentation of the faces themselves. Though Whitman's persona "complain[s] not" and is "content with all," the poem, at least in later editions, appears to contrast the negative images of the deformed and diseased faces of sections 2 and 3 with the positive images of health and life in sections 4 and 5. There we find the "healthy honest boy" who is the "programme of all good"; the "mother of many children" who makes the poet "fully content"; and the Quaker woman whose portrait ends the poem, an icon of wholesome beauty, an earth-mother figure associated with an idealized rural domesticity. Whitman even confers religious significance on the idealized faces of the final sections: they are descended "from the Master himself," they are accompanied by "the Lord," and they appear in a version of the Edenic paradise on "First-day morning." The ideology of moral and aesthetic indifference promoted in "Song of Myself" and in the other poems of the first editions is replaced after

1871 by a subtly but importantly more conservative ideology, one informed by the very distinctions Whitman appears elsewhere to reject: between real and ideal, evil and good, diseased and healthy, urban and pastoral, secular and sacred. Whitman does not delete the disturbing passage from "Faces" in its entirety, as he does with the slavery passage in "The Sleepers," but he does weaken its message with the removal of his summation.

A personal subtext appears in section 3, where Whitman relates the story of his mentally defective brother Eddy. In caring for Eddy, Whitman had learned to see beneath the face, even that of the "smear'd and slobbering idiot" he sees at the asylum.[32] Whitman later told Burroughs that he blamed his father's alcoholism for Eddy's condition. Eddy's plight is not an exclusively urban one (although Whitman does identify alcoholism as an urban vice in *Franklin Evans*), but it is connected metaphorically with the rapidly decaying condition of cities like New York:

> I knew of the agents that emptied and broke my brother,
> The same wait to clear the rubbish from the fallen tenement,
> And I shall look again in a score or two of ages,
> And I shall meet the real landlord perfect and unharm'd, every
> inch as good as myself.

> (42–45)

In comparing his defective brother to a tenement on the verge of collapse, Whitman signals the deeper social reality underlying the poem. By the mid-1850s, he was acutely aware of the lack of decent affordable housing in the city; he was to argue in one of his *Life Illustrated* editorials of the following year for the replacement of New York's decaying tenements, which, as Emory Holloway puts it, constituted "a rapidly spreading fungus growth" that threatened to destroy the urban environment (*NYD,* 89). Spann documents the existence of four hundred such tenant houses in the Greenwich Village area alone, buildings originally intended for private dwellings but which had degenerated into overcrowded, unsanitary, and badly maintained tenements, each housing several poor families (109–110). These low-income urban dwellings, which Whitman would characterize in his editorial as examples of "Architectural Wickedness," were, he wrote, "the most striking type of that condition of social morals which is the fertile hot-bed for evils the most enormous" (*NYD,* 92). As Spann suggests, these tenements were not only "the seeds from which future slums would often grow" (110) but also areas that were avoided at all costs by those who could afford to do so.

Whitman's use of the tenement image is particularly resonant in a poem intended to bring to the reader's consciousness the discomforting existence of those "faces" that are commonly passed over, ignored, or denied. Whitman would no doubt have concurred with the sanitary inspector who wrote in the 1860s that the wealthy resident of Fifth Avenue would do well to take heed of the houses and populations of less desirable neighborhoods: "if he can read certain results in these causes, he will see enough to diminish his sense of security in his own house" (Spann, 110).

Throughout the earlier sections of "Faces," we have the sense of an urban landscape, though it is not clearly foregrounded as such. Section 3 in particular, with its depiction of a "creas'd and cadaverous march" (the pedestrian march through city streets or to and from the "ceaseless ferry"), evokes the city strongly; the asylum and the fallen tenement are the joint markers of the negative side of urban reality, synecdoches for a discourse of poverty, madness, and death.[33]

Whitman's poem, and especially its title, may also contain an intertextual reference to Wordsworth's discussion of the city in book 7 of *The Prelude*. Two separate passages in Wordsworth's poem make direct reference to faces: first, as he begins to walk the streets of London, he finds "The comers and the goers face to face— / face after face" (172–73); then, toward the end of book 7, he makes the crucial discovery that "the face of every one / That passes me by is a mystery," and he finds the blind beggar, "who, with upright face, / Stood propped against a wall, upon his chest / Wearing a written paper, to explain / The story of the man, and who he was" (612–15). Whitman's poem can be read as a direct response to Wordsworth: where the earlier poet despaired of understanding the mystery behind each face, Whitman is determined to "see neath the rims of your haggard and mean disguises," to "unmuzzle" the faces of the people he encounters. Wordsworth cannot read the beggar's face or delve into the mysteries of his life beyond what he finds written on a piece of paper attached to the man's chest; for him, this "label" is not only more revealing than the man's face, but it becomes a metaphor for our limited knowledge of "ourselves and of the universe." Whitman, whether inspired by his belief in the science of phrenology, by his confidence in his own powers of observation, or by his faith in the expressiveness of every human spirit, reads a great deal into each face he encounters, conferring on it properties that have nothing to do with its apparent social status.

The intertextual connection with the blind beggar episode of *The Prelude* emphasizes the importance the city was beginning to have for Whitman as a location and subject for poetry. Though social issues such as the rise in urban poverty were never at the center of Whitman's poems, they remained present in the background. In an unpublished notebook poem ("To the Poor"), written in the period before the 1855 poems, Whitman declares his solidarity with the poor more directly than he ever would in his published poems: presenting himself as one who "preferred to be poor—rather than to be rich," he declares that, "The road to riches is easily open to me, / But I do not choose it / I choose to stay with you." Such pronouncements as this were long on rhetoric and short on practical consideration; however, the best indication of Whitman's social awareness is the poems of the first edition themselves, which provided a view of the city never before seen in poetry and never even approached in American verse.

The timing of their publication was itself significant, following what Spann calls "one of the hardest and most terrifying winters ever experienced by New York" (309). That winter, as unemployment rose, wages fell, the cost of basic necessities soared, the temperature dropped to minus ten degrees Fahrenheit, and charities ran out of money to help the poor, Whitman would have witnessed an intensification of the city's problems, marking the dawn of a new era for the city of New York. The strikes of longshoremen, the anger of urban working men, and the mass meetings of the unemployed all constituted, according to Spann, a "dark prophecy of the social earthquakes which periodically were to shake urban America after the Civil War" (312). How direct a correlation can be established between the onset of these new urban realities and the beginnings of a new, socially conscious mode of poetry can only be a matter for critical surmise, but the historical coincidence of these two events is certainly compelling.

Like other poems in the 1855 edition, "Song of Myself" and "The Sleepers" in particular, "Faces" is only partially a city poem, drifting out toward the end to the less threatening space afforded by a suburban or rural topos and reinstalling the dichotomy Whitman had dislodged. Anticipating the open road poem of the following year—and well aware of "[h]ow it deadens one, this living in a city!"—Whitman's speaker will abandon the metropolis and its problems for a scene resembling the pastoral Long Island of his boyhood. Here he finds the image of his maternal grandmother "in an armchair under the shaded porch of the farmhouse" and the young woman embracing her "limber-hipp'd" lover by the "garden pickets." In the most lyrical moment of the poem, the frenetic urgency and ugly realities of city life are perfectly counterbalanced by a static, idyllic scene:

Lull'd and late is the smoke of the First-day morning,
It hangs over the rows of trees by the fences,
It hangs thin by the sassafras and wild-cherry and cat brier under them.

(70–72)

The poem traces a psychological progression from the purgatory of everyday street life to the inferno of urban degradation and finally to the paradise of the pastoral retreat. "Faces" is a poem about the city, yet it saves its most sublime poetic moment for the country.

"Crossing Brooklyn Ferry" and the Changing Metropolis

No sooner had Whitman published the first edition of twelve poems than he began compiling a notebook in which he sketched out the substance of several more—most notably the poem that would become "Crossing Brooklyn Ferry." About half the lines in "Sun-Down Poem," as it was called in its original 1856 incarnation, can be found in their rough form in the notebook, where they were crossed out as they were incorporated within *Leaves of Grass*. Here Whitman first formulates the idea of a poem that will take as its locale the city itself, or rather the two cities, New York and Brooklyn, between which the ferry travels. Whitman's poem will capture "the scenes on the river as I cross the Fulton ferry" and will present them not only for the benefit of contemporary readers but for those of the future: "A hundred years hence others will see them. Two hundred years—many hundred years hence others will enjoy the flow [of the river]" (*N*, 5).

Whitman's comments suggest that he knew this was to be a major poem, and a poem different in tone and substance from the recently published poems of the first edition—more obviously lyrical, tending toward the sublime of the Romantic ode or nature poem. Critical readers of Whitman's poetry have underscored the status of this poem as a central, even groundbreaking work of the Whitman canon, a work establishing him both as the preeminent poet of the American city and as the foremost poet of expansive lyric consciousness in nineteenth-century America. If the effect of Whitman's poem was still confusing to readers like Barrett Wendell, who in 1900 claimed that the concluding stanzas of "Crossing Brooklyn Ferry" were "inarticulate, and surging in a mad kind of rhythm which sounds as if hexameters were trying to bubble through sewage," the poem was also hailed as a "wonder" and a "miracle" in which Whitman "breathed ennobling imaginative fervour" into "what seemed utterly sordid"—the crowded, urban, polluted East River.[34] It is this "idealizing" of common reality to which Wendell refers that signals a change in Whitman's poetic stance at the very moment when he attempts to embrace the urban experience most fully. As William Sharpe argues, "Crossing Brooklyn Ferry" initiates a poetry—later followed up in the *Calamus* sequence—that presents "an urban landscape thronging with crowds, permeated with longing, and insatiate for continual self-consummation" (70–71). However, it is also possible to read the poem as an initial phase of a move away from the attitudes that mark the poems of the first edition—specifically Whitman's doctrine of indifference, a totally egalitarian and nonjudgmental empathy for the common man.

In a notebook entry placed between the pages of his drafts for "Crossing Brooklyn Ferry"—and thus presumably contemporaneous with them—we find the following principle of poetic composition: "*The newer better principle through all my poems.*—(dramas, novels, compositions of any sort.) Present only great characters, good, loving characters.—Present the best phases of character, that any one, man or woman is eligible to. Present noble phases of character for young men" (*N*, 5–6). The language and sentiment of such a passage, albeit only a notebook entry and not part of a published work, is clearly at odds with the openness and democratic fervor of his 1855 poems, and its aesthetic program is antithetical to the depiction of human life we find in poems such as "Faces," "The Sleepers," and "Song of Myself." Whitman's embrace of a "newer better principle" so soon after the publication of his first poems implies a dissatisfaction with the tone of moral and aesthetic indifference they contain (and perhaps also with their disappointing public reception). The progression in his thought from "good, loving characters" to "the best phases of character" and finally to "noble phases of character" presents an increasingly hierarchical notion of distinction, a distinction based fundamentally on personal characteristics but which takes on aspects of class or nobility as well. How does such a project relate to Whitman's claim in "Song of Myself" to be "the poet of wickedness also" and to "moisten the roots of all that has grown"?

Whitman had ended his original (1855) version of "Song of the Answerer" with a radical program for the democratic American poet—the "answerer" to all personal and social needs:

> The gentleman of perfect blood acknowledges his perfect
> blood,

The insulter, the prostitute, the angry person, the beggar, see
    themselves in the ways of him. . . . he strangely transmutes
    them,
They are not vile any more. . . . they hardly know themselves
    they are so grown.

You think it would be good to be the writer of melodious verses,
Well it would be good to be the writer of melodious verses;
But what verses beyond the flowing character you could have? . . .
    or beyond beautiful manners and behaviour?
Or beyond one manly or affectionate deed of an apprenticeboy?
    . . . or old woman? . . . or man that has been in prison or is
    likely to be in prison?

(CP1855, 131–32)

Here Whitman presents a list that moves in the opposite direction from that of the notebook entry: away from aesthetic, moral and social distinction. From the "writer of melodious verses"—the exemplar of high literary culture—he moves to the realm of the socially acceptable manifestations of character, manners, and behaviour, and finally to the socially marginal world of the apprenticeboy and the ex-convict.

But as his notebook plans for "Crossing Brooklyn Ferry" indicate, Whitman *was* interested in becoming the "writer of melodious verses," at least more so than he had been in the poems of the first edition. His second entry concerning the ferry poem presents one of the poem's central images—the seagulls bathed in the transforming light of sunset: "I too many and many a time have crossed the ferry[.] I have watched the sea-gulls flapping their wings—I have seen them floating with motionless wings high in the air at sunset, just oscillating their bodies, I have seen the glistening yellow light parts of their bodies and the rest in strong shadow[.] I have seen them high up slowly wheeling in circles edging slowly to the south" (*N*, 6). The diction and syntax of this passage indicate that Whitman was already experimenting with a different poetic register from the more colloquial and declarative style he had exploited in the first edition. The notebook version anticipates larger stylistic changes in the poem itself, both in its more elevated and abstract diction and in its more self-consciously poetic syntax—especially in the final, apotheosizing section. Such syntactic inversions as "drench with your splendor me," "being than which none else is perhaps more spiritual," and "not you any more shall be able to foil us"—all from section 9 of the poem—suggest both the heightened affective state and the defamiliarized language of lyric poetry in the Sublime tradition.

These phrases may be idiosyncratic enough to resist categorization as "melodious verses," at least within the context of nineteenth-century American poetry, but they would certainly appear to contradict Whitman's claim never to have written "poetry as such." If "Crossing Brooklyn Ferry" is Whitman's most significant poem of the city, as most critics and readers would agree it is, it achieves that status less through the mimetic representation of social or topographic reality than through a transcendent rhetoric that aligns it with a more generic mode of post-Romantic poetic discourse. Sharpe argues that the poem differs from the usual "delocalized encounter" in lyric poetry by "situat[ing] the reader as part of a specific urban landscape, the poet's own" (93). Yet the landscape of "Crossing Brooklyn Ferry" is no more "localized" than that of Romantic poems such as "Tintern Abbey" and "Mont Blanc." In fact, the liminality of the poem's setting (suspended between east and west, sky and river, city and country, and day and night), combined with the hazy, vaporous, shimmering quality of the visual picture presented and the abstraction of much of its language, contribute to a sense of confusion about the exact details of physical setting. It is true that the poem presents a good deal of geographic detail, but it also offers passages like the following from section 2:

> The impalpable sustenance of me from all things at all hours of
>   the day,
> The simple, compact, well-join'd scheme, myself disintegrated,
>   every one disintegrated yet part of the scheme,
> The similitudes of the past and those of the future,
> The glories strung like beads on my smallest sights and
>   hearings, on the walk in the street and the passage over the
>   river,
> The current rushing so swiftly and swimming with me far away,
> The others that are to follow me, the ties between me and them,
> The certainty of others, the life, love, sight, hearing of others.
>
> (6–12)

It is easy to see how early readers of the poem might have been confounded by the vagueness of such passages. Unlike many of Whitman's other city poems—"Faces," "To a Common Prostitute," "The City Dead-House,"

"Give Me the Splendid Silent Sun," and "Sparkles from the Wheel," for example—this poem is not clearly in dialogue with the social realities of the city or even with the sociolectic discussion of those realities. According to Spann, thirty-three million passengers rode the East River ferries in 1860, making Whitman's Brooklyn Ferry, along with his Broadway, the ideal synecdoche for the city's massive and constantly moving populace. M. Wynn Thomas's social reading of the poem takes this argument further, suggesting that the ferry served as a potent symbol for America's democracy since it gave the populace at large a means of transportation that would have been available only to a privileged few in earlier periods. Yet a close reading of the language of the poem undermines a sense of its explicitly social force. Though Whitman evokes the "hundreds and hundreds that cross, returning home," he seems far less interested in discussing the actual lives or appearances of those people (or of the places they return home to) than in establishing an "orgasmic union" (Sharpe) between poet, reader, and city. The use of abstraction ("impalpable sustenance of me," "similitudes of the past and those of the future"), simile ("glories strung like beads"), and generalized diction ("the walk in the street") detract from the poem's importance as social or historical commentary.

Sharpe's more persuasive reading of the poem finds central the apotheosis in which "poet, reader, and citizens of Mannahatta become members of a harmoniously pastoralized city of the Saved" (98). Within this vision of a "New Jerusalem," Whitman creates "an urban-pastoral synthesis, the prosperous, industrialized new garden city of the West." In linking the poem to Emerson, Wordsworth, and the Bible, Sharpe underscores the literary intertextuality that distinguishes it from Whitman's earlier work, while also emphasizing the poet's now distanced perspective on the city and its people and language. Philip Fisher relates the poem's central image of "fine spokes of light, from my head" to the tradition of Christian iconography as represented in the works of Giotto and Fra Angelico—another appropriation of the high cultural code.[35] "Crossing Brooklyn Ferry," then, is less a sociolectic *crossing* than an idiolectic, intertextual, and highly personal *meditation* on place and time. The original title, "Sun-Down Poem," is perhaps more accurately descriptive of the poem's contents, referring specifically neither to country nor city but to a universal natural phenomenon.

In the climactic final section of the poem, Whitman does adumbrate the sights of the growing city—(the ships in the bay, the tall buildings of Manhattan, the "foundry chimneys" of industry)—but he also invokes a more transcendental set of objects: the "necessary film" that "envelop[s] the soul," the "divinest aromas" that encircle the body, and the "dumb, beautiful ministers" that bear some undetermined relationship to both. We learn far more about the ferry itself from an essay like "A General Dash at the Ferries," from George Foster's *Fifteen Minutes around New York*, than we do from Whitman's poem. In Foster's humorous sketch we are told of various people who ride the ferry—including a voluptuous but badly dressed lady, a "thin, intellectual-looking woman," a Bowery boy and "gal," a "nervous old gentleman," and an English tourist—and we are given a taste of the ferry ride itself, during which one "large, fat woman" falls into the river, and the passengers have just enough time for a few "great mouthfuls of fresh sea air, enough to supply the city deficit of oxygen for the remainder of the day" (201–6). Despite Foster's irreverent attitude toward the city, the ferry, and its passengers, he at least attempts to deal with the physical and sociohistorical realities of this characteristic New York phenomenon: the pollution and congestion of the city, the scandal sheets, the different strata of social life, the uncaring attitude toward personal disaster.

How much Whitman's poem is concerned with the kinds of social or historical issues Foster treats, and which he himself had treated more forthrightly in earlier poems, is not clear. I am not entirely convinced by Thomas's suggestion that Whitman "translates the dollar sign, the money figure which actually stimulated economic activity, into the poetic figures of water and sun," and thus asserts "an exalted faith in the masses" (109). If Whitman expresses a love for the masses in many of his writings, he also evinces a certain degree of anxiety about the effects of the crowd on the life of the individual. In a prose commentary on the ferries, Whitman presents the boat as a symbol not so much of democratic optimism as of the "great business of the mass," which travels back and forth "like iron-willed destiny," unaware of the suffering of individuals. In a frightening vision of the coincidence of the new urban masses and new technologies, Whitman imagines one man jumping overboard and drowning in the river and another being "crushed between the landing and the prow"; both are quickly forgotten by the "curious crowd," who look "so unshudderingly on the scene" (*UPP*, 1:168).

Whitman, as Thomas himself points out, was experiencing increasing difficulty in justifying an optimistic faith in radical democracy. The changes in Whitman's poetic stance appear to parallel changes in his engagement with the social realities of the city. When he is most interested in promoting a vision of radical social equality, as he is in the poems of the 1855 edition, he eschews a high cultural or transcendent poetic code that would mark his own distinction from the urban masses he describes. But when his commitment to facing such difficult social problems begins to flag, as it does in "Crossing Brooklyn Ferry," he embraces a high poetic style more commensurate with the elevation of urban reality than with indifference to its darker side.

By the time of "Democratic Vistas" (1871), Whitman's program of indifference appears to him so suspect that he is forced to make what he himself recognized as a paradoxical claim for socioeconomic distinction. The underpinnings of American democracy, he now argues, are less an unprejudiced acceptance of the common man than "a more universal ownership of property, general homesteads, general comfort—a vast, intertwining reticulation of wealth" (*PW,* 383). The nation will be "firmest held and knit by the principle of the safety and endurance of the aggregate of its middling property owners." Democracy, once Whitman's champion of the lowly and the socially marginal, now "looks with suspicious, ill-satisfied eye upon the very poor, the ignorant, and on those out of business": "She asks for men and women with occupations, well-off, owners of houses and acres, and with cash in the bank—and with some cravings for literature, too; and must have them, and hastens to make them." As if feeling the need to justify his assertion further, Whitman adds that "the extreme business energy, and this almost maniacal appetite for wealth prevalent in the United States, are parts of amelioration and progress, indispensibly needed to prepare the very results I demand." Whitman's "theory" of democracy, he writes, "includes riches, and the getting of riches."

Yet as Whitman also knew, a system that privileges wealth and business above all else, that supports only those with "cash in the bank," is not easily reconcilable either with the principle of democracy or with the reality of urban life. We find an increasing strain in Whitman's attempts to deal with the socioeconomic situation of urban America. In 1856, the same year as the publication of "Crossing Brooklyn Ferry," Whitman provided in his "New York Dissected" sketches an almost naturalistic portrait of the diversity of midcentury New York life. Two articles in particular document Whitman's reaction to the growing immigrant population, an aspect of the urban experience that he practically ignores in his poetry despite the fact that by 1855 one in every two New Yorkers was foreign born, and thousands more were arriving every month.[36]

In "Broadway," Whitman presents a prose catalogue of the ethnic poor that includes "dirty looking German Jews," "sturdy, brown-cheeked, hard-featured German peasant women," Frenchmen who "gesticulate and gabble," and an Irishman "killed by falling from his house" (*NYD*, 123). What is striking here is not only the bluntly realized portraits but the absence of Whitman's characteristically sympathetic attitude toward the underprivileged. The German women have "unnaturally stupid faces, almost as if they were blind drunk"; "beggar-women" have "bad faces" and "hypocritical, twisted features"; prostitutes are "hideous women of the night . . . bawdy, hateful, and foul-tongued"; gamblers are "whiskered, down-looking, debauched villains." Absent from the sketch is any indication that Whitman empathizes or identifies with their plight; he ends the piece with a half-serious suggestion that both evil and good spirits move through the crowd, alternately corrupting and redeeming the city's inhabitants.

The final essay in the series, "Advice to Strangers," is even more surprising when viewed in the light of the indifferent Whitman of "Song of Myself." Here Whitman warns visitors to the city not to "go wandering about the streets or parks unnecessarily in the evening," since New York "is one of the most crime-haunted and dangerous cities in Christendom." Whitman assigns the blame for this urban violence to a "floating population"—composed primarily of immigrants—that contains "hundreds—thousands—of infernal rascals . . . street boys, grown into rowdies, and the brutal scum of vile city ignorance and filth; shoulder-hitters and thieves" (*NYD*, 140). Whitman's advice sounds like the sensationalist rhetoric of reactionary forces in the city and unlike both the reformist discourse of Fourierist journals and his own earlier statements of indifference, reception, and universal eligibility.[37]

Whitman would continue to write city poetry after 1856, but the strain of what Thomas calls trying to "weld the quotidian to the transcendental" (165) was to prove too great at a time when material and spiritual realities were "diverging rather than converging." Even the 1860 poem "Mannahatta," the well-known paean to his city, seems to be a rehashing of material from previous writings rather than a spontaneous and sincere response to the urban environment; the "aboriginal name" of Mannahatta counts for more in the poem than the contemporary city's people and language do. In "To a Common Prostitute" (1860) Whitman can claim not to "exclude" the woman he encounters, but the changes he made in the manuscript before publishing the poem (from "my love" to "my girl" in line 4, and from "kiss on your lips" to "significant look" in line 6) indicate that this was no longer the provocatively egalitarian Whitman of the 1855 poems. He uses the idealized figure of the prostitute (and not the hideous harlot of his newspaper essay) to celebrate his own "liberal and lusty" nature rather than to make any comment on prostitution itself. "The City Dead-House" of 1867, despite Whitman's sympathetic stance toward the "poor dead prostitute," is a far more sentimental poem than most critics have acknowledged; as in "Faces," Whitman uses the metaphor of the decaying tenement to describe the woman's fallen condition, but here he weights the portrait with so much excess verbiage that it loses its initial impact. Finally, "Sparkles from the Wheel," from the 1871 edition, is not only a highly sentimentalized portrait of an old knife grinder in the city but is indebted to the kind of narrative genre painting popular in the late nineteenth century. Each of these poems, while important reminders to Whitman's readership that the city was still a viable subject for poetry, fails to achieve the subversive or disturbing effect of a poem like "Faces," an effect commensurate with the reality of the urban situation and with the tenor of contemporary urban discourses.[38]

Whitman left New York during the war to settle first in Washington and then later in Camden, thereafter returning to visit "Mannahatta" on several occasions, three of which are recorded in *Specimen Days* (June 1878, May 1879, and August 1881). When away from New York, Whitman expresses a belief in the pastoral hygiene of nature. "Democracy most of all affiliates with the open air," he writes in *Specimen Days:* "It is sunny and hardy and sane only with Nature. . . . must either be fibered, vitalized, by regular contact with out-door light and air and growth, farm-scenes, animals, fields, trees, birds, sun-warmth and free skies, or it will certainly dwindle and pale." No longer indifferent to the positive effects of nature or to the potentially devastating effects of the city, the poet who had witnessed all forms of human misery was still "amazed," in February 1879, by the sight of "three quite good-looking American men, of respectable personal presence . . . carrying chiffonier-bags on their shoulders, and the usual iron hooks in their hands, plodding along, their eyes cast down, spying for scraps, rags, bones, &c" (*PW,* 528–29).[39] It was this scene, and others like it, that prompted his growing fears that the "vast crops of poor, desperate, dissatisfied, nomadic, miserably-waged populations, such as we see looming over us in late years," would eat away at the United States "like a cancer of lungs or stomach" (528). In an 1889 conversation with Horace Traubel, Whitman referred to Camden as "an ever larger and larger congregation of maggots, human maggots," and pointed to "underflowing currents of life . . . so low, so vile, so dirty, so mean" (*WWC*, 5:423).

Despite his latent fears, however, Whitman would continue to maintain, as on his 1878 visit to the "Human and Heroic New York," that "an appreciative and perceptive study of the current humanity of New York gives the directest proof yet of successful Democracy, and of the solution of that paradox, the eligibility of the free and fully developed individual with the paramount aggregate" (*PW*, 172). And in 1881 he made the seemingly paradoxical claim that "despite the suffocating crowding of some of its tenement houses," the city of New York "comprises the most favorable health-chances in the world" (*PW*, 274).

At this point, Whitman's social comments are only intermittent bursts of concern upon a colorful background of carnivals, boat trips up the river, walks in Central Park, and the procession of horses and carriages down Fifth Avenue and Broadway. Instead of the trenchant social criticism of his *Daily Eagle* and "New York Dissected" articles, we now find a seemingly naive vision of New York, one dominated by the discourse of urban boosterism ("the most favorable health-chances in the world") and informed by the *flâneur*'s self-indulgent love for the urban spectacle. In his postwar descriptions of the city, such as the letter to a Broadway stage conductor that serves as an epigraph for this chapter, Whitman's language appears to be saturated with the icons of sociocultural distinction: the "first-class teams," the splendor of the "great street," and the "tall, ornamental, noble buildings" of white marble. In these later encounters with the city, Whitman appears to experience something of what Walter Benjamin describes as the phantasmagoria of the urban experience, a flooding or intoxication of the senses common to the nineteenth-century *flâneur*, who finds himself anaesthetized by the overwhelming flow of sensations, even as he has the impression of experiencing a heightened awareness of his surroundings.[40]

In these later writings, Whitman's indifference to all aspects of the city has been replaced by extremes of rejection or idealization, as he moves back and forth between the peaceful enjoyment of nature and the more turbulent and stimulating interaction with urban life. When confronted once more with the excitement of the city, Whitman cannot accept his earlier arguments for the pleasures of nature. "I can no more get along without horses, civilization, aggregations of humanity, meetings, hotels, theatres," he writes, "than I can get along without food": "Have I, too, somewhere in my writings been shallow enough to speak of living absolutely alone? of how good it were to hear nothing but silent Nature in woods, mountains' far recesses? to see no tormenting sights, reeking presence of men, women, children?" (*PW*, 355).

Whitman's sentiments are certainly hyperbolic; he may still have been able to tolerate the "tormenting sights" and "reeking presences" of the city in small doses, but his primary focus was never again to remain on them. He makes a valiant attempt to infuse the city with the praise he feels on one level it deserves, but he fails to add in any substantive way to the postwar discourse of the city, a discourse just beginning to develop in the work of younger realists like James and Howells, and which would reach its most concentrated expression in the urban naturalism of Crane and Dreiser.

Through Whitman's eyes, the city seemed little changed; yet in the space of the poet's literary career, his beloved New York had been transformed from a relatively small and fast-growing metropolis to an urban magnet with a population in the millions. The effects such changes in New York and other cities would have on American literature and culture are inestimable. For the first time, an American writer had at his disposal the considerable human, social, and discursive resources of a large city. With the exciting new visual and social panorama the city provided came new responsibilities and new aesthetic choices. In order to be America's poet, one had to confront disturbing, even frightening realities, including the reality most difficult of all for Whitman to accept: that not all of America's people were good, or even acceptable citizens. As an editorial in *Harper's* put it as early as 1857, a "decent and orderly town of moderate size" had been transformed into a "a huge and barbarous metropolis" (Spann, 315). Such reactions would come to seem less exaggerated as the century wore on; the rapidity of changes in the city explains, to some degree, Whitman's own inability to deal with the new urban environment. Much as he might have wished to remain "one of the roughs," there were aspects of the city that were rougher than even he could tolerate or condone. If in the 1840s and early 1850s Whitman could still "[pass] freely in and about those parts of the city which are inhabited by the worst characters" (Bucke) and could identify himself with the poor and often dangerous inhabitants of the urban ghetto, he lost much of that remarkable openness to experience in his later years, years spent attempting to deal with the material forces of change that had been poetically unleashed onto the pages of the first edition.

Translating and Answering

In "Song of the Answerer," Whitman had declared that the purpose of the poet was to resolve social distinctions by "translating" all forms of human experience into a universal poetic language:

> Every existence has its idiom, every thing has an idiom and
>   tongue,
> He resolves all tongues into his own and bestows it upon men,
>   and any man translates, and any man translates himself also,
> One part does not counteract another part, he is the joiner, he
>   sees how they join.
>
> He says indifferently and alike *How are you friend?* to the
>   President at his levee,
> And he says *Good-day my brother*, to Cudge that hoes in the
>   sugar-field,
> And both understand him and know that his speech is right.
>
> (31–36)

Whitman is explicit about whose idiom he will "translate," and whom he will join to whom: the joining of the "President at his levee" to the "Cudge that hoes in the sugar-field" is only the most dramatic example. But as much as he is committed to the democratic act of joining and translating on behalf of the people at large, Whitman is equally concerned with the poet's universal acceptance *by* the people. In his fantasy of both embracing and being embraced by all, he portrays the poetic vocation as translatable to the terms of any profession, trade, or circumstance. In his role of poet, or "Answerer," Whitman can "walk with perfect ease in the capitol," but he can also be (mis)taken for a mechanic, a soldier or sailor, an engineer or deckhand, a "gentleman of perfect blood," a prostitute, or a beggar.

Whitman includes in his catalogue of professions and social types the "author" and the "artist," as if to distance his own status as poet (the 1856 title was "Poem of the Poet") from these two categories. His version of the poet in 1855 still appears to have been that of the direct mouthpiece of the people, the one who could maintain an unmediated relationship to all forms of language, all aspects of the sociolect. But as Whitman's poetic career continued, he began to see his own work much more in terms of the interdependent functions of art and authorship. After the disastrous public reception of the first edition, he saw that he would need a distinctive "art" both in order to mark himself as a poet for the ages and to legitimate himself within his own culture as a serious "author" and not merely a literary eccentric. What Whitman came to realize—even if he would not have articulated it consciously—was that to "translate" human discourses into poetry would mean in some sense to transform them into an acceptably high cultural mode, into an idiolect that reflected the exigencies of "art" as much as the pressures of "reality." Publishing second, third, and fourth editions, and continually revising his original poems in the process, required a degree of self-reflexivity that, in turn, inevitably implied a different relationship to (poetic) language. The poetic function—which involved "translating" the language of others in order to be universally admired by them—produced not simply one language among others but a distinctive form of language, one suited to the "higher" aims for which he felt he was ordained as America's bard. Whitman's poetic relationship to the city changed not only in relation to social and historical changes in New York but in relation to the requirements and pressures of his own career, a career increasingly defined by the conventionalizing persona of the Good Gray Poet rather than by the rebelliously "indifferent" persona of the first edition.[41]

CHAPTER FOUR

Figuring the Body in Leaves: Whitman and the Discourse of Corporeality

O my body! I dare not desert the likes of you in other men
and women, nor the likes and the parts of you,
I believe the likes of you are to stand or fall with the
likes of the soul, (and that they are the soul,)
I believe the likes of you shall stand or fall with my
poems, and that they are my poems,
Man's, woman's, child's, youth's, wife's, husband's,
mother's, father's, young man's, young woman's poems.
    —Walt Whitman, "I Sing the Body Electric"

There are aspects of writing that we can call idiolectic; there is
an idiolect, which is the presence of the body. . . . The body passes
in a certain way into writing. Consequently, there are [different]
idiolects for each writer.
    —Roland Barthes, conversation with Maurice Nadeau[1]

The Body as Idiolect

The idea that the most palpable evidence of an authorial idiolect is the imprint of the physical body on the text does not originate in the late twentieth-century writings of Roland Barthes. As Elaine Scarry notes in her introduction to *Literature and the Body*, there exists a long-standing tradition of "directly tying language to the body itself" and of viewing the writer's voice as "a prolongation of the body."[2] What interests me in Barthes's formulation of the relationship between the body and the idiolect, however, is his more particular notion that the idiolect, the author's individual style or expression, can be located most firmly in those places where the body has passed directly into language.

This is not to deny that the human body has a social function quite apart from its presence as a marker of human individuality; Scarry herself acknowledges the significance of the body as a social unit by dividing the entries in her collection into "Essays on Populations" and "Essays on Persons." However, in high cultural forms of literature, and especially in lyric poetry, it is the author's idiolectic presence and not his or her social context that is most vividly signaled through a foregrounded interaction of body and text.

In the essays on literature and the body collected by Scarry, John Donne serves as the privileged example of a poet who, in a variety of ways, "lifts the body into language" (15). Whether he is reflecting postcoital sadness in his poetic closure (Ricks) or establishing a connection between the anatomical body and the physical book or page (Scarry), Donne stretches to breaking points the metaphorical relationships between the body and language; it is in these metaphorical conceits, these alchemical verbal formulations, that Donne's idiolect most forcefully expresses itself.

Whitman shares with Donne some of the means of bringing the body into poetry—for example, the overarching conceit of the book or page as living entities (the poet's body or "leaves of grass"), and the poetic engagement with the contemporary discourses of science and medicine. But the two poets also differ in several important ways. First of all, Whitman's poems resist the consistently allegorical or metaphorical figuration through which Donne moves from the physical to the metaphysical, aesthetic, or spiritual plane. Secondly, Whitman is aware of and engaged with class differences as they are reflected within discourses of the body in a way that Donne does not seem to be: as we shall see, Whitman attempts to use the poem as a vehicle for effecting a change in sociocultural attitudes toward the body and sexuality. Finally, the American poet, unlike his English predecessor, is concerned to a striking degree with creating within the literary text a symbolic space in which the physical presence of the writer can come into direct contact with that of readers.[3]

How can these various trajectories of the body through Whitman's poetry be read in terms of an interaction between the sociolect and the idiolect? Let us retrace the rhetorical steps of Whitman's engagement with the areas of social and literary discourse discussed in this book. Slavery is a subject for which the sociolect provided only a highly inadequate means of understanding or empathy, and thus the poet needed to create through an imaginative involvement with the slave a convincingly idiolectic expression. The city, on the other hand, is the quintessential site of the sociolect, but as such it can provide only the raw materials out of which the poet must shape an idiolectic vision. Finally, the body is the privileged site of personal or idiolectic expression, a site that must be enlarged, in Whitman's terms, to provide for a more democratic or all-embracing understanding of the relationship between private physical and public social realities. Although at times it is highly idiolectic, Whitman's poetic treatment of the body is not only a personal or lyric one; it is also informed by current discourses of hygiene and medical science, and even more significantly by Whitman's desire to give voice to a social body as well as an individual body, to "contain multitudes." If Whitman's "largeness" is physical and corporeal, it is, as we have already seen, simultaneously aesthetic and sociopolitical. The body is, for Whitman, the master trope that can contain or comment on all other areas of society and discourse. This discursive capacity of the body is reflected in the very etymologies of corporeality: through the poetry of the body and of sexuality, Whitman can *in-corporate* all citizens, he can *em-body* all of America, past, present, and future. As seen in such poems as "The Sleepers," "I Sing the Body Electric," and "Faces," it is through the body that Whitman comments most effectively on political and social issues ranging from race and slavery to urban poverty and the growth of the city.

One of the most striking examples of Whitman's all-inclusive use of the body is in the 1856 poem "Salut Au Monde!" In section 10, he embraces the bodies not only of all Americans but of all the world's peoples. Amidst a catalogue that ranges across the continents of Asia, Africa, Europe, and the Americas, he places a hymn to the bodies of the world's unfortunate:

> I see all the menials of the earth, laboring,
> I see all the prisoners in the prisons,
> I see the defective human bodies of the earth,
> The blind, the deaf and dumb, idiots, hunchbacks, lunatics,
> The pirates, thieves, betrayers, murderers, slave-makers of the earth,
> The helpless infants, and the helpless old men and women.

> (151–56)

Unlike a more typically lyric appropriation of the body such as that of Donne—whose poetic energies focus on an inward revelation of the poet's own body, a body which can then be analogized to various psychic states—

Whitman's poem moves outward to grasp the complexity of the body in all its physical and social forms. Rather than imagine all physical states as possible within his own body, he identifies with all physical states and physical variations as they occur in the (social) world.[4] Whitman's reference in the poem to a series of bodily states, states normally circumscribed in accepted social discourses, heightens the reader's perception of the most powerfully liminal points in his texts: in Michael Moon's terms, "those moments which invite the reader to assume the subject-position of a stable self dissolving under pressure of overwhelming fears and desires" (15). But where Moon stresses the dissolution of the individual poet or reader through bodily identifications—the dispersal of individual subjectivity into a shared (homo)social experience—I want here to stress the way in which the presentation of the poem as physical body defines Whitman's individual idiolect. No longer able to base a sense of self on the well-ordered discursive paths of the sociolect— the socially sanctioned and "safe" discussions of excessive drinking, sexual promiscuity and indulgence, and the evils of masturbation, prostitution, or homosexuality—the reader confronts the closest approximation of the authorial and physical presence of the writer himself. That the title of "Song of Myself" in the editions from 1860 to 1881 was simply "Walt Whitman" is itself significant; what the reader will encounter, Whitman suggests through a powerful metonymic conversion, is not a poem but a person and, ultimately, a body. "For every atom belonging to me as good belongs to you," Whitman writes in the third line of the poem. The word, the poet's idiolect, passes not only into the text but into the reader as well, as if circumventing the need for a sociolectic medium of exchange between literary and ordinary usage. The poem too is a living thing with its own life trajectory; like Whitman himself, it is born at the age of thirty-seven and hopes "to cease not till death."

Where, then, is the presence of the sociolect in the opening lines of "Song of Myself"? Such a question is impossible to answer, since the sociolect is itself the shared medium through which we understand each other; the poet's words would be nonsense without it. The presence of the poet's body, and the idiolectic linguistic presence it brings with it, can only remain in their seemingly crystalline form for a brief moment, and that moment is itself illusory. Gradually the social world, the world of political contingencies and cultural meanings and distinctions, must reenter the poem. It becomes increasingly clear in the course of the poem that the idiolect is but a personalized reordering of the sociolect, a mode of juxtaposing sociolectic elements rather than any kind of "personal language" of the poet's invention.

In the opening section of the poem, Whitman seems at pains to hold off the social and cultural in favor of an unadulterated physicality, but he is never entirely able to do so. In the lines dealing with his own origins, for example, he presents two rival versions of the same event, one stressing his status as a child of nature—"My tongue, every atom of my blood, form'd from this soil, this air"—and one stressing his human genealogy—"Born here of parents born here from parents the same, and their parents the same." The latter genealogy is itself syntactically ambiguous; it is at once a rejection of differ-ence (each generation is the same as the last) and a celebration of historical specificity (the speaker is himself a fourth-generation American, perhaps even a fourth-generation New Yorker, depending on the as yet unspecified referent of "here"). The quatrain ending the first section is similarly am-biguous:

> Creeds and schools in abeyance,
> Retiring back a while sufficed at what they are, but never forgotten,
> I harbor for good or bad, I permit to speak at every hazard,
> Nature without check with original energy.
>
> (10–13)

Here the lack of syntactic clarity in the first and final verses may reflect a real ambivalence about the poet's relationship to "nature without check" on the one hand and to "creeds and schools" on the other. Is it the creeds and schools he permits to speak at every hazard, or nature, or both? Are these creeds "never forgotten" by him or by the society in general?

The same ambivalence appears to permeate the opening lines of section 2, in which the "perfumes" enter as the first real sign of a human culture in com-petition with nature's "original energy." Here we find houses, rooms, and shelves all "crowded with perfumes"; Whitman appears to celebrate the sen-sual excess represented by these perfumes ("I breathe the fragrance myself and know it and like it") but he stops short of letting himself become "intoxi-cated" by their "distillation" and thereby of losing control of the body's senses. The houses, rooms, and shelves in which the perfumes are held indi-cate the social or economic level on which they operate. Such perfumes may be sensuous, but they are also rare or expensive commodities—markers of a new bourgeois materialism. Susan Buck-Morss has pointed to the important status of perfumeries in the nineteenth-century city: in Paris, for example, perfumes were used to overpower "the olfactory sense of a population already besieged by the smells of the city." At the same time, perfumes represented part of the world of commodities described by Marx as the phantasmagoric: they epitomized the commodity that conceals every trace of the labor used to produce it. On one level, then, Whitman's resistance to "intoxication" by the perfumes may also represent a resistance to the urban phantasmagoria and the mass commodification of which it is part.[5]

Yet rather than address this level of sociocultural distinction directly, Whitman moves on to contrast the perfumes with the "atmosphere" itself and with the natural habitat in which that atmosphere can be found. Unlike the perfume, the ultimate seduction of which he resists, the sensual world of nature is allowed to intoxicate him, as the flow of language and image move forward in a kind of synaesthetic whirl:

> The smoke of my own breath,
> Echoes, ripples, buzz'd whispers, love-root, silk-thread, crotch
>   and vine,
> My respiration and inspiration, the beating of my heart, the
>   passing of blood and air through my lungs.
> The sniff of green leaves and dry leaves, and of the shore and
>   dark-color'd sea-rocks, and of the hay in the barn,
> The sound of the belch'd words of my voice loos'd to the eddies
>   of the wind,
> A few light kisses, a few embraces, a reaching around of arms,
> The play of shine and shade on the trees as the supple boughs
>   wag,
> The delight alone or in the rush of the streets, or along the fields
>   and hill-sides,
> The feeling of health, the full-noon trill, the song of me rising
>   from bed and meeting the sun.

>   (21–29)

This is one of the most evocative and idiolectically charged passages of *Leaves of Grass,* combining Whitman's characteristic catalogue style with a heightened lyrical intensity. The passage gains much of its poetic force through different types of vocal utterance, each of which intersects with "natural" process in a way that remains highly personal, highly idiolectic. Images of breath and life process are brought together with images of nature and, simultaneously, with instances of language, voice, or song: "echoes," "buzz'd whispers," "the sound of the belch'd words of my voice," "the full-noon trill, the song of me rising from the bed." Despite the single evocation of "the rush of the streets," this is a passage that remains at a certain remove from the social or sociolectic level. Everything in the passage is invested with the sense of a personal language—whether an Emersonian language of nature or Whitman's own more physically located language of life, breath, and the body. The "smoke of my own breath" becomes a personal signature on the air, just as the "belch'd words" are loosed to the winds and the "song of me" rises to meet the sun.

Rhetorically, the passage works to set up the critique with which Whitman will end this section of the poem, and with which he will establish an implicit antithesis that informs not only "Song of Myself" but all subsequent poems in at least the first three editions:

> Have you reckon'd a thousand acres much? have you reckon'd
>   the earth much?
> Have you practis'd so long to learn to read?
> Have you felt so proud to get at the meaning of poems?
> Stop this day and night with me and you shall possess the origin
>   of all poems,
> You shall possess the good of the earth and sun, (there are
>   millions of suns left,)
> You shall no longer take things at second or third hand, nor look
>   through the eyes of the dead, nor feed on the spectres in
>   books,
> You shall not look through my eyes either, nor take things
>   from me,
> You shall listen to all sides and filter them from your self.
>
> (30–37)

The opening equation, between "a thousand acres" and "the earth," picks up on the earlier opposition of "perfumes" and "atmosphere," but the underlying economic metaphor—"have you reckon'd"—makes even clearer Whitman's critique of society's drive for quantification and ownership. Once more he stresses that the earth, like the meaning of a poem, cannot be bought and sold; only the directly physical, personal, and presumably sexual presence of Whitman ("Stop this day and night with me") can convey "the origin of all poems," just as only the all-encompassing presence of nature, and not money or books, can supply "the good of the earth and sun." Whitman is clear in his preference for the natural, the intimate, and the physical over the learned and the literary, yet he backs away from the extreme personalism of the opening lines: he urges the reader not to "take things from me" or to "look through my eyes" but instead to "listen to all sides" and to "filter them from your self." Indeed, such lines may seem to contradict the earlier claim that every atom of the poet belongs to the reader. Now the reader is presented as an autonomous agent who, rather than directly absorbing the idiolect of the poet, must filter the poet's language through the various registers of the internalized sociolect in order to arrive at a personal set of ideas or beliefs.

But it is important to consider who Whitman's intended reader is. This is a reader who has "practis'd so long to learn to read" and who feels "so proud to get at the meaning of poems." Unlike the assumed readership of Emerson or the fireside poets, for whom reading books, and even reading and understanding poems, would have been considered a normal or expected accomplishment, Whitman's implied reader is a member of a class for whom reading is still difficult, for whom poetry is a challenge and perhaps a source of confusion or uncertainty. Thus when Whitman proposes to "belch" the words of his voice or to send his "barbaric yawps" over the rooftops, it is as much an attempt to send a reassuring message of physicality to his working-class brethren as to *épater le bourgeois*. By section 5, this message has been fully relayed; the identity of the reader has been merged with that of the speaker's lover. The writer/reader relationship is no longer a literary one but an expressly physical one:

> Loafe with me in the grass, loose the stop from your throat,
> Not words, not music or rhyme I want, not custom or lecture,
>   not even the best,
> Only the lull I like, the hum of your valvèd voice.
>
> (84–86)

Whitman appears to reject the need for cultural distinction, asking his reader/addressee/lover to engage him in a wordless conversation whose only value lies in its physical sensation—"the hum of your valvèd voice." Here, perhaps, is the idiolectic taken to its ultimate extreme—a language only of the voice itself, a resonance without the sociocultural framework of words, music, rhyme, custom, or lecture. Yet even in the process of disavowing cultural distinction, Whitman cannot escape the distinctive flavor imparted by poetic tradition. In the last line we find clearly foregrounded instances of alliteration (on both l and v), as well as onomatopoeia ("lull" and "hum"), and even archaic poeticism in the Romantic vein ("valvèd voice"). Finally, the relationship of idiolect and sociolect becomes highly complex in the poem, even, or perhaps especially, where the body is concerned. As we shall see below, it will ultimately be the interaction of the public discourses of corporeality with the more private attempts to figure the body in the poem that will produce Whitman's most resonant passages.

Bodily Distinctions, Bodily Hexis

In the 1855 edition, Whitman addressed two of the central issues at stake in current politics: slavery, an issue that culminated in the violent social upheaval and massive human slaughter of the Civil War; and urbanization, with its tremendous repercussions in the various spheres of social, cultural, and economic life. Yet in exploring these discourses, Whitman appears either to have exhausted their creative potential (in his treatment of slavery in the 1855 poems, for example) or to have ceased to be actively engaged with them (in his growing personal and aesthetic distance from the problems of the city).

In each of the first three editions, Whitman puts increasing emphasis on developing poetic forms for responding to yet another area of discourse: that of the physical and sexual body. If Whitman began his poetic examination of the body in his 1855 edition, he both expands and intensifies that examination in later editions. In 1856 he adds to the already potent presence of the body in first-edition poems—in particular "The Sleepers," "I Sing the Body Electric," and sections of "Song of Myself"—several new poems specifically addressing the poet's sexuality and corporeality: "Song of the Broad-Axe," "By Blue Ontario's Shore," "Spontaneous Me," "Song of the Rolling Earth," "This Compost," and "A Woman Waits for Me" as well as the new concluding section of "I Sing the Body Electric" with its remarkable anatomical inventory. The 1860 edition continues this tendency with the two sequences on the sexual body—*Calamus* for homosexual love or "manly attachment" and "Enfans d'Adam" for heterosexual love—in addition to the poems "As I Ebb'd with the Ocean of Life" and "Starting from Paumanok." And in the early 1860s Whitman begins work on a new group of poems—to be published as *Drum-Taps* in 1865 and later reincorporated into *Leaves of Grass*—which takes as its central motif the living, dead, and wounded bodies of soldiers in the Civil War.

Since several recent critics have explored the question of Whitman and the body in some detail, my discussion will focus on certain aspects of his use of the body as a means of resisting traditional modes of poetic figuration that sought to distinguish the poetic image of the body from the sociocultural realities of human physicality, health, and sexuality.[6] This, then, will be the final movement in Whitman's poetic struggle with distinction: the avoidance of sociocultural distinction in the poems will find its analogue in the effort to achieve a solidarity—both personal and textual—with the somatic presence of all people.[7] In order to avoid the co-optation of the body by a conventional poetic system of figuration, Whitman adopts various rhetorical and formal strategies for maintaining the somatic imprint of the body on the poetic text. In doing so, he also rejects modes of poetic figuration that seek to deny the corporeal substance of the body by repressing its physical and sexual functions. For Whitman, the body's figural status in the work of both English and American contemporaries only works to obfuscate the real pressures of corporeality and sexuality on the poet, his language, and his social existence.

Whitman's most passionate attack on the sexual attitudes typical of modern literature comes in his 1856 letter to Emerson, where he writes of a total repression of the body's sexuality in contemporary cultural and literary discourse:

> To the lack of an avowed, empowered, unabashed development of sex . . . and to the fact of speakers and writers fraudulently assuming as always dead what every one knows to be always alive, is attributable the remarkable non-personality and indistinctness of modern productions in books, art, talk. . . . By silence or obedience the pens of savans, poets, historians, biographers, and the rest, have long connived at the filthy law, and books enslaved to it, that what makes the manhood of a man, that sex, womanhood, maternity, desires, lusty animations, organs, acts, are unmentionable and to be ashamed of, to be driven to skulk out of literature with whatever belongs to them. This filthy law has to be repealed—it stands in the way of great reforms. . . . This tepid wash, this diluted deferential love, as in songs, fictions, and so forth, is enough to make a man vomit; as to manly friendship, everywhere observed in The States, there is not the first breath of it to be observed in print. I say that the body of a man or woman, the main matter, is so far quite unexpressed in poems; but that the body is to be expressed, and sex is. Of bards for These States, if it come to a question, it is whether they shall celebrate in poems the eternal decency of the amativeness of Nature, the motherhood of all, or whether they shall be the bards of the fashionable delusion of the inherent nastiness of sex, and of the feeble and querulous modesty of deprivation. (*LG*, 737–38)

If we are to accept the terms of Whitman's polemic, the midcentury discourses of poetry and other literatures acted either as vehicles for the censorship of the physical or, even worse, as vehicles for spreading antisexual propaganda—"the fashionable delusion of the inherent nastiness of sex." Of course, Whitman was not alone in identifying what Peter Gay has called the "bourgeois hypocrisy" of Victorian middle-class values in the sexual arena; in fact, complaints about sexual hypocrisy themselves became part of a familiar discourse in the late nineteenth century.[8]

Whether Whitman's desire to represent the body is part of a more general tendency in American literary culture is a question that must be asked, although a definitive answer is difficult. Sharon Cameron has argued that nineteenth-century American literary texts differed from their English counterparts precisely in their more foregrounded presentation of the body and the physical self. In *The Corporeal Self*, Cameron distinguishes the nineteenth-century American literary texts, with their concern for the body as a palpable entity in its own right, from an English literary tradition that treats the body primarily as a figure or image "for the world's complexity, whether cosmic, political, or architectural."[9] According to Cameron, American literature presents the body not anagogically—"in the service of something else" (9)—but mimetically or metonymically, as a concrete entity with a significance apart from its place in a larger political or metaphysical scheme. While Cameron's privileged examples are Hawthorne and Melville, she also finds the tendency to foreground the body's palpable presence in the works of Charles Brockden Brown as well as Poe, Emerson, Thoreau, Whitman, and Dickinson.[10]

Clearly, it would not have occurred to Whitman himself or to his immediate contemporaries that "the impulse to define the body and its palpable boundaries" is "at the heart of the American literary tradition" (Cameron, 11, 3). The works of Brockden Brown and Dickinson were presumably unknown to him; the gothic writings of Poe and Hawthorne would not have struck him as particularly revolutionary in their treatment of the body. Emerson was hardly a spokesman for the direct representation of the body in literature; he tried to persuade Whitman to take out the most sexually frank poems in the "Enfans d'Adam" cluster and gradually withdrew his support for Whitman's poetry altogether in response to what he felt was a too candid treatment of the body and sex. And even Thoreau, who generally approved of *Leaves of Grass*, found "two or three pieces" to be "disagreeable, to say the least. . . . as if the beasts spoke."[11] Finally, the mainstream prose and poetry of the 1840s and 1850s was even less engaged with the body than these selective examples from the currently fashionable canon of American literature would suggest. If the dominant literary discourse of the period was that established by Emerson and the fireside poets, Whitman's characterization of a "tepid wash" of language about the body must be seen as an accurate one. More adventurous writers like Melville and Thoreau did exist, but they were far outnumbered by poets and novelists who avoided any but the most decorous and conventionalized treatment of human anatomy.

Of all American writers of his era, it is Whitman who departs most radically from both literary and sociolectic conventions in his discussion of the body. If Thoreau's understanding of the body's materiality represents an important revision of Emerson's transcendental Romanticism, Whitman's celebration of the sexual body represents a far more decisive break in discursive practice, one that can be compared with breaks effected in other cultures by Baudelaire, Nietzsche, and Freud. Whitman's recognition of the body goes beyond Emerson's, and even Thoreau's, because he posits not only a balance between body and soul but an identity between the two.[12] It is this refusal to represent somatic existence as either secondary to or separate from ethical, social, or cultural levels of existence that characterizes Whitman's departure from the sociolectic view of the body and sex. As M. Jimmie Killingsworth has stated, Whitman's work was at the origin of an American liberal tradition that recognized the importance of "erotic energy as a powerful force in shaping individuals and societies" (46). Whitman's desire to merge the social and the sexual was indicative of what was beginning to happen in the political realm (Killingsworth allies Whitman's stance to that of the liberal "Locofocos" of the 1830s and 1840s), but it remained far more unusual, and perhaps unique, within the realm of literary and cultural discourse.

Various critics have hinted at sociolinguistic readings of the body in Whitman's poetry. Paul Zweig has observed, for example, that "Whitman experienced public crises [like the outbreak of the Civil War] in his flesh."[13] Killingsworth has commented on this same phenomenon, suggesting that Whitman takes the crisis of the war as a moment to deny or control the body. In an often-cited notebook entry written near the beginning of the war, Whitman writes that he will "inaugurate for myself a pure, perfect, clean-blooded, robust body, by ignoring all drinks but water and pure milk, late suppers—a great body, a purged, cleansed, spiritualized, invigorated body."

Whitman's vocabulary of purgation and spiritualization indicates an effort to repress bodily impulses at a moment of political and social threat to the

Union—as if he is willing at a time of extreme crisis to make an uncharacter-istic gesture of solidarity with sociopolitical forces of control. For Michael Moon, however, Whitman's relationship to systems of power is far more complex and ambivalent than such an interpretation would suggest. Writing, according to Moon, in the period "of the most intense political conflict and social transformation in American history to date" (5), Whitman faced the almost insurmountable task of attempting to reconcile his own poetic im-pulses both with disturbing historical events and with the psychosexual dy-namics underlying literature and social history. It is clear that for Whitman the distinctions between body and soul, body and mind, or body and lan-guage were not unrelated to traditional distinctions between socioeconomic classes or cultural orders. In a passage from the 1855 preface, later to appear in somewhat different form in "By Blue Ontario's Shore," Whitman displays his awareness of these connections. The poet, Whitman claims, should con-cern himself neither with "rhyme and uniformity" nor with "fluency and or-naments" but exclusively with those qualities that engender "beautiful blood and a beautiful brain":

> Love the earth and sun and the animals, despise riches, give alms to every one that asks, stand up for the stupid and crazy, devote your in-come and labor to others, hate tyrants, argue not concerning God, have patience and indulgence toward the people, take off your hat to nothing known or unknown or to any man or number of men, go freely with powerful uneducated persons and with the young and with the mothers of families, read these leaves in the open air every season of every year of your life, re-examine all you have been told at school or church or in any book, dismiss whatever insults your own soul, and your very flesh shall be a great poem and have the richest fluency not only in its words but in the silent lines of its lips and face and between the lashes of your eyes and in every motion and joint of your body. (*LG*, 714–15)

What is most interesting in this passage is Whitman's linkage of a radical social equality not only with the writing of poetry but with a kind of corpo-real well-being that in Whitman's mind is the prerequisite of effective writing. He seeks a form of extreme organicism that also suggests the radically idio-lectic potential to be found in writing from the body: "your very flesh shall be a great poem." It is significant, however, that he does so within the larger context of a cultural and societal framework—that of the leveling of sociocul-tural distinctions. What Whitman grasps intuitively is the notion of what

Bourdieu has called "bodily hexis," or the body's innate sense of social dispositions. As John Thompson writes in the introduction to Bourdieu's *Language and Symbolic Power*, bodily hexis can be seen in "the differing ways that men and women carry themselves in the world, in their differing postures, their differing ways of walking and speaking, of eating and laughing, as well as in the differing ways that men and women deploy themselves in the more intimate ways of life."[14] It is precisely this sense of the body as "the site of incorporated history" that Whitman appears to propose in his preface and that he continues to develop in his poetry.

Whitman's own life experience made him intensely aware of social and educational differences between himself and others, both those with more formal education and cultural background (Emerson and the Boston literati, for example) and those with far less. Charley Shively, in his groundbreaking *Calamus Lovers,* has collected letters Whitman received from various working-class men and boys who, if not the "illiterates" Whitman sometimes claimed them to be, certainly lacked the culture and education necessary to write perfect standard English.[15] As Shively notes, Whitman's academic admirers have often repressed his lower-class ties, seeking to elevate him above the very masses from whom he came and with whom he chose throughout his life to associate. Not surprisingly, Whitman sought the companionship of men and boys who reminded him of his own working-class background. Nevertheless, Richard Stoddard wrote upon Whitman's death that he "always wondered why [Whitman] was interested in the class of men whom he visited," and modern scholars have devoted the vast majority of their attention to Whitman's relationship with middle-class friends and associates (Traubel, O'Connor, Bucke, and Burroughs) rather than to his working-class lovers and "comrades." Our knowledge of Whitman's "other" life of working-class contacts has come primarily through hints rather than scholarly research. Much of the scholarly attention to Whitman's friendships has been a misguided attempt to conceal the truth: "Whitman admired the common people because he was one. He sought his sexual partners among the workers. . . . Whitman's boy-loving has been even less popular among the learned than his homosexuality. He acted as both mother and father to his lovers, many of whom were orphans, poor and lost in the great world" (Shively, 18–19).

Shively's observations are extremely significant in terms of Whitman's unique sense of the body's importance as a locus of social and linguistic energies. In the opening section of "Song of Myself," when Whitman writes

"I loafe and invite my soul," repeating the word *loafe* in the following line, he is already employing a notion of bodily hexis to communicate a complex of social and personal attitudes that will be further developed in the course of the poem. By informing the reader that he will "lean and loafe," he is adopting a posture antithetical to that of the conventionally decorous and earnest demeanor of the nineteenth-century poet. His relaxed and somewhat impudent pose suggests that he will resist any form of censorship by the dominant class or the dominant discourse, either of his language or of his body. As Bourdieu makes clear, the linguistic gesture and its accompanying physical gesture cannot be separated; they bear the same relationship to forms of socioeconomic distinction: "It is no coincidence that bourgeois distinction invests the same intention in its relation to language as it invests in its relation to the body. The sense of acceptability which orients linguistic practices is inscribed in the most deep-rooted of bodily dispositions: it is the whole body which responds by its posture . . . to the tension of the market" (*Language*, 86).

Whitman's poetic use of bodily hexis to rebel against the normative social codes of midcentury literary America was part of his larger attempt to encompass physical attitudes or characteristics within language. For Whitman, not only individual expression but entire languages could be understood in terms of the kind of relationship to the physical they convey. The English language, which Whitman viewed as a language of political and cultural resistance against a French-based aristocracy, already contained the essence of what his poems would attempt to express: "The English tongue is full of strong words native or adopted to express the blood-born passion of the race for rudeness and resistance, as against polish and all acts to give in: robust, brawny, athletic, muscular, acrid, harsh, rugged, severe, pluck, grit, effrontery, stern, resistance, bracing, rude, rugged, rough, shaggy, bearded, arrogant, haughty. These words are alive and sinewy—they walk, look, step with an air of command" (*DN*, 738).

The words Whitman chooses to display in this entry from "The Primer of Words" derive their evocative power from a strong consonantal presence and a tendency toward closed or dark vowels which gives them a marked sonic thickness or density—what he himself calls a "rude" or "sinewy" character—and an almost onomatopoeic suggestiveness of the physical world. Here Whitman adumbrates on the most basic level the way in which somatic structures can be embedded within language, on the level of what Robert Frost would later call "the sound of sense." But what Whitman reads as the inherent rejection in the language of "polish" and of "all acts to give in" is also an ideological statement about the capacity of the English language to reflect an oppositional physical attitude or a state of "nature" in reaction to cultural distinction and co-optation. The language itself contains a kind of bodily hexis that stands metonymically for the poet's own stance, although it is a relationship at several removes: England to France; American English (an even more "shaggy" version of the vernacular) to British English; Whitman's "barbaric yawp" to the "standard" American speech of Webster's dictionary.

Whitman's preference for "unpolished" words over more polished or refined ones is also a way of expressing, in Bourdieu's terms, a "whole relation to the social world, and [a] whole socially informed relation to the world":

> There is every reason to think that . . . the bodily hexis characteristic of a social class determines the system of phonological features which characterizes a class pronunciation. . . . Thus, in the case of the lower classes, articulatory style is quite clearly part of a relation to the body that is dominated by the refusal of "airs and graces" (i.e., the refusal of stylization and the imposition of form) and by the valorization of virility—one aspect of a more general disposition to appreciate what is "natural." . . . On the one hand, domesticated language, censorship made natural, which proscribes "gross" remarks, "coarse" jokes and "thick" accents, goes hand in hand with the domestication of the body which excludes all excessive manifestations of appetites or feelings . . . and which subjects the body to all kinds of discipline and censorship aimed at denaturalizing it. (*Language*, 86–87)

The "rudeness" or "resistance" Whitman seeks in language, and the thickness and coarseness of the words he chooses to illustrate his argument, represent not only an aesthetic agenda but a class-based refusal to adopt the linguistic decorum of more genteel writers. For Whitman, an acceptance of the dominant style—in this case that of the fireside poets and their literary contemporaries—would represent a denial of both social and sexual identities and realities, in Bourdieu's words "a repudiation of the virile values which constitute class membership" (*Language*, 86). As Whitman makes clear in his 1856 letter to Emerson, what concerns him most about the current state of American culture is "the stinging fact that in orthodox society today, if the dresses were changed, the men might easily pass for women and the women for men" (*LG*, 737).

If Shively is correct that Whitman's social class has been as taboo a subject in biographical and critical studies as his sexual practices, many of his poems and statements need to be reevaluated in terms of such a class dynamic, one that is related to a social sense of the physical body. Shively's assessment and the related arguments of Killingsworth, Moon, and others are supported by Foucault's contention in *The History of Sexuality* that it was the late nineteenth century that saw the fullest development of the relationship between social power and sexuality. According to Foucault, by the end of the eighteenth century the control of sexuality had moved outside the realm of the church and into the dominion of the state through medical, pedagogical, and demographic axes. But it was not until the nineteenth century that a discourse of sexuality was sufficiently developed to encompass the lower and working classes, to "spread through the entire social body."[16] In fact, it was also not until that time that the bourgeois classes became aware of the fact that other classes had bodies at all. Not until a system of controls could be developed through the agency of schools, housing, hygiene, medicine, and health insurance did it become possible "to safely import the deployment of sexuality into the exploited classes" (126).

Foucault's analysis of sociosexual hegemony in nineteenth-century France would certainly have been applicable, with minor revisions, to American society as well. As Robert Wiebe makes clear in *The Opening of American Society*, the 1840s and 1850s saw an increasing division along class lines in all aspects of social, economic, and physical life. The expanding institutions of midcentury American society "mobilized the values of the new culture into a nationwide standard for inclusion and exclusion, a class line that separated those who were qualified to participate in a democracy of free choices from those who were not."[17] The two classes—the haves and the have-nots of American life—moved on "parallel tracks," tracks that grew further apart as the century went on, and as "respectable Americans found themselves devoting more and more attention to the maintenance of this crucial distinction." The American social body was increasingly divided into two or possibly three bodies, with a group of upper- and middle-class citizens expressing an ever greater aversion to the physicality, violence, and sickness of the poor, while at the same time showing almost total disregard for the bodies of the blacks and Native Americans who stood at the lowest rung of the social order: "A long cycle that originated in the gentry hierarchy and traced the rising expectations and democratized prospects of the early 19th century preserved a culture of equality in its upper half at the expense of its lower half. Below the class line lived an agglomeration of white Protestant floaters and outcast religious sects, white Catholics, blacks in and out of slavery, and native Americans" (Wiebe, 346).

The "propertyless poor" were represented more often than not as disreputable, vice-ridden, and dangerous, in contrast to the cherished respectability and sobriety of the middle class. The poor and migrant populations of lower-class whites engaged in physical behavior no longer acceptable to "respectable" Americans. Their form of bodily hexis included such activities as fighting and brawling, wife and child beating, swearing, carousing, and drinking. The only site of connection between the two classes was increasingly reduced to the various institutions of reform: prisons, schools, asylums, hospitals, poorhouses, and temperance groups. The legal profession also contributed to the social and physical disenfranchisement of the lower class: rather than represent the rights of poor families, courts would split families up, send sick or old members to other areas, bind the children through apprentice laws, and put youngsters to work at physically dangerous jobs.

Whitman's poems and other writings address this divided and exclusionary situation in various direct and metaphorical ways. When Whitman figures himself as a poet embracing the nation as a body, he not only literalizes the metaphorical construction of the social body or body politic, but he also destroys any notion of such differences in class orientation as Foucault describes. Whitman's recognition that all bodies—from whatever social class, ethnic background, or racial type—are essentially equal, his claim in "The Sleepers" to have "averaged" all ("one is no better than the other, / The night and sleep have liken'd them and restored them"), allows him to circumvent any bourgeois hegemony that could exercise its control over the bodies of lower-class citizens. Yet it is significant that it is only through the trope of sleep, a shared and passive form of bodily hexis, that Whitman is able to destabilize the kinds of social distinctions that are rigidly maintained in waking activities.

Bodies and Parts of Bodies

In sections 7 and 8 of "The Sleepers," Whitman provides his most radically destabilizing catalogue, one that combines social types from various strata of society ("the ennuyé," "the money-maker," "the criminal") with an equally wide range of physical types ("the stammerer, the sick, the perfect-form'd, the homely"). Here, more than anywhere else in Leaves of Grass, physical distinction and sociocultural distinction are brought together in crucible-like juxtaposition.

Whitman's recognition that such a utopian "averaging" of all of these individuals can only occur in a dream state is clear in his depiction of a nighttime scene. "Every thing in the dim light is beautiful," he declares, but it seems unlikely that it would appear so by the light of day. Darkness hides both physical and social differences; it disguises both ugliness and violence. Whitman's vision, however unrealistic it may be, is nonetheless powerful; the final catalogue of bodies in "The Sleepers" is worth quoting in its entirety:

> The sleepers are very beautiful as they lie unclothed,
> They flow hand in hand over the whole earth from east to west
>   as they lie unclothed,
> The Asiatic and African are hand in hand, the European and
>   American are hand in hand,
> Learn'd and unlearn'd are hand in hand, and male and female
>   are hand in hand,
> The bare arm of the girl crosses the bare arm of her lover, they
>   press close without lust, his lips press her neck,
> The father holds his grown or ungrown son in his arms with
>   measureless love, and the son holds the father in his arms
>   with measureless love,
> The white hair of the mother shines on the white wrist of the
>   daughter,
> The breath of the boy goes with the breath of the man, friend is
>   inarm'd by friend,
> The scholar kisses the teacher and the teacher kisses the scholar,
>   the wrong'd is made right,
> The call of the slave is one with the master's call, and the master
>   salutes the slave,
> The felon steps forth from the prison, the insane becomes sane,
>   the suffering of sick persons is reliev'd,
> The sweatings and fevers stop, the throat that was unsound is
>   sound, the lungs of the consumptive are resumed, the poor
>   distress'd head is free,
> The joints of the rheumatic move as smoothly as ever, and
>   smoother than ever,
> Stiflings and passages open, the paralyzed become supple,

The swell'd and convuls'd and congested awake to themselves in
  condition,
They pass the invigoration of the night and the chemistry of the
  night, and awake.

(161–76)

That no poet contemporaneous with Whitman would have been capable
of writing such a passage goes without saying. Even had another writer taken
enough interest in the various maladies Whitman catalogues to put them in
poetic form—not as metaphors, but for their own sake—the kinds of juxtapositions and rapid shifts in discursive register he achieves here broke every rule
of poetic decorum. How could a poet of the Victorian era have combined the
white-haired mother and her fair daughter with the bodies of the felon and
the insane? Do the scholar and the teacher really belong in the same poem,
not to say the same passage, with the sick and deformed? Even Thoreau, despite his democratic openness to bodily experience, is careful in *Walden* to
distinguish "the animal in us . . . reptile and sensual" from our "divine being."
Unlike Whitman, who could so unhesitatingly celebrate all aspects of the
physical, Thoreau expresses the hegemonic view in his traditionally Christian
concern that the "inferior and brutish" aspects of human nature "cannot be
wholly expelled," and that as "creatures of appetite . . . our very life is our disgrace."[18] For Whitman, the notion of any form of life as a "disgrace" is an
alien one, at least in the mid-1850s. As he makes clear in section 24 of "Song
of Myself," he is "divine" precisely in proportion to how much he can participate in the physical:

Turbulent, fleshy, sensual, eating, drinking and breeding,
No sentimentalist, no stander above men and women or apart
  from them,
No more modest than immodest.

(498–500)

Whitman's goal will be to record not only his own voice but "forbidden
voices" as well, "voices of sexes and lusts . . . voices indecent by me clarified
and transfigured."
    Two poems first published in 1860 give expression to these same connec-
tions between body and social orientation. "In Paths Untrodden," the first
poem of the *Calamus* sequence, begins with a striking image of Whitman's
own separation from various forms of bourgeois distinction:

In paths untrodden,
In the growth by margins of pond-waters,
Escaped from the life that exhibits itself,
From all the standards hitherto publish'd, from the pleasures,
    profits, conformities,
Which too long I was offering to feed my soul . . .

(1–5)

In lines that serve as an entry into what Killingsworth has called the "substratum of nineteenth-century sexual life," Whitman finds a descriptive image that serves as an allegorical figure for that which is both socially marginal and palpably physical: an untrodden path through the luxuriant growth at the margins of a pond. Whitman finds himself in what for him is a new kind of space, one in which he can experience a new sense of bodily hexis. Here he can be simultaneously alone—"Here by myself away from the clank of the world"—and together with his male friends and lovers, his "comrades." The site is clearly suggestive of a hidden or repressed sexuality—"No longer abashed, (for in this secluded spot I can respond as I would not dare elsewhere)"—and it is one where physical experience replaces the sociocultural realm of "standards" and "profits." It is here that the physical responsiveness to sexuality and the idiolectic potential of poetic language to capture a private, personal, or socially repressed aspect of experience are most closely joined.

Whitman's sexual marginality interarticulates with a sense of social marginality. He can neither accept the bourgeois values of educated or dominant classes from which he is at least partially excluded by his background, nor can he become fully a part of the working class to which his "cameradoes" belong. As an aspiring poet, he represents the cultural capital associated with one group; as a former tradesman and lover of working-class men and boys, he embodies the denial of sociocultural distinction typical of the other group.

In this poem Whitman sets forth the plan for the entire sequence: to "sing no songs . . . but those of manly attachment" and to make those songs about "that substantial life." The "substantial life" I take in its root form: a life of substance, of the physical. This physicality or sensuality is further suggested by the synecdochic figure of "talk'd to here by tongues aromatic." Not only is the tongue a part of the body that serves an ambiguously sexual and linguistic purpose, but the "aromatic" tongue is also related to the calamus plant from which the entire sequence takes its name—a plant known, according to Whitman, for its "fresh, aquatic, pungent bouquet" (*Corr.* 1:347). Thus the first phallic image of the poem and of the sequence occurs simultaneously with the first linguistic figure, a coupling that will be a trademark of the Calamus poems as a whole. The use of the calamus as a central figure within a personal symbolic code also represents the use of the idiolectic register to foreground the physical and sexual body.

Whitman establishes a further tension in the poem between the public life of business and publishing—"the life that exhibits itself"—and the private life of (homo)sexuality—"the secrets of my nights and days." Though Whitman would later deny that these "secrets" were specifically homoerotic and would be at pains to argue that the significance of the *Calamus* poems was more political than sexual—(that the "adhesive" love of men for each other would work for the "counterbalance and offset of our materialistic and vulgar American democracy")—my own reading of the poet suggests that in his work sexuality and politics are not easily untwined.

In the final section of "Starting from Paumanok" (most of which was later removed from the poem), Whitman again articulates his utopian vision of sexual expression in terms of egalitarian social relations:

> O my comrade! O you and me at last—and us two only;
> O power, liberty, eternity at last!
> O to be relieved of distinctions! to make as much of vices as of
>   virtues!
> O to level occupations and the sexes! O to bring all to common
>   ground! O adhesiveness!
> O the pensive aching to be together—you know not why, and I
>   know not why.

Once again Whitman returns to his key term of *distinctions*—distinctions that in this case can be avoided only through physical, and presumably sexual, contact. As the climactic moment in the introductory poem of the 1860 edition—then called "Proto-Leaf"—this passage must have had great importance for Whitman, and it is all the more significant that he removed it from the 1867 edition. In the passage, Whitman collapses together the personal level of "In Paths Untrodden" with the larger social and political frame of many of his earlier poems. In the briefest possible space, he moves from the extremely personal, almost confessional level of "O you and me at last—and us two only" to the grandly general proclamation "O power, liberty, eternity at last!"—a line that can be read neither as wholly idiolectic nor wholly sociolectic. The operatic swell of Whitman's apostrophes continues through the next two lines, as we move from the more personal or ethical level of radical democracy—"to make as much of vices as of virtues"—to the sociopolitical leveling of the occupations and the sexes ("to bring all to common ground") and finally to the sociosexual means of achieving such common ground—"adhesiveness." The passage ends with a return to the personal— "O the pensive aching to be together"—and to the uncontrollable and mysterious level of magnetic attraction—"you know not why, and I know not why." Sexual attraction, it would seem, is ultimately a highly personal matter that resists the controlling influence of any social hegemony; sex is itself democratic. Following Whitman's logic, male homoerotic bonding must be considered even more democratic, since it occurs outside of the socioeconomic sphere of marriage and thus outside the "conformities" of the "life that exhibits itself."[19]

If this passage and "In Paths Untrodden" provide significant instances of Whitman's attempt to figure the body poetically, a more extreme example of his attempt to avoid conventional uses of the body as a means of poetic figuration can be seen in his catalogues of the body's parts and functions. The most exhaustive example of these bodily catalogues, one which exemplifies both Whitman's resistance to abstract or metaphorical figuration of the body and his interest in the concrete expression of the body's physical existence, is the concluding section of "I Sing the Body Electric." What is most interesting about this passage, aside from the sheer bravado of its unadorned presentation of the body, is its extremely diverse mixture of discursive levels: in fact, the passage can be read as a repository of all of society's disparate constructions of the body through language.

Whitman's notebook entries demonstrate an unusual interest in the details of anatomy and medical practice. In his unfinished project "The Primer of Words," Whitman calls attention to the discursive riches contributed by medicine and its attendant technologies: "Medicine has hundreds of useful and characteristic words—new means of cure—new schools of doctors— the wonderful anatomy of the body—the names of a thousand diseases— surgeon's terms—hydropathy—all that relates to the great organs of the body. The Medical art is always grand—nothing affords a nobler scope for superior men and women. It, of course, will never cease to be near to man, and add new terms" (DN, 734).

For a nineteenth-century American poet to interest himself in "the names of a thousand diseases" already signals a surprising openness to an area of the sociolect usually ignored by literary writers. Bryant, for example—who shared with Whitman an interest in homeopathy, gave lectures on the subject, and even served as president of the board of directors of the Homeopathic College in New York in 1869—would maintain a firm distinction between his poetic writing and the discourses of nonpoetic interests like homeopathic medicine. Equally striking in Whitman's notebook is the importance he gives to the "new terms" generated by medicine, an importance seemingly as great as that of the health benefits themselves. Whitman is awed not so much by the scientific advances in medical technology as by the linguistic expression of those advances, by the increasing complexity of the sociolect. This mid-nineteenth-century sociolect incorporated society's increasing fascination with the medical sciences, including not only traditional medicine but also such unorthodox schools as allopathy, homeopathy, hydropathy, Thomsonianism, phrenology, and mesmeric and spiritual healing, not to mention the various medical imposters and advertisers of spurious cures who competed for the growing medical business.[20]

Elsewhere in his notebooks and journalistic writings, Whitman shows a considerable awareness of—and interest in—scientific and pseudoscientific discourses relating to medicine, health, and hygiene. In the late 1850s, we find him writing on insanity and on personal hygiene, clipping articles from medical texts, and transcribing portions of books like *The Science of Swimming* and *Fowler on Hereditary Descent*.[21] Whitman was in personal contact with a number of New York physicians in the 1840s and 1850s, among them Edward Dixon, a well-known genito-urinary surgeon who wrote articles on such current medical issues as onanism and "spermatorrhea."[22] Whitman knew enough about medicine to argue with some of Dixon's more ridiculous medical suggestions, though he shared the physician's fundamental belief that nature's forces—fresh air, water, sleep, healthy food, and exercise—were the best cure for most ailments. In his articles for the *Daily Eagle* and later for the *Brooklyn Times*, Whitman addresses such topics as insanity, surgery, druggists, public health, bathing and the public baths, female health and exercise, abortion, the medical profession, the health of children in the city, and "manly exercise"; Whitman gained much of his knowledge of medicine and public health firsthand from his frequent visits to Brooklyn hospitals. In the early 1860s, he displayed an even stronger commitment to these same issues, proposing to write a series of articles on the "science of a sound and beautiful body."[23] Finally, the Civil War provided Whitman with the opportunity to perform a more active medical role, as a volunteer hospital aide. From all accounts, Whitman's preoccupation with doctors and medical discourse continued throughout his later life; in Camden, he professed a wish to have been a doctor himself, citing medicine as the profession that best combined "science and the emotional elements."[24]

When Whitman documents the body in the final section of "I Sing the Body Electric," his juxtapositions of discursive registers and his use of personal coinages to supplement the existing sociolect result in a poetry that remains characteristically his own. After an introductory passage of four lines—in which he introduces the idea of an identity between the body and the soul, and between the body and the poem—Whitman begins with a seemingly straightforward cataloguing of the body from top to bottom, and then shifts to various kinds of internal organs before ending the poem with a final group of lines that achieve their heightened lyrical effect through an increased mixing of discursive modes.

> Head, neck, hair, ears, drop and tympan of the ears,
> Eyes, eye-fringes, iris of the eye, eyebrows, and the waking or
>   sleeping of the lids,
> Mouth, tongue, lips, teeth, roof of the mouth, jaws, and the
>   jaw-hinges,
> Nose, nostrils of the nose, and the partition,
> Cheeks, temples, forehead, chin, throat, back of the neck,
>   neck-slue,
> Strong shoulders, manly beard, scapula, hind-shoulders, and
>   the ample side-round of the chest,
> Upper-arm, armpit, elbow-socket, lower-arm, arm-sinews,
>   armbones,
> Wrist and wrist-joints, hand, palm, knuckles, thumb, forefinger,
>   finger-joints, finger-nails,
> Broad breast-front, curling hair of the breast, breast-bone,
>   breast-side,
> Ribs, belly, backbone, joints of the backbone,
> Hips, hip-sockets, hip-strength, inward and outward round,
>   man-balls, man-root,
> Strong set of thighs, well carrying the trunk above,

Leg-fibres, knee, knee-pan, upper-leg, under-leg,
Ankles, instep, foot-ball, toes, toe-joints, the heel;
All attitudes, all the shapeliness, all the belongings of my or your
    body or of any one's body, male or female,
The lung-sponges, the stomach-sac, the bowels sweet and clean,
The brain in its folds inside the skull-frame,
Sympathies, heart-valves, palate-valves, sexuality, maternity.

(133–50)

In his reading of the passage, Tenney Nathanson criticizes what he sees as Whitman's "encyclopaedic" listing of the body's parts, an "obsessive enumeration" which only manages to catalogue "the *disjecta membra* which the alienated body subjected to cultural encoding has become," rather than "re-animating . . . the body by means of pneumatic energies endowed with restorative force" (288). Nathanson, however, gives insufficient attention to the formal, rhetorical, and stylistic means by which Whitman achieves his unique and memorable conclusion to "I Sing the Body Electric." Whitman's catalogue is not simply an encyclopaedic enumeration but an ecstatic celebration of the body, which allows us to share with the poet in a linguistic recreation of the body itself, a recreation unmediated by a history of the use of the body for poetic figuration.

The most striking stylistic feature of the section is the number of hyphenated words identifying parts of the body. A partial listing of such words gives a sense of the verbal energy and the directness of somatic impact the words convey: eye-fringes, jaw-hinges, neck-slue, hind-shoulders, upper-arm, elbow-socket, lower-arm, arm-sinews, arm-bones, wrist-joints, finger-nails, breast-front, breast-bone, breast-side, hip-sockets, hip-strength, man-balls, man-root, leg-fibres, knee-pan, upper-leg, under-leg, foot-ball, toe-joints, lung-sponges, stomach-sac, skull-frame, heart-valves, palate-valves. Although some of these were expressions in common use in Whitman's day, and most are at least easily understood, others are more obscure: Whitman's coinage *neck-slue*, for example, relies on a nautical term meaning "to turn on its axis" (and normally used only as a verb) to convey a precise movement of the neck. Other expressions rely on a subtle displacement of normal usage. In the 1853 Webster's dictionary, sockets exist for eyes but not for elbows; fringes are reserved for hair or thread and not for eyes; there are eye-balls but no "man-balls." "Man-root," denoting the penis, is a highly imagistic coinage, as are "lung-sponges," and "skull-frame." At the opposite end of the linguistic spectrum, "heart-valves," "palate-valves," and "stomach-sac" are terms of medical usage, specialized enough not to be found in Webster's. The richness of Whitman's linguistic palette is emphasized further by the juxtaposition of Anglo-Saxon words (arm-sinews, hind-shoulders), with Latinate ones (*scapula* for the shoulder-blade, *tympan* for ear-drum). Each of these neologisms, unusual verbal combinations, and technical terms serves to emphasize the body's materiality. The body is essentially irreducible to language of any kind, but it is completely irreducible, Whitman makes clear, to the kinds of vague and euphemistic vocabulary traditionally used by poets to describe physical functions and characteristics. In his aggressive mixing of technical or medical diction with a level of more intimate and personal observation ("the ample side-round of the chest," "strong set of thighs, well carrying the trunk above," "inward and outward round," "the bowels sweet and clean") and a level of more abstract meditation on the body's aptitude for its various functions ("attitudes," "shapeliness," "sympathies"), Whitman rhetorically elides the difference between social and personal forms of discourse, making possible a further synthesis, in the form of the poem itself, of poetic language (rhythmically varied, imagistically dense, linguistically creative) and the precision of scientific or anatomical discourse. The curious melange of discourses, along with the physicality of the hyphenated words, prevents the body itself from becoming marked by any kind of social or cultural distinctions: treated as a function of their raw materials, all bodies are represented as truly equal or identical.

The final lines of the poem shift registers once again, this time from the catalogue of body parts to an ecstatic appreciation of the physical body in all its aspects, culminating in the apotheosizing leap from body to soul:

> The continual changes of the flex of the mouth, and around the
>   eyes,
> The skin, the sunburnt shade, freckles, hair,
> The curious sympathy one feels when feeling with the hand the
>   naked meat of the body,
> The circling rivers of the breath, and breathing it in and out,
> The beauty of the waist, and thence of the hips, and thence
>   downward toward the knees,
> The thin red jellies within you or within me, the bones and the
>   marrow of the bones,
> The exquisite realization of health;

O I say these are not the parts and poems of the body only, but
    of the soul,
O I say now these are the soul!

(156–64)

Whitman ends his poem with some of the most potent lines ever written about the human anatomy, despite what Killingsworth calls the "deemphasis of sexuality" inherent in his abstract references to the soul in the final two lines. Having established through his exhaustive catalogue the concreteness and social impermeability of the body, Whitman now finds an expansiveness of expression that can bridge the sensual reality of the physical body and the electric charge of the spiritualized body. The catalogue, relatively unmarked by idiolectic expression (except in the unusual diction contained in the hyphenated words), is replaced by an idiolectic register that allows the poet to express himself through images that are simultaneouly highly physical and outlandishly personal: the description of blood as "thin red jellies" or of the breath as "circling rivers"; the unusually detailed and sensual observations of "the flex of the mouth" and "the naked meat of the body." It is the ending of "I Sing the Body Electric," more than anything in *Leaves of Grass*, that exemplifies the tremendous idiolectic potential of the body in Whitman's poetry. It is the desire to represent the palpable forms of the body rather than to explore its metaphorical or figurative possibilities that allows Whitman to break with previous poetic practice and to produce what is essentially a new poetic language of the body, one that resists any reappropriation by a discourse of socioeconomic distinction.

A Triumphant Life and a Triumphant Death

The catalogue of the body ending "I Sing the Body Electric" may be socially fluid, but the bodily hexis Whitman represents throughout the poem is clearly marked as one of working-class or lower-class origin. In section 2, we find "The group of laborers seated at noon-time with their open dinner-kettles" and "The wrestle of wrestlers, two apprentice-boys, quite grown, lusty, good-natured, native-born, out on the vacant lot at sun-down after work." Section 3 introduces a more extended physical portrait of the "common farmer, the father of five sons," who sails, hunts, and fishes with "wonderful vigor, calmness, beauty of person." And in sections 7 and 8, as we have already seen, Whitman represents the class-marked body in its most extreme

Figuring the Body in Leaves   179

form: that of slaves at auction. But it is in the final section that the poet most forcefully evokes a physical activity that mirrors the bodily hexis of the working-class "rough":

> Food, drink, pulse, digestion, sweat, sleep, walking, swimming,
> Poise on the hips, leaping, reclining, embracing, arm-curving
>   and tightening.

(154–55)

The identification of the "body electric" with a particular social class is clear, without any overt declaration of class-based sympathies. Whitman presents a scene of working-class homosocial activity in which the exercising, feasting, and frolicking are completely undifferentiated from the most basic of bodily processes: pulse, digestion, and sweat. Here working-class men are showing off their physiques and their muscles in an unabashed and frank display of both physicality and sexuality.

Like his sixteenth-century predecessor Rabelais, Whitman presents in *Leaves of Grass* a literary text that articulates a constant struggle between what Bakhtin has characterized as the "closed body" of the bourgeoisie and the "carnivalesque" body of the other classes. Alone among American poets writing in the wake of Romanticism, Whitman approximates the Rabelaisian gesture of combining in his poem the various tropes of corporeal existence (sex, food and drink, laughter) with the traditional poetic trope of death. Bakhtin, who may have been unaware of Whitman's work, claims that the Rabelaisian chronotope of carnivalesque physicality is lost in subsequent works of literature, especially those in the Romantic and post-Romantic mode:

> The wholeness of a triumphant life, a whole that embraces death, and laughter, and food and sexual activity, is lost. Life and death are perceived solely within the limits of the sealed-off individual life (where life is unrepeatable, and death an irremediable end), and, therefore, within the limits of life taken in its internal and subjective aspect. Thus, in the artistic imagery of the Romantics and the Symbolists, these matrices are transformed into sharp, static contrasts and oxymorons that are either not resolved at all (since there is no all-encompassing, larger real "whole") or resolved on the plane of mysticism. (*Dialogic Imagination*, 199)

The Romantic lyric poet typically achieved a sense of distinction from the everyday world precisely through the kind of oxymoronic contrasts that attempt to deny, or at least circumvent, the existence of any real social context, any palpable physical world, or the physical reality of death. Among nineteenth-century American authors, it is Melville in prose fiction and Whitman in poetry who come closest to satisfying the Rabelaisian paradigm and to rejecting the Romantic literary mode. Whitman often brings into unusual and startling juxtaposition the same group of elements identified by Bakhtin: in "A Song of the Rolling Earth," for example, he writes within a single line of "Persuasions of lovers, curses, gasps of the dying, laughter of young people, accents of bargainers" (39). Taken as a whole, *Leaves of Grass* presents a large enough context to provide "the wholeness of a triumphant life" rather than the "sealed-off individual life" of the typical Romantic lyric. If the earlier editions concentrate more on the life-affirming properties of laughter, food, and especially sex, the poems published in Whitman's third and subsequent editions make death a process equal in importance to life itself.[25]

"Song of Myself" already contains a significant meditation on death and its relation to life. Some of the most revealing moments in the poem occur when Whitman attempts to reconcile the dual pulls of life and death, as he does in sections 6–7, in section 24, and especially in section 49, where he imagines the allegorical figures of Death, the Corpse, and Life. Fundamental to Whitman's vision of death are its corporeality and its sensuality, especially when contrasted with the sentimentality and abstraction characteristic of the treatment of death by Whitman's poetic contemporaries.[26] As with Whitman's candid depictions of the sexual encounter and of the anatomical body, the body here is the subject, not merely a figure for another plane of existence, whether social or metaphysical. Whitman writes:

> And as to you Corpse I think you are good manure, but that
>   does not offend me,
> I smell the white roses sweet-scented and growing,
> I reach to the leafy lips, I reach to the polish'd breast of melons.
>
> (1294–96)

What is most extraordinary in this passage is the inversion of readerly expectations that prevents Whitman's representation of death from ever reaching the static point of traditional allegorical or prosopopoeic figuration. The personified and apostrophized Corpse is immediately reduced to the physical status of "good manure." Whitman proceeds to produce out of this manure not the agricultural crops that we might expect but "white roses sweet-scented," with their associations of purity and courtly tradition in stark contrast to the antipoetic crudity of manure. Finally, Whitman shifts discursive registers again: from the traditionally iconographic poetic image of white roses to the corporeal and sexualized "leafy lips" and "polish'd breast of melons." The lips and breast would normally be coded as signs of female sexuality, though within Whitman's sexual economy they remain more ambiguous. Given the nongendered but presumptively male nature of the Corpse here, death and (homo)sexuality are combined in a powerful and highly destabilizing way, reminiscent of the statement in section 24 that "Copulation is no more rank than death is."

Yet Whitman does not pursue this approach to death in later poems. By the time of his postwar elegy for Lincoln, "When Lilacs Last in the Dooryard Bloom'd," the poet's treatment of death has shifted from the voice-based discursiveness in section 49 of "Song of Myself" to the poetically figured form of the elegy itself, a convention that stands at a far remove from the generically open poems of the first edition. Whitman's Lincoln elegy was one of his best-known poems by the late nineteenth century and was generally accepted as one of the poet's central works; it was anthologized along with other "safe" Whitman poems like "O Captain! My Captain!" and "Come Up from the Fields Father." It is significant that all three of these poems deal more directly with death than they do with life: two with the death of the political and spiritual leader Lincoln, and one with the death of a soldier and the only son of an Ohio farming couple. Apparently death was a more acceptable topic to many nineteenth-century readers than was life, especially in the terms with which Whitman chose to celebrate life as a bodily function. Unlike the processes of physical labor and sexuality, death, especially as represented in the elegiac mode of these poems, was a well-established high cultural topos, one treated by such nineteenth-century poets as Poe, Longfellow, Bryant, Wordsworth, and Tennyson. It was a topos within which sociocultural distinctions were generally made clear, both in terms of the social positioning of the dead subject and in terms of the more exalted language presupposed by the decorum of the ode or elegiac poem. Whitman's highly symbolic rendering of Lincoln's death in "When Lilacs Last in the Dooryard Bloom'd" may have helped ensure the poet's own fame, but such fame would come only at great expense: he had to cast aside his earlier reticence to insert his poetry into a canon of lyric utterance that marked itself so clearly as a product of high cultural distinction. The subject of death, it appears, becomes a catalyst for Whitman's poetic repudiation of many of the principles that guided his first two editions; by 1867, he would write to William Rossetti of a cluster of poems "born of thoughts on the deep themes of Death and Immortality" (*Corr.* 2:350), which would eventually become the "Whispers of Heavenly Death" cluster. These poems of the 1860s were concerned with the soul as transcendent figure for a spiritual or divine order, not as marker of a personal or bodily identity.

In 1856, Whitman had still maintained a sense of the fundamental inefficacy of language, of a language that could never "tell the best," as he writes in "A Song of the Rolling Earth":

> When I undertake to tell the best I cannot,
> My tongue is ineffectual on its pivots,
> My breath will not be obedient to its organs,
> I become a dumb man.
>
> (104–7)

The most profound moment of uncertainty in Whitman's ambition to "sing [him]self" as a poet occurs in this passage, when he contemplates the earth in its mute and concrete expansiveness. Yet such resolutions by Whitman to "leave the best untold," however sincerely felt, would not last long.

Increasingly, Whitman attempted to impose on his poetic texts a weight of cultural distinction they could not sustain. No longer ambivalent about his ability or desire to "tell the best," Whitman sought in later editions a form of poetic distinction much more in line with the dominant poetic ideology of nineteenth-century Romanticism. His new poetic, after 1860, was one predicated more on the Romantic discourse of transcendence and less on the contemporary social discourses articulating the "collective substratum" whose underlying presence, as Theodor Adorno suggests, is essential to the construction of authentic lyric poetry.[27] Whitman's aesthetic and political agenda of the early editions, conceived largely as a response to the pressures of various forms of distinction—social, cultural, racial, national, physical, and historical—would eventually give way before new pressures that came to bear on him. As David Reynolds has noted, in the latter part of his career Whitman felt a profound ambivalence about his own attempts to seek literary and cultural recognition. This ambivalence is perhaps best exemplified in his complex attitude toward "O Captain! My Captain!"—a poem that clearly embarrassed him (at times causing him to wish he had never written it), but which he recited on every possible occasion, even appending it to the end of his popular Lincoln lecture.[28] Whitman could no longer easily differentiate his increasing popular success from the quality of his writing, which grew more conventional, patriotic, and even religious in concert with evolving middle-class tastes and expectations. Rather than the raw social substratum reflected in a poem like "Faces," Whitman would too often turn to the kind of nostalgic sentimentality exploited in "What Best I See in Thee," an 1881 poem dedicated to Ulysses S. Grant on his return from a world tour. In the third line of this poem, "Ever undimm'd by time shoots warlike victory's dazzle," we find an extreme example of Whitman's desire in his later poetry to achieve poetic distinction through what he once would have considered superficial means: syntactic inversion, assonance and alliteration worthy of Tennyson or Swinburne, and a post-Romantic appeal to heroic grandeur. By the 1880s, Whitman's textual politics have become a politics of socio-cultural distinction, supplanting the politics of ironic detachment and aes-thetic irreverence that inform his most important poems of the early editions.

Surely there are biographical explanations for this change—for example, the pain and disillusionment occasioned by the Civil War, the identification with Lincoln as a political and spiritual leader, and the attempt to conceal or to deflect attention from his homosexual orientation—all of which may have contributed to a rhetoric capitulating to conventional tastes. But we might also associate the transformation of Whitman's rhetoric with the dynamics of the literary field of his time. When it became clear to Whitman that he had failed to gain sufficient symbolic capital within his literary field, he chose to abandon his earlier strategies of difference and to adopt a position closer to that which had already been carved out by his more successful contemporar-ies. Ironically, the double logic of distinction whereby the younger Whitman had established a uniquely important place in American poetic history was abandoned when it did not provide him with the access to literary fame he in-creasingly desired. While he would remain thoroughly American in his role as a cultural icon, he would cease to contribute significantly to the ongoing development of American literature. American readers would have to wait several decades before another generation would recognize in Whitman the thoroughly *distinct* poet who expressed the "American keynote" more suc-cessfully than any other, who managed to translate into powerful and lasting poetry the discourses of his time and nation.

NOTES

Introduction

1 C. Carroll Hollis, *Language and Style in "Leaves of Grass"* (Baton Rouge: Louisiana State University Press, 1983), 234.

2 Paul Zweig, *Walt Whitman: The Making of the Poet* (New York: Basic Books, 1984). The biographical explanations show relatively widespread agreement. In a more schematic rendering of the same trajectory traced in greater detail by Zweig, Richard Chase identifies three hypotheses for Whitman's "transformation": his sexual "liberation" by an octaroon woman in New Orleans in 1848; the discovery of his own latent homosexuality; and a mystical experience which led him to a "cosmic consciousness." Jerome Loving concurs with the last two of these and adds the discovery of Emerson. See Richard Chase, *Walt Whitman Reconsidered* (New York: William Sloane, 1955) and Jerome Loving, *Emerson, Whitman, and the American Muse* (Chapel Hill: University of North Carolina Press, 1982), 67–69.

3 See in particular Pierre Bourdieu, *Distinction: A Social Critique of the Judgement of Taste* (Cambridge: Harvard University Press, 1984) and his *The Field of Cultural Production: Essays on Art and Literature*, ed. Randal Johnson (New York: Columbia University Press, 1993).

4 In Mikhail Bakhtin, *Speech Genres and Other Late Essays*, trans. Vern McGee, ed. Caryl Emerson and Michael Holquist (Austin: University of Texas Press, 1986), 60–102.

5 Roland Barthes, *Elements of Semiology*, trans. A. Lavers and C. Smith (New York: Hill and Wang, 1977).

6 Michael Riffaterre, *Semiotics of Poetry* (Bloomington: Indiana University Press, 1978), 21.

7 Michael Riffaterre, "Textuality: W. H. Auden's 'Musée des Beaux Arts,'" in *Textual Analysis: Some Readers Reading*, ed. Mary Ann Caws (New York: Modern Language Association, 1986), 1.

8 Whitman's other titles for the poems in the 1856 edition share this naive quality of directness, a quality that is often supplanted by more self-consciously literary titles in the later editions. See for example "Poem of the Body" ("I Sing the Body Electric" after 1867), "Poem of Procreation" ("A Woman Waits for Me"

after 1867), "Poem of Women" ("Unfolded Out of the Folds" after 1871), and "Poem of Salutation" ("Salut au Monde" after 1860).

9　Quoted by Laurent Jenny, "The Strategy of Form," in *French Literary Theory Today: A Reader,* ed. Tsvetan Todorov (New York: Cambridge University Press, 1984), 36.

10　See Bourdieu's *The Field of Cultural Production* for a discussion both of the more general process through which works of literature and the arts interact with a larger "economy of symbolic goods" and of the specific nineteenth-century context in which French authors such as Gustave Flaubert negotiated within such an economy.

11　Fredric Jameson, *The Political Unconscious: Narrative as Socially Symbolic Act* (Ithaca: Cornell University Press, 1981), 57–58.

12　Riffaterre's definition of *textuality* is a more restrictive one than I would apply, but I quote it here for the sake of clarity: "the complex of formal and semantic factors that characterize the self-sufficient, coherent, unified text and legitimize its forms, however aberrant they may be, by removing any hint of the the gratuitous" ("Textuality," 1). For Riffaterre, these defining factors are the poem's idiolect, its closure, and its overall "significance" as a work of art.

13　See Richard Terdiman, *Discourse/Counter-Discourse: The Theory and Practice of Symbolic Resistance in Nineteenth-Century France* (Ithaca: Cornell University Press, 1985).

14　Stephen Greenblatt, *Learning to Curse: Essays in Early Modern Culture* (New York: Routledge, 1990), 112.

15　I exempt Emily Dickinson's poetry from these general statements about Whitman's contemporary poetic milieu. Dickinson's work represents an equally radical but entirely different rearrangement of discursive parameters, but since it was unknown to Whitman, it bears only a tangential relevance to an analysis of Whitman's sociolect.

16　See David S. Reynolds's discussion of the growing inequality between the rich and the poor in *Walt Whitman's America: A Cultural Biography* (New York: Knopf, 1995), 141. The gap in wealth and buying power between the wealthiest and least wealthy sectors of the population widened rapidly in the period of Whitman's childhood and poetic development, 1825–60, thereby imposing greater class differences on a society that had been relatively more egalitarian earlier in the century.

17　Whitman uses well over thirteen thousand words, almost seven thousand of them only once. Although I cannot perform a word count on all British and American poets, my selective comparisons indicate that Whitman's word use is extremely diverse relative to that of other poetic writers. His notebooks on language, and especially his *American Primer,* would substantiate what appears to have been a tremendous interest in words, discourses, dialects, and languages. Whitman's extensive poetic vocabulary not only underscores his inclusive ambitions but also distinguishes him from other Romantic and post-Romantic poets (Wordsworth and Tennyson, for example), who sought to decrease or economize poetic vocabulary, to limit the intrusion of the sociolect into the poetic text.

18 Robert Creeley, "Introduction to Whitman," in *Walt Whitman: The Measure of His Song,* ed. Jim Perlman, Ed Folsom, and Dan Campion (Minneapolis: Holy Cow, 1981), 198.

19 In citing Whitman's notebook entries, I have silently corrected his confusing punctuation.

CHAPTER ONE   Intertextuality and the Poetics of Distinction

1 See Floyd Stovall, *The Foreground of "Leaves of Grass"* (Charlottesville: University Press of Virginia, 1974), 294.

2 Recent books by Kenneth Price and Ezra Greenspan provide a useful background for my attempt to answer these questions. Price's *Whitman and Tradition: The Poet in His Century* (New Haven: Yale University Press, 1990) is more narrowly focused on Whitman's literary intertext—specifically that of English Romantic and post-Romantic poetry—and how the literary tradition provides "norms within which Whitman worked and from which he deviated" (4). Greenspan's *Walt Whitman and the American Reader* (New York: Cambridge University Press, 1991) explores the issue of "reader-writer relations" in Whitman's work, concentrating both on the biographical record of Whitman's career as a printer and journalist and on the "reader-addressed quality of Whitman's poetry" (viii).

3 Shelley Fisher Fishkin, *From Fact to Fiction: Journalism and Imaginative Writing in America* (Baltimore: Johns Hopkins University Press, 1985). While Fishkin provides some indication of the role Whitman's journalistic writing played as a prefiguration of his poetic enterprise, she stops short of any rigorous analysis of the way in which the two forms intersect, shedding no new light on the mystery surrounding Whitman's sudden entry into the sphere of poetry, and instead relying on an overly schematic opposition between "fact" and "art." She concludes that Whitman's "success as a poet came only when he stopped trying to be 'artistic' and circled back to the subjects, style, stance, and strategies he had first developed as editor of the New York *Aurora* [in 1842]" (29).

4 Bourdieu, *Distinction,* 491.

5 David S. Reynolds, *Beneath the American Renaissance: The Subversive Imagination in the Age of Emerson and Melville* (New York: Knopf, 1989), 444–45.

6   See the discussion in Price, *Whitman and Tradition*. Citing Whitman's own as-
    sertion that "no one will get at my verses who insists upon viewing them as a lit-
    erary performance, or attempt at such a performance," Price writes: "The sheer
    energy of Whitman's denials of connectedness with literary high culture, par-
    ticularly in his great early phase, suggests that more attention should be paid to
    his defensive strategy. Only by placing the poet in the literary context he so often
    tried to expunge can we comprehend the nature of his adversarial side" (4). Of
    course what Price proposes is exactly what Harold Bloom has done, albeit in
    limited form.

7   Leo Spitzer, "*Explication de texte* Applied to Walt Whitman's Poem 'Out of the
    Cradle Endlessly Rocking,'" in *A Century of Whitman Criticism,* ed. E. H.
    Miller (Bloomington: Indiana University Press, 1969), 273–74. Spitzer writes: "I
    am convinced that [Whitman's] 'bird or demon' is a descendant of Shelley's
    'Sprite bird,' that the brother mocking-bird is one of Saint Francis' brother crea-
    tures, that his 'feathered guests from Alabama' is a derivative from Arnold's
    'wanderer from a Grecian shore,' that the conception of 'a thousand singers,
    a thousand songs . . . and thousand echoes' all present in the poet is a re-
    elaboration of Victor Hugo's 'ame aux mille voix' and 'echo sonore.' Be this as it
    may, the basic motifs in which the idea of world harmony has taken shape in
    Europe must be in our mind when we read Whitman's poem, which becomes
    greater to the degree that it can be shown as ranking with, and sometimes excel-
    ling, the great parallel poems of world literature."

8   Harold Bloom, *Poetry and Repression* (New Haven: Yale University Press, 1976),
    257.

9   See, for example, the following books: Betsy Erkkila, *Whitman the Political Poet*
    (New York: Oxford University Press, 1989); Byrne Fone, *Masculine Landscapes:
    Walt Whitman and the Homoerotic Text* (Carbondale: Southern Illinois Uni-
    versity Press, 1992); M. Jimmie Killingsworth, *Whitman's Poetry of the Body:
    Sexuality, Politics, and the Text* (Chapel Hill: University of North Carolina
    Press, 1989); Michael Moon, *Disseminating Whitman: Revision and Cor-
    poreality in "Leaves of Grass"* (Cambridge: Harvard University Press, 1991);
    Tenney Nathanson, *Whitman's Presence: Body, Voice, and Writing in "Leaves of
    Grass"* (New York: New York University Press, 1992); and David S. Reynolds,
    Walt Whitman's America.

10 David Reynolds's analysis suggests that aspects of the carnivalesque may in fact
    inform Whitman's stance, particularly his use of the "b'hoy" motif to define his
    persona of "independent loafer" and "rowdy mystic" (*Renaissance*, 465–66).
    Whitman had clearly read Rabelais and may have been directly influenced by
    his version of the carnivalesque: he specifically mentions Rabelais among the
    great writers of "Democracy and Nature," along with Juvenal, Cervantes, and
    the Hebrew prophet. Whitman mentions Rabelais on two other significant occa-

sions, once citing him as a writer who would have appreciated the vitality of the Broadway omnibus drivers and once listing him as one of the "four mighty and primal hands" who would be capable of composing a portrait of President Lincoln. Thus for Whitman, Rabelais appears to stand as one of the central emblems of democratic writing.

11   Walt Whitman, *Complete Writings,* ed. Richard M. Bucke et al. (New York: Putnam, 1902), 9:35–36.

12   See Price, *Whitman and Tradition,* 20.

13   See *NUPM,* 1773–76, 1797, and 1799.

14   For an interesting discussion of British material culture that could be usefully applied to American culture of the period as well, see Tom Richards, *The Commodity Culture of Victorian England: Advertising and Spectacle 1851–1914* (Stanford: Stanford University Press, 1990), especially chap. 1, "The Great Exhibition of Things."

15   Raymond Williams, *Marxism and Literature* (Oxford: Oxford University Press, 1977), 51.

16   A more sincere statement of his opinion of these writers may be found in anonymous interviews of the period (in the *St. Louis Post-Dispatch* on October 17, 1879, and the *London Advertiser* [Ontario, Canada] on June 5, 1880; both reprinted in *WOT*). Speaking in a less official capacity, Whitman is more honest (and generally more negative) about the relative strengths of the "mighty four": "Our greatest man is Emerson. Bryant, I think, has a few pulsations. Whittier is a puritan poet without unction—without justice. I hardly know what to say about Longfellow" (*WOT,* 15). Unlike in the *Specimen Days* article, where he is careful not to discriminate among the four poets, he claims that "Emerson is by far the greatest of American authors" (*WOT,* 22), and he chastises the others for their inability to capture the "strength and rankness" of human nature.

17   In *Whitman the Political Poet,* Erkkila locates the difference between the two theories of culture in Whitman's embrace of democracy and his challenge to the hegemonic dominance of an elite class, a class Arnold embraced as the preserver of cultural authority: Whitman's essay is "a full-scale attack on the genteel as a system of power no less class based than the feudal products of Europe." Where Erkkila focuses her attention on the political implications of Whitman's stance, Trachtenberg examines Whitman's interest in redefining the word *culture,* as well as the related concepts of "democracy" and "America." For Trachtenberg, the key issue is not the aristocratic legacy of feudalism, but rather the word *culture* itself, one which Whitman wishes to preserve for his own purposes: "His rage against 'the word Culture' is a rage against what he considers a fatal flaw in the prevailing definition, especially with its colonial mentality, its self-abasement before a sanctified Old World tradition" (Alan Trachtenberg, "American Studies as a Cultural Program," in *American Renaissance Reconsidered,* ed. Walter Benn

Michaels and Donald Pease [Baltimore: Johns Hopkins University Press, 1985], 175). For yet another comparison of Whitman and Arnold, see Robert Weisbuch, *Atlantic Double-Cross: American Literature and British Influence in the Age of Emerson* (Chicago: University of Chicago Press, 1986), 83–108.

18 Thorstein Veblen, *The Theory of the Leisure Class* (New York: Penguin, 1979), 391.

19 Larzer Ziff, *Literary Democracy: The Declaration of Cultural Independence* (New York: Viking, 1981), 58–59.

20 Oliver Wendell Holmes, *The Autocrat at the Breakfast Table* (New York: Sagamore, 1957), 244.

21 Interestingly, Holmes's satirical portrait, though written from the inside position of social privilege, corresponds in some respects to Whitman's own feelings toward the inner circle of Boston intellectuals and writers. Holmes disparages in his own "aristocracy" a "cheap dandyism" corresponding to a lack of "manhood" and "gallantry."

22 Roy Harvey Pearce, *The Continuity of American Poetry* (Princeton: Princeton University Press, 1961), 251. A third group of poets, largely neglected by Pearce's study, is that of nineteenth-century women poets (often dismissed as "sentimental" poets) such as Lydia Sigourney, Helen Hunt Jackson, and Lucy Larcom. Their cultural position differed from Whitman's both in their identification with a tradition of women's writing and in their primary focus on the domestic sphere. As Cheryl Walker has pointed out, these poets often failed to achieve a poetry that transcended societal and literary conventions because they were "so deeply trapped in their own powerlessness that they were afraid to disappoint the very critical expectations that kept them mired in mediocrity" (*The Nightingale's Burden: Women Poets and American Culture before 1900* [Bloomington: Indiana University Press, 1982], 57). Unlike Whitman, who used his working-class background to aesthetic advantage in fashioning a poetry that could move experimentally between high and low registers of poetic expression, nineteenth-century women poets were too often trapped in a limited aesthetic and cultural space that allowed neither high literary aspirations nor a radicalized sociopolitical consciousness.

23 William Charvat, *The Profession of Authorship in America, 1800–1870* (Columbus: Ohio State University Press, 1968).

24 Despite Whitman's claim, in his note to Emerson at the end of the 1856 edition, that the thousand copies of his first edition had "readily sold" and that he was about to "print several thousand copies" of the second, it is clear that this was a flagrant exaggeration—if not an outright lie, as Whitman's literary executor and biographer M. R. Bucke claimed. According to Bucke, there was "no sale" of the first edition, and "little or no sale" of the second, a fact substantiated by Whitman himself, who later admitted to doubting "if even ten were sold." See

Justin Kaplan, *Walt Whitman: A Life* (New York: Simon and Schuster, 1980), 207–8.

25 The relative popularity of Longfellow can be understood as a middle-class imitation of high taste at a time when a large segment of the evolving middle class was still in a state of social flux, its members aspiring to a higher class identification than their background and education had previously allowed. The mainstream literary culture of the day, as represented by magazines like *Harper's* and *Putnam's,* by the various poetry anthologies, and by the books of Longfellow and Whittier, provided relatively easy access for many middle-class Americans to a form of seemingly high culture accessible to a less elite readership.

26 Dana wrote to the editor George Putnam in 1852: "You are not going to put in a spade to help dig the ditch . . . between our literature and that of the Fatherland?" (Ziff, 48). It would appear that the boundaries between "nationalists" and "universalists" were drawn largely along class lines: the embrace of English tradition occurs most frequently within the patrician class and can be seen as an attempt to maintain cultural standards in the face of a growing and less educated middle class.

27 The role played by Evert Duyckinck and the Young America movement in defining America's literary nationalism cannot be explored here, but it has been covered by various commentators. See, for example, Rush Welter, *The Mind of America, 1820–1860* (New York: Columbia University Press, 1975), Russel Nye, *Society and Culture in America, 1830–1860* (New York: Harper and Row, 1974), and Perry Miller, *The Raven and the Whale: The War of Words and Wits in the Era of Poe and Melville* (New York: Harcourt, Brace, 1956).

28 Henry Wadsworth Longfellow, *Kavanagh: A Tale* (Boston: Ticknor, Reed and Fields, 1849), 115.

29 The two entries, both reprinted in *The Gathering of the Forces,* are "'Home' Literature" (July 11, 1846) and "Independent American Literature" (February 10, 1847). In "'Home' Literature," Whitman decries European literature as an "evil influence" which is "not to be endured much longer." He rejects European and particularly English literature on two grounds: the antidemocratic politics expressed by those works with some literary merit, and the "trash" and "vulgar coarseness" propagated by the rest (*GF,* 2:242–45).

30 Leon Chai, *Romantic Foundations of the American Renaissance* (Ithaca: Cornell University Press, 1987), 7.

31 Lawrence Buell, *New England Literary Culture* (New York: Cambridge University Press, 1986), 106.

32 See, for example, Whitman's unpublished poetic fragment, "I am the poet of reality," from an 1847 notebook.

33 William Cullen Bryant, *Prose Writings,* ed. Parke Godwin (New York: Russell and Russell, 1961), 34.

34 William Cullen Bryant, *Poetical Works* (1903; New York: AMS, 1969), 130–33.

35 See Walt Whitman, *A Child's Reminiscence,* ed. Thomas Mabbott and Rollo Silver (Seattle: University of Washington Press, 1930), 19.

36 See Robert Schonick, "Whitman and the Magazines: Some Documentary Evidence," in *On Whitman: The Best from American Literature,* ed. Edwin Cady and Louis Budd (Durham: Duke University Press, 1987), 161–85.

37 *Walt Whitman's Workshop: A Collection of Unpublished Prose Manuscripts,* ed. Clifton Furniss (Cambridge: Harvard University Press, 1928), 245–46.

38 The extent of this aesthetic and cultural consensus (a consensus from which Whitman was excluded), is evidenced by the increasing acceptance of Emerson by the fireside group after 1850. In *Literary Culture* Buell cites the facts that Longfellow put a picture of Emerson in his study, Lowell dedicated a book to him, and Holmes wrote one of his biographies. Significantly, it was just as Emerson achieved a *rapprochement* with the fireside poets and other members of the Boston literati that he and Whitman drifted apart.

39 See Charvat, *Profession,* 101.

CHAPTER TWO   The Invisible Discourse: Slavery and Subjectivity in *Leaves of Grass*

1 V. N. Volosinov, *Marxism and the Philosophy of Language,* trans. Ladislav Matejka and I. R. Titunik (Cambridge: Harvard University Press, 1986), 21–22.

2 Jürgen Link, "Interdiscourse, Literature, and Collective Symbols: Theses Towards a Theory of Discourse and Literature," *Enclitic* 8, no. 1/2 (1984): 157–65.

3 Albert Boime, *The Art of Exclusion: Representing Blacks in the Nineteenth Century* (Washington, D.C.: Smithsonian Institution Press, 1990), 4.

4 For a discussion of the way in which Melville's novel reflected political discourses and issues of his day, see Alan Heimert, "*Moby-Dick* and American Political Symbolism," *American Quarterly* 15 (1963): 498–534. For readings of the novel that link it more specifically to the slavery issue, see Carolyn Karcher, *Shadow over the Promised Land: Slavery, Race, and Violence in Melville's America* (Baton Rouge: Louisiana State University Press, 1980), 62–91.

5 Michael Rogin, *Subversive Genealogy: The Politics and Art of Herman Melville* (Berkeley: University of California Press, 1985), 142–43.

6 Charles Glicksburg, ed., *Walt Whitman and the Civil War* (Philadelphia: University of Pennsylvania Press, 1933), 9.

7 Ken Peeples, "The Paradox of the 'Good Gray Poet' (Walt Whitman on Slavery and the Black Man)," *Phylon* 35 (1974): 22, 32.

8 For a seminal discussion of heteroglossia, see Mikhail Bakhtin, *The Dialogic Imagination: Four Essays,* ed. Michael Holquist, trans. Caryl Emerson and Michael Holquist (Austin: University of Texas Press, 1981). The concept of a

"social semiotics" has begun to achieve currency in post-Bakhtinian critical discussion; see, for example, Terdiman, *Discourse/Counter-Discourse* and Robert Hodge and Gunther Kress, *Social Semiotics* (Ithaca: Cornell University Press, 1988).

9　To quote from Michael Holquist's introduction to *The Dialogic Imagination*, "the homogeneity of the [poetic] genre corresponds to ideas about the privileged status of a unitary, centripetalizing language" (xxx).

10　Karen Sanchez-Eppler's article, "To Stand Between: A Political Perspective on Whitman's Poetics of Merger and Embodiment" (*ELH* 56.4 [1989]: 923–49), treats Whitman's relation to slavery in specifically corporeal, even psychosexual terms. Claiming that "Whitman locates the poet in the sexually charged middle space between masters and slaves," Sanchez-Eppler goes on to explore, through a reading of Whitman's slavery passages, "the political sources and implications of his corporeal poetry" (923). Yet despite her central argument that the "choice and manipulation of poetic style can exert political force" and that "Whitman's conception of the poet as mediator itself establishes connections between literary and social practices" (939), Sanchez-Eppler provides little of the historical specificity that would be necessary to establish such "links between poetry and politics" (940). Further, her unquestioning acceptance of Whitman's own equation of the physical body with the body politic prevents her from interrogating more deeply his commitment to a radical political and poetic agenda. My discussion is situated between historically based readings of Whitman and slavery, such as Betsy Erkkila's, and nonhistorical (semiotic/corporeal/interpersonal) readings such as that proposed by Sanchez-Eppler; I differ from both of these critics in remaining more skeptical of Whitman's own rhetorical claims and more concerned with his responses to literary and sociocultural discourses.

11　See Sean Wilentz, *Chants Democratic: New York City and the Rise of the Working Class, 1788–1850* (New York: Oxford University Press, 1984), 263–64.

12　Houston Baker, *The Journey Back: Issues in Black Literature and Criticism* (Chicago: University of Chicago Press, 1980), 37–43. Gregory Jay concurs with Baker in finding a "Transcendentalist cast" to Douglass's rhetoric, although he identifies in Douglass's later writings a movement away from Garrisonian abolitionism and toward a more militantly confrontational stance (see "American Literature and the New Historicism: The Example of Frederick Douglass," *Boundary 2* 17.1 [1990]: 211–42). Priscilla Wald has identified Douglass's authorial struggle in two different versions of the narrative (the 1845 *Narrative of the Life of Frederick Douglass, an American Slave* and the 1855 *My Bondage and My Freedom*) as a negotiation between the highly prescribed conventions of the slave narrative as literary form and the nationalistic desire "to represent himself as . . . a more comfortably and recognizably American self" (*Constituting Americans: Cultural Anxiety and Narrative Form* [Durham: Duke University

Press, 1995], 73–75). Of course, at the time of his most important poetic engagement with slavery, Whitman would have been aware of the 1845 *Narrative* only. Although he never mentions having read Douglass's book, Whitman did hear Douglass speak at the Buffalo Free-Soil Convention of 1848. Given the general popularity of the *Narrative*, it is likely that Whitman was at least passingly familiar with it, but it was probably not of major importance as an influence on his own depictions of slavery.

13 For Walker's and Garnet's essays, as well as other radical antebellum writings by black nationalists, see Sterling Stuckey, ed., *The Ideological Origins of Black Nationalism* (Boston: Beacon, 1972).

14 David Van Leer, "The Anxiety of Ethnicity in Douglass's *Narrative*," in *Frederick Douglass: New Literary and Historical Essays,* ed. Eric Sundquist (New York: Cambridge University Press, 1990), 133.

15 Whether the curiously flawed attempt at black dialect in a single stanza of the 1867 "Ethiopia Saluting the Colors" can be said to constitute the direct quotation of black speech is debatable.

16 John Greenleaf Whittier, *The Complete Poetical Works* (Boston: Houghton Mifflin, 1984), 377.

17 The two most widely disseminated literary representations of the slave auction were Douglass's *Narrative* (1845) and Stowe's *Uncle Tom's Cabin* (1853), but the scene was represented in the visual arts as well. Two examples are the group sculpture "The Slave Auction" (1859) by John Rogers and the painting "The Last Sale of Slaves in St. Louis" (1865) by Thomas Noble.

18 Thomas Andrews, "Walt Whitman and Slavery: A Reconstruction of One Aspect of His Concept of the American Common Man," *CLA Journal* 9 (1966): 225–33. In the first period, 1842–46, Whitman has little to say about slavery itself but is against the slave trade, which by that time had been illegal in this country for several decades. The second period, 1846–48, covers the years immediately after the Wilmot Proviso; here Whitman is most clearly against the extension of slavery into the western territories. In 1848–58, the third and most active period, Whitman sees the problem largely in terms of a contest between white working men and slave owners. Finally, after 1858, the issue of slavery becomes of secondary importance to the preservation of the Union. The period of Whitman's most overtly political antislavery activity was fairly brief, lasting from the summer of 1848—during which Whitman acted as a delegate to the Free-Soil Convention in Buffalo—through 1850, the year of the Compromise and of the Fugitive Slave Law. During this time, Whitman founded the weekly *Freeman*, wrote several poems dealing with slavery, and may even have lectured on the subject.

19 Daniel Aaron, *The Unwritten War: American Writers and the Civil War* (Madison: University of Wisconsin Press, 1987), 62.

20 See George Frederickson, *The Black Image in the White Mind: A Debate on Afro-American Character and Destiny 1817–1914* (Middletown: Wesleyan University Press, 1971). Fredrickson argues that many moderate northerners saw colonization for American blacks as the "only practical long range solution to the menace of slavery" (9), and the only short-term means of ending the threat of violence or insurrection.

21 Whitman did, however, commemorate Brown's hanging in the 1865 poem "Year of Meteors."

22 Ralph Waldo Emerson, *Works* (Boston: Houghton Mifflin, 1904), 11:281.

23 If Emerson did indeed end a lecture with these words, as Whitman later claimed (*WWC*, 4:161), his meaning was presumably that slavery should not be seen as an isolated problem that could be solved by abolitionist fervor alone but rather as part of a larger oppression of democratic spirit in America.

24 See Thomas Brasher, *Whitman as Editor of the Brooklyn Daily Eagle* (Detroit: Wayne State University Press, 1970), 162. Other indications are that Whitman felt the slavery debate had simply gone on too long and that it had taken up attention that could have been directed toward less divisive issues. Whitman believed that the tone set by abolitionists had actually hindered the cause of freedom. In the *Eagle*, Whitman accused "red-hot fanatics" of preventing other states from following Delaware's lead in ending slavery.

25 It is significant that the beginning of Whitman's career as a literary reviewer (with the *Daily Eagle*) coincided with the period of his most frequent writings on slavery. Despite his involvement with such questions of national importance as the Wilmot Proviso and the Mexican War, Whitman found time during 1846 and 1847 to review over four hundred books in the *Eagle*, many of them literary. For him, literary reviewing and political activity were not mutually exclusive activities: an involvement with the history of western thought could not help but provoke a concurrent assessment of contemporary sociopolitical events and discourses. It was precisely this intersection of literary and extraliterary discourses that was crucial to Whitman's poetic development.

26 Whitman's predecessor at the *Daily Eagle*, William Marsh, had printed one of Longfellow's antislavery poems in the paper. Whitman also mentions two of the poems—"The Quadroon Girl" and "The Witnesses"—in his *Specimen Days* article on the death of Longfellow (*PW*, 285).

27 Longfellow, *Complete Poetical Works*, 22. John Greenleaf Whittier's "The Slave-Ships" is in his *The Complete Poetical Works* (Boston: Houghton Mifflin, 1894), 44–45.

28 Several factors have been proposed as explanatory of Whitman's heightened interest in slavery during this period. It may have been set off by the revolutionary fervor that followed the events in Europe in 1848, or by Whitman's firsthand observation of slavery in New Orleans in the spring of 1848, when he may even

have witnessed the kind of slave auctions he later envisions in "I Sing the Body Electric." Another plausible explanation for Whitman's change in attitude is a lecture he heard in December 1847 on "The Worth of Liberty." Whitman's review of the lecture in the *Eagle* indicates the depth of his own response: "The lecturer's picture of a slave, the *thing* without the feelings of a man—*not* a husband, *not* a parent, *not* a wife, *not* a patriot—and impossible to be either, in its proper sense—was burningly fearful and true" (Brasher, *Whitman as Editor,* 164–65).

29 It was a belief growing increasingly prevalent among certain nativist groups like the Know-Nothings, whose political power reached an all-time peak in the mid-1850s.

30 Whitman himself expressed strong feelings about both the rights of slaves to seek their freedom and the rights of individuals like himself to help them. In "As of the Orator," Whitman offers his own services to any escapees he might have the "privilege" to assist, and he attacks the weakness and the hypocrisy of those who would defend fugitives only when it is easy or popular to do so.

31 If some critics have found parallels with Christ and the last supper in the speaker's treatment of the slave, I am inclined to read this narrative as an understated account of what Whitman would consider an act of natural human kindness. The language of the passage, despite the somewhat stereotypical details of the slave's "revolving eyes" and "awkwardness," is strikingly direct: it seems to owe little to either the sensationalism or the sentimentality of conventionalized versions of the runaway, such as the famous scenes in *Uncle Tom's Cabin.*

32 Edwin Havilland Miller, *Walt Whitman's "Song of Myself": A Mosaic of Interpretations* (Iowa City: University of Iowa Press, 1989), 114.

33 In "As of the Orator," he writes: "It is not events of danger and threatening storms that I dread. Give us turbulence, give us excitement, give us the rage and disputes of hell, all this rather than this lethargy of death that spreads like a vapor of decaying corpses over our land" (*NUPM,* 2197).

34 In an epigram to one of Whittier's antislavery poems, he quotes from a speech by Samuel May: "Genius of America! Spirit of our free institutions! where art thou? How art thou fallen, O Lucifer! son of the morning—how art thou fallen from Heaven! Hell from beneath is moved for thee, to meet thee at thy coming!" (Whittier, *Complete Poetical Works,* 45). Whitman himself had worked on the idea of a "black portrait" of "Lucifer . . . the denied God" in the poem "Pictures." In anticipation of the "Black Lucifer" passage, he wrote: "But I do not deny him—though cast out and rebellious, he is my God as much as any."

35 See, for example, the painting "The Devil and Tom Walker" (1838) by Charles Deas, which represents a black man as a devil with horns and glowing eyes. As Guy McElroy comments in his gloss of the painting, "the cursed state of the black race was supported by theologians, who, quoting scripture (particularly

the descent of Ham in the book of Genesis), extended this punishment to include the mark of dark skin as an indicator of evil." See Guy McElroy, *Facing History: The Black Image in American Art, 1740–1940* (Washington: Corcoran Gallery/Bedford Arts, 1990).

36 These white fears were not entirely unfounded; despite attempts to suppress or censor accounts of negro uprising, there were over two hundred and fifty reported revolts and attempted revolts in the United States. Whitman's passage may in fact have been even more topical than it at first appears: according to Herbert Aptheker, the decade of the 1850s, and especially the period 1854–56, was one of "very great concerted slave unrest." The year 1856 alone, in what amounted "very nearly to positive insurrection," saw slave revolts in Kentucky, Arkansas, Tennessee, Mississippi, Louisiana, Texas, Maryland, Alabama, North and South Carolina, Georgia, and Florida (*Essays in the History of the American Negro* [New York: International, 1945], 54–57). Whitman would certainly have been aware of the most publicized incidents of unrest, such as Nat Turner's bloody rebellion of 1831, but how cognizant he was of more contemporary uprisings is unclear.

37 James Warren, *Walt Whitman's Language Experiment* (University Park: Pennsylvania State University Press, 1990), 86.

38 See Erkkila, *Political Poet*, 122–24.

39 Bryant, "The Death of Lincoln," *Poetical Works*, 316–17.

40 In *Memoranda during the War*, also from 1875, Whitman comments that "black domination, but little above the beasts" in certain southern states was "a temporary, deserved punishment for their Slavery and Succession sins" (*PW*, 66).

41 Whitman goes on to write: "That our national democratic experiment, principle, and machinery, could triumphantly sustain such a shock, and that the Constitution could weather it, like a ship a storm, and come out of it as sound and whole as before, is by far the most signal proof yet of the stability of that experiment, Democracy, and of those principles, and that Constitution" (*PW*, 431).

CHAPTER THREE   The Aesthetics of "Indifference": Whitman and the American City

1 Morton and Lucia White, *The Intellectual versus the City: From Thomas Jefferson to Frank Lloyd Wright* (first published 1962; Oxford University Press, 1977), 2.

2 Whitman finds the same shortcomings in Thoreau as in Emerson. "I do not think it was so much a love of woods, streams and hills that made [Thoreau] live in the country, as a morbid dislike of humanity," he told Anne Gilchrist. Whitman also complained to Traubel: "The great vice in Thoreau's composition was his disdain of the universe—his disdain of cities, companions, civiliza-

tions." For these quotes and a discussion of Whitman and Thoreau, see Kaplan, *A Life,* 366, and M. Wynn Thomas, *The Lunar Light of Whitman's Poetry* (Cambridge: Harvard University Press, 1987), 148.

3 Timothy Sweet, *Traces of War: Poetry, Photography, and the Crisis of the Union* (Baltimore: Johns Hopkins University Press, 1990), 59.

4 Bakhtin, *Dialogic Imagination,* 243.

5 See Leo Marx, "Pastoralism in American Literature," in *Ideology and Classic American Literature,* ed. Sacvan Bercovitch and Myra Jehlen (New York: Cambridge University Press, 1986), 36–65.

6 See Brasher, *Whitman as Editor,* for a brief discussion of Whitman's attitudes toward both New York and Brooklyn, especially as reflected in his journalism of the 1840s.

7 See Theodor Adorno, "Veblen's Attack on Culture," in *Prisms,* trans. Samuel and Shierry Weber (Cambridge: MIT Press, 1981), 78.

8 James Machor, "Pastoralism and the American Urban Ideal: Hawthorne, Whitman, and the Literary Pattern," *American Literature* 54.3 (1982).

9 I am also indebted to varying degrees to several recent discussions of Whitman and the city, the most interesting of which are Thomas's *The Lunar Light of Whitman's Poetry,* Kristiann Versluys's chapter on Whitman in *The Poet in the City* (Tübingen: Narr Verlag, 1987), and William Sharpe's chapter entitled "Walt Whitman's Urban Incarnation," in *Unreal Cities: Urban Figuration in Wordsworth, Baudelaire, Whitman, Eliot, and Williams* (Baltimore: Johns Hopkins University Press, 1987). Each of these critics views Whitman's relationship to New York in quite different terms. Versluys reads Whitman's poetry as a Romantic or metaphysical idealization of the city, an idealization that largely fails to come to terms with the city's darker elements; Sharpe stresses Whitman's interaction with the city as that of a desiring body who uses his poems to build a "poetic city of the self"; Thomas takes an essentially sociohistorical approach, tracing both Whitman's "passionate involvement" with the city and his growing ambivalence about it through reference to the cultural and historical moment in which the poetry was written.

10 William Wordsworth, *The Prelude: 1799, 1805, 1850* (New York: Norton, 1979), 262–64.

11 Raymond Williams, *The Country and the City* (New York: Oxford University Press, 1973), 215.

12 Priscilla Ferguson, "Reading Revolutionary Paris," in *Literature and Social Practice,* ed. Philippe Desan, Priscilla Ferguson, and Wendy Griswold (Chicago: University of Chicago Press, 1989), 46.

13 Michael Cowan, *City of the West: Emerson, America, and Urban Metaphor* (New Haven: Yale University Press, 1967), 18.

14 See Ralph Waldo Emerson, *The Early Lectures,* ed. Robert Spiller and Stephen Whicher (Cambridge: Harvard University Press, 1972), 3:347.

15 Bryant, *Poetical Works,* 130.

16 Edward Spann, *The New Metropolis: New York City, 1840–1857* (New York: Columbia University Press, 1981), 242, 249.

17 My information about population growth is taken from Spann, *New Metropolis.* The population of New York proper (present-day Manhattan) grew by 160 percent during the same period, to over eight hundred thousand.

18 Whittier, *Complete Poetical Works,* 86.

19 See Janis Stout's *Sodoms in Eden: The City in American Fiction Before 1860* (Westport, Conn.: Greenwood Press, 1976) and Adrienne Siegel's *The Image of the American City in Popular Literature: 1820–1870* (Port Washington, N.Y.: Kennikat Press, 1981).

20 George Foster, *New York in Slices, by an Experienced Carver* (New York, 1848), 4–5.

21 See Stuart Blumin's introduction to George Foster's *New York by Gas-Light* (Berkeley: University of California Press, 1990), 33–34. Blumin documents the fact that Foster wrote for the paper in 1842–43, but he fails to mention the interesting fact that Whitman had been editor in the spring of 1842.

22 Blumin's introduction to *New York by Gas-Light,* 38. Foster, a jack-of-all-trades in the New York world of literary journalism—not to mention his stint as a professional flute player in Mobile and St. Louis—seems to have exceeded even Whitman in his mobility between high and low culture. In addition to his city novel and sketches, he published stories and poems in *Graham's Magazine* as well as a history of the French revolution of 1848, and he edited the first American edition of Shelley's poems in 1845. He also edited a satirical weekly magazine, *John-Donkey,* in 1848; another magazine, *The Verdict,* in 1851; and was described after his death in 1856 as "a genuine bohemian." The dearth of biographical record on Foster will probably prevent his contribution to New York cultural life at midcentury from being adequately explored, but he was certainly an interesting figure in what we can roughly describe as Whitman's circle.

23 America's urban novels were themselves indebted to a genre of European city pseudofiction beginning with eighteenth-century accounts like *London Unmasked* (1787) and continuing into nineteenth-century books like Pierce Egan's *Life in London* (1821) and Eugene Sue's *The Mysteries of Paris* (1842–43). If the social context for the rash of urban novels in the United States was the phenomenal growth of and rapidly changing nature of life in America's cities, the seminal event within literary culture was certainly the publication of Sue's novel, which appeared in its American translation even before French serialization of the novel was completed. It is no mere coincidence that many of the urban

American novels of the 1840s and 1850s contained the word *mysteries* in their titles. Sue's book, arguably France's first bestseller, had an important influence on the novels of Victor Hugo and Émile Zola and may even have contributed to the revolution of 1848; it also figures prominently in Marx's critique of bourgeois socialist fiction in *The Holy Family* (1845).

24 Exact sales figures for the book are unknown, but it may have sold as many as twenty thousand copies.

25 See the discussion of Dickens and Whitman in Graham Clarke, *Walt Whitman: The Poem as Private History* (London: Vision/St. Mark's, 1991), 113–17.

26 *Walt Whitman of the "New York Aurora,"* eds. Joseph Jay Rubin and Charles Brown (State College, Penn.: Bald Eagle, 1950), 19.

27 See the *Oxford English Dictionary,* which lists several other definitions along with these two. The OED lists these as the first two meanings, in the order given; in common use today, the second has probably superseded the first. Though this would not have been the case in Whitman's day, both meanings were clearly in current use.

28 See Stout, "The opposition remained narrowly, if spectacularly, moral. . . . The novels of sensationalists did make clear the availability of a wide range of urban topics for realistic fiction, but, again, their exaggerations and conventionality prevented their becoming in any way a fiction of realism" (*Sodoms in Eden,* 42).

29 During the same visit, Conway was struck by the way in which Whitman greeted as friends and equals many of the "laboring class" whom they met on the roads and the ferry: "He says he is one of that class by choice, that he is personally dear to some thousands of such" (Kaplan, *A Life,* 213).

30 Killingsworth, *Whitman's Poetry of the Body,* 14.

31 Graham Clarke has called attention to "The Sleepers" as an important urban poem. This "quintessential poem of New York City" presents "an urban habitat rarely pictured in Whitman's 'Manhattan'" (109, 100). Like "Faces," "The Sleepers" contains an "underside" of New York life, with its prisons, asylums, and hospitals that in their ensemble "establish an alternative urban map of American meaning" (109).

32 In his notebook draft for the poem, Whitman writes: "I should think poorly of myself if I should be even a few days with any community either of sane or insane people, and not make them convinced, whether they acknowledge it or not, of my truth, my sympathy, and my dignity" (*DN,* 767).

33 The number of inmates in New York's asylums for the insane increased dramatically throughout the nineteenth century, as capacity was increased by facilities on Blackwell's (1848), Ward's (1871), and Hart's (1878) islands (see Clarke, 115). Urban poverty was also increasing at an alarming rate, as were related urban problems such as vagrancy, prostitution, and mortality. Fifty-two percent of chil-

dren under five died in the city in the 1850s, and the overall mortality rate of one in twenty-seven was far higher than those of London or Paris. See Christine Stansell, *City of Women: Sex and Class in New York, 1789–1860* (New York: Knopf, 1986), 199.

34 In E. H. Miller, ed. *A Century of Whitman Criticism* (Bloomington: Indiana University Press, 1969), 109.

35 Philip Fisher, "Democratic Social Space: Whitman, Melville, and the Promise of American Transparency," in *The New American Studies*, ed. Philip Fisher (Berkeley: University of California Press, 1991), 81.

36 See Spann, *New Metropolis*, 21. Though Whitman recognized America's need as a generous democracy to embrace the various peoples of the world—as evidenced by his claim, cited in chapter 2, to welcome all "fugitives" and by his argument that "the opulence of race-elements is in the theory of America" (Erkkila, 85)—his aesthetic reaction to the waves of immigrants appears to have been less than entirely positive. As we have already seen in "I Sing the Body Electric," he writes unflatteringly of the "dull-faced immigrants just landed on the wharf."

37 Spann quotes one example of such anti-immigrant rhetoric from the *New York Tribune* of 1847: "Every hole and corner under a roof, down to the very vaults and cellars within the jurisdiction of the city, have become resting places for the swarms of foreign paupers and idiots emptied daily upon our shores by the governments of a portion of Europe" (71). The problem of increasing crime was a very real one in the city, along with the increase in immigration and the general growth of the city's population. There were fifty-six murders in 1852 versus only nine in 1847. This startling rate of increase prompted the *New York Times* to comment in 1854 that "stabbing and shooting are in vogue in the public streets," and caused *Harper's Weekly* to ask in 1857, the year after Whitman's article, "whether it is not necessary to carry sword-canes, dirks, bowie-knives, and revolvers to protect us free citizens from other free citizens" (Spann, 314–15).

38 I think here of the various discourses of urban reform, ranging from the more extreme anti-urban rhetoric of Fourierists and radical groups to the more generic critiques of the city summarized by Spann.

39 Whitman does not designate a location for this scene, but we must assume it to be either Camden, his home after the war, or Philadelphia, where he was a regular visitor. In an article of March 8, 1879, printed in the *Philadelphia Progress*, he notices "plenty of hard-up folks along the pavements" (*PW*, 188). According to urban historians such as Christine Stansell, the sight of such "rag-pickers" was no longer unusual in certain parts of the American city, as the number of homeless people grew in proportion to the increasing influx of immigrants. See Stansell, *City of Women*, 198.

40 See Susan Buck-Morss, "Aesthetics and Anaesthetics: Walter Benjamin's Art-work Essay Reconsidered," *October* 62 (1992): 22.

41 See Reynolds, *Walt Whitman's America,* for a discussion of Whitman's move toward conventionality in his later life.

CHAPTER FOUR   Figuring the Body in Leaves: Whitman and the Discourse of Corporeality

1 My translation.

2 Elaine Scarry, ed. *Literature and the Body: Essays on Populations and Persons* (Baltimore: Johns Hopkins University Press, 1988), xiv.

3 See Moon, *Disseminating Whitman,* 14.

4 Michael Moon proposes "embodiment" as a central trope or gesture in Whitman's poems. According to Moon, Whitman achieves in many of his poems an indeterminate and "fluid" form of embodiment that breaks down the barriers between the bodies represented in the text. In doing so, he is able to "produce texts more radical than his culture officially permitted writers to produce" and to "exploit the subversive potential inherent in the densely figurative public discourse of his time" (14). Thus it is through the portrayal not only of his own body but of radically "other" bodies that Whitman is able to depart from, to resist, and at times even to challenge or comment on the prevailing sociolect.

5 See Buck-Morss, "Aesthetics and Anaesthetics."

6 See Moon, *Disseminating Whitman,* as well as Killingsworth, *Whitman's Poetry of the Body,* Fone, *Masculine Landscapes,* and Nathanson, *Whitman's Presence.* Earlier studies that still provide useful discussion and information include Harold Aspiz, *Walt Whitman and the Body Beautiful* (Urbana: University of Illinois Press, 1980), and Robert K. Martin, *The Homosexual Tradition in American Poetry* (Austin: University of Texas Press, 1979). Since the books by Fone and Nathanson appeared after my project was well under way, they have had little direct impact on my argument in this chapter.

7 In "I Sing the Body Electric," for example, he apostrophizes the body ("O my body!"), but only in order to compare his body with those of others ("I dare not desert the likes of you in other men and women"). This radically democratizing gesture is brought to its conclusion when he reincorporates all bodies as poems. Thus, rather than relying on traditional poetic figuration, he establishes an identity with all other bodies through the equation my body = other bodies, bodies = poems, other bodies (poems) = my body (my poem).

8 See Peter Gay, *The Bourgeois Experience: Victoria to Freud,* 3 vols., especially vol. 1, *Education of the Senses* (New York: Oxford University Press, 1984).

9 Sharon Cameron, *The Corporeal Self: Allegories of the Body in Melville and Hawthorne* (Baltimore: Johns Hopkins University Press, 1981), 9.

10 Statistical analysis does not bear out Cameron's contention about a heightened interest in the body, at least among *poets* of the nineteenth century; the difference in frequency between Whitman's evocation of the body and related images and that of other poets is quite striking. Whitman uses the word *body* about 110 times in *Leaves of Grass*, as compared with 7 citations in all of Emerson's poetry and 10 in Dickinson's. The words *blood* (60 usages) and *flesh* (22 usages) also appear far more frequently in Whitman's writing than in that of his contemporaries.

11 Quoted in Kaplan, *A Life*, 222.

12 See Jeffrey Steele's reading of Whitman in *The Representation of Self in the American Renaissance* (Chapel Hill: University of North Carolina Press, 1987), 70–72, where he characterizes the essentially transgressive nature of Whitman's understanding of the body, one which "avoids ethical perspectives that stigmatize bodily and sexual functions."

13 Paul Zweig, *Walt Whitman: The Making of the Poet*, 324.

14 Pierre Bourdieu, *Language and Symbolic Power*, ed. John Thompson, trans. Gino Raymond and Matthew Adamson (Cambridge: Harvard University Press, 1991), 13.

15 Charley Shively, ed. *Calamus Lovers: Walt Whitman's Working Class Camerades*, (San Francisco: Gay Sunshine Press, 1987).

16 Michel Foucault, *The History of Sexuality*, vol. 1: *An Introduction*, trans. Robert Hurley (New York: Pantheon, 1978), 122.

17 Robert Wiebe, *The Opening of American Society: From the Adoption of the Constitution to the Eve of Disunion* (New York: Knopf, 1984), 321.

18 Henry David Thoreau, *Walden and Other Writings* (New York: Bantam, 1962), 267–68.

19 Whitman's rationale for cutting this passage is not altogether clear (although it is consistent with a pattern of such cuts in the later editions); nothing in the passage is particularly compromising either to him or to his overall message, and what he says here he also says in various forms elsewhere. Certainly the poem as it stands without the excised passage is less forceful, more abstract, and less political in its message; perhaps Whitman hesitated about introducing *Leaves of Grass* (the poem follows the "Inscriptions" and precedes "Song of Myself" in later versions) with such a strong statement of sexual politics.

20 For a more complete discussion of Whitman's relation to medicine and doctors, see Aspiz, *Body Beautiful*.

21 See *NUPM*, 2246–59.

22 See Aspiz, *Body Beautiful*, 59–61.

23 There is no evidence that Whitman actually proposed such a series to a publisher; however, his notebook entries suggest that the idea was more than just a passing whim.

24 Grace Gilchrist, "Chats with Walt Whitman," *Temple Bar Magazine* 103 (1898): 210. Reprinted in Aspiz, *Body Beautiful,* 37.

25 In fact, the word *death* occurs far more often than even the word *body* in *Leaves of Grass* (180 times), belying the common image of Whitman as a predominantly affirmative poet of life.

26 We might think, for example, of one of the most famous poems by Whitman's American contemporaries, Bryant's "Thanatopsis." "Thanatopsis" presented death and burial as a threefold process: a physical return of the body to the "Earth, that nourished thee"; a historical return to join with the dead of past ages who lie beneath the earth; and finally a spiritual journey, "sustained and soothed / By an unfaltering trust," into an everlasting sleep that will be filled with "sweet dreams."

27 See Adorno's discussion of this dialectic in "Lyric Poetry and Society," *Telos* 20 (1974): 56–71.

28 Reynolds, *Walt Whitman's America,* 531.

☙WORKS CITED

Aaron, Daniel. *The Unwritten War: American Writers and the Civil War*. Madison: University of Wisconsin Press, 1987.

Adorno, Theodor. "Lyric Poetry and Society." *Telos* 20 (1974): 56–71.

———. *Prisms*. Trans. Samuel and Shierry Weber. Cambridge: MIT Press, 1981.

Andrews, Thomas. "Walt Whitman and Slavery: A Reconstruction of One Aspect of His Concept of the American Common Man." *CLA Journal* 9 (1966): 225–33.

Aptheker, Herbert. *Essays in the History of the American Negro*. New York: International, 1945.

Arnold, Matthew. From a letter to W. D. O'Connor. *Walt Whitman: The Measure of His Song*. Ed. Jim Perlman, Ed Folsom, and Dan Campion. Minneapolis: Holy Cow, 1981.

Aspiz, Harold. *Walt Whitman and the Body Beautiful*. Urbana: University of Illinois Press, 1980.

Baker, Houston. *The Journey Back: Issues in Black Literature and Criticism*. Chicago: University of Chicago Press, 1980.

Bakhtin, Mikhail. *The Dialogic Imagination: Four Essays*. Ed. Michael Holquist. Trans. Caryl Emerson and Michael Holquist. Austin: University of Texas Press, 1981.

———. *Speech Genres and Other Late Essays*. Trans. Vern McGee. Ed. Caryl Emerson and Michael Holquist. Austin: University of Texas Press, 1986.

Barthes, Roland. *Elements of Semiology*. Trans. A. Lavers and C. Smith. New York: Hill and Wang, 1977.

Barthes, Roland. and Maurice Nadeau. *Sur la littérature*. Grenoble: Presses Universitaire de Grenoble, 1980.

Baudrillard, Jean. *America*. Trans. Chris Turner. London and New York: Verso, 1988.

Bloom, Harold. *Poetry and Repression*. New Haven: Yale University Press, 1976.

Boime, Albert. *The Art of Exclusion: Representing Blacks in the Nineteenth Century*. Washington, D.C.: Smithsonian Institution Press, 1990.

Bourdieu, Pierre. *Distinction: A Social Critique of the Judgement of Taste*. Trans. Richard Nice. Cambridge: Harvard University Press, 1984.

———. *The Field of Cultural Production: Essays on Art and Literature*. Ed. Randal Johnson. New York: Columbia University Press, 1993.

———. *Language and Symbolic Power.* Ed. John Thompson. Trans. Gino Raymond and Matthew Adamson. Cambridge: Harvard University Press, 1991.

Brasher, Thomas. *Whitman as Editor of the Brooklyn Daily Eagle.* Detroit: Wayne State University Press, 1970.

Bryant, William Cullen. *Poetical Works.* 1903. New York: AMS, 1969.

———. *Prose Writings.* Ed. Parke Godwin. New York: Russell and Russell, 1961.

Buck-Morss, Susan. "Aesthetics and Anaesthetics: Walter Benjamin's Artwork Essay Reconsidered." *October* 62 (1992): 3–41.

Buell, Lawrence. *New England Literary Culture.* New York: Cambridge University Press, 1986.

Cameron, Sharon. *The Corporeal Self: Allegories of the Body in Melville and Hawthorne.* Baltimore: Johns Hopkins University Press, 1981.

Chai, Leon. *Romantic Foundations of the American Renaissance.* Ithaca: Cornell University Press, 1987.

Charvat, William. *The Profession of Authorship in America, 1800–1870.* Columbus: Ohio State University Press, 1968.

Chase, Richard. *Walt Whitman Reconsidered.* New York: William Sloane, 1955.

Clarke, Graham. *Walt Whitman: The Poem as Private History.* London: Vision/ St. Mark's, 1991.

Cowan, Michael. *City of the West: Emerson, America, and Urban Metaphor.* New Haven: Yale University Press, 1967.

Creeley, Robert. "Introduction to Whitman." *Walt Whitman: The Measure of His Song.* Ed. Jim Perlman, Ed Folsom, and Dan Campion. Minneapolis: Holy Cow, 1981.

Emerson, Ralph Waldo. *The Early Lectures.* Ed. Robert Spiller and Stephen Whicher. 3 vols. Cambridge: Harvard University Press, 1959–72.

———. *Works.* Ed. James Elliot Cabot. 12 vols. Boston: Houghton Mifflin, 1899–1904.

Erkkila, Betsy. *Whitman the Political Poet.* New York: Oxford University Press, 1989.

Ferguson, Priscilla. "Reading Revolutionary Paris." *Literature and Social Practice.* Ed. Philippe Desan, Priscilla Ferguson, and Wendy Griswold. Chicago: University of Chicago Press, 1989.

Fisher, Philip. "Democratic Social Space: Whitman, Melville, and the Promise of American Transparency." *The New American Studies.* Ed. Philip Fisher. Berkeley: University of California Press, 1991.

Fishkin, Shelley Fisher. *From Fact to Fiction: Journalism and Imaginative Writing in America.* Baltimore: Johns Hopkins University Press, 1985.

Fone, Byrne. *Masculine Landscapes: Walt Whitman and the Homoerotic Text.* Carbondale: Southern Illinois University Press, 1992.

Foster, George. *Fifteen Minutes around New York.* New York: c. 1854.

———. *New York by Gas-Light.* Ed. Stuart Blumin. Berkeley: University of California Press, 1990.

———. *New York in Slices, by an Experienced Carver.* New York, 1848.

Foucault, Michel. *The History of Sexuality,* vol. 1: *An Introduction.* Trans. Robert Hurley. New York: Pantheon, 1978.

Frederickson, George. *The Black Image in the White Mind: A Debate on Afro-American Character and Destiny 1817–1914.* Middletown: Wesleyan University Press, 1971.

Gay, Peter. *The Bourgeois Experience: Victoria to Freud.* 3 vols. Vol. 1: *Education of the Senses.* New York: Oxford University Press, 1984.

Gilchrist, Grace. "Chats with Walt Whitman." *Temple Bar Magazine* 103 (1898).

Glicksburg, Charles, ed. *Walt Whitman and the Civil War.* Philadelphia: University of Pennsylvania Press, 1933.

Greenblatt, Stephen. *Learning to Curse: Essays in Early Modern Culture.* New York: Routledge, 1990.

Greenspan, Ezra. *Walt Whitman and the American Reader.* New York: Cambridge University Press, 1991.

Heimert, Alan. "*Moby-Dick* and American Political Symbolism." *American Quarterly* 15 (1963): 498–534.

Hodge, Robert, and Gunther Kress. *Social Semiotics.* Ithaca: Cornell University Press, 1988.

Hollis, C. Carroll. *Language and Style in "Leaves of Grass."* Baton Rouge: Louisiana State University Press, 1983.

Holmes, Oliver Wendell. *The Autocrat at the Breakfast Table.* 1858. New York: Sagamore, 1957.

Jameson, Fredric. *The Political Unconscious: Narrative as Socially Symbolic Act.* Ithaca: Cornell University Press, 1981.

Jay, Gregory. "American Literature and the New Historicism: The Example of Frederick Douglass." *Boundary* 2 17.1 (1990): 211–42.

Jenny, Laurent. "The Strategy of Form." *French Literary Theory Today: A Reader.* Ed. Tsvetan Todorov. New York: Cambridge University Press, 1984.

Kaplan, Justin. *Walt Whitman: A Life.* New York: Simon and Schuster, 1980.

Karcher, Carolyn. *Shadow over the Promised Land: Slavery, Race, and Violence in Melville's America.* Baton Rouge: Louisiana State University Press, 1980.

Killingsworth, M. Jimmie. *Whitman's Poetry of the Body: Sexuality, Politics, and the Text.* Chapel Hill: University of North Carolina Press, 1989.

Link, Jürgen. "Interdiscourse, Literature, and Collective Symbols: Theses Towards a Theory of Discourse and Literature." *Enclitic* 8, no. 1/2 (1984): 157–65.

Longfellow, Henry Wadsworth. *The Complete Poetical Works.* Boston: Houghton Mifflin, 1894.

————. *Kavanagh: A Tale.* Boston: Ticknor, Reed and Fields, 1849.

Loving, Jerome. *Emerson, Whitman, and the American Muse.* Chapel Hill: University of North Carolina Press, 1982.

Machor, James. "Pastoralism and the American Urban Ideal: Hawthorne, Whitman, and the Literary Pattern." *American Literature* 54.3 (1982): 329–53.

Martin, Robert K. *The Homosexual Tradition in American Poetry.* Austin: University of Texas Press, 1979.

Marx, Leo. "Pastoralism in American Literature." *Ideology and Classic American Literature.* Ed. Sacvan Bercovitch and Myra Jehlen. New York: Cambridge University Press, 1986.

McElroy, Guy. *Facing History: The Black Image in American Art, 1740–1940.* Washington: Corcoran Gallery/Bedford Arts, 1990.

Melville, Herman. *Moby-Dick.* New York: Library of America, 1991.

Miller, Edwin Havilland. *Walt Whitman's "Song of Myself": A Mosaic of Interpretations.* Iowa City: University of Iowa Press, 1989.

Moon, Michael. *Disseminating Whitman: Revision and Corporeality in "Leaves of Grass."* Cambridge: Harvard University Press, 1991.

Nathanson, Tenney. *Whitman's Presence: Body, Voice, and Writing in "Leaves of Grass."* New York: New York University Press, 1992.

Pearce, Roy Harvey. *The Continuity of American Poetry.* Princeton: Princeton University Press, 1961.

Peeples, Ken. "The Paradox of the 'Good Gray Poet' (Walt Whitman on Slavery and the Black Man)." *Phylon* 35 (1974): 22–34.

Pound, Ezra. *Selected Prose, 1909–1965.* New York: New Directions, 1973.

Price, Kenneth. *Whitman and Tradition: The Poet in His Century.* New Haven: Yale University Press, 1990.

Reynolds, David S. *Beneath the American Renaissance: The Subversive Imagination in the Age of Emerson and Melville.* New York: Knopf, 1989.

————. *Walt Whitman's America: A Cultural Biography.* New York: Knopf, 1995.

Richards, Tom. *The Commodity Culture of Victorian England: Advertising and Spectacle 1851–1914.* Stanford: Stanford University Press, 1990.

Riffaterre, Michael. *Semiotics of Poetry.* Bloomington: Indiana University Press, 1978.

————. "Textuality: W. H. Auden's 'Musée des Beaux Arts.'" *Textual Analysis: Some Readers Reading.* Ed. Mary Ann Caws. New York: Modern Language Association, 1986.

Rogin, Michael. *Subversive Genealogy: The Politics and Art of Herman Melville.* Berkeley: University of California Press, 1985.

Sanchez-Eppler, Karen. "To Stand Between: A Political Perspective on Whitman's Poetics of Merger and Embodiment." *ELH* 56.4 (1989): 923–49.

Scarry, Elaine, ed. *Literature and the Body: Essays on Populations and Persons.* Baltimore: Johns Hopkins University Press, 1988.

Schonick, Robert. "Whitman and the Magazines: Some Documentary Evidence." *On Whitman: The Best from American Literature*. Ed. Edwin Cady and Louis Budd. Durham: Duke University Press, 1987.

Sharpe, William. *Unreal Cities: Urban Figuration in Wordsworth, Baudelaire, Whitman, Eliot, and Williams*. Baltimore: Johns Hopkins University Press, 1987.

Shively, Charley, ed. *Calamus Lovers: Walt Whitman's Working Class Cameradoes*. San Francisco: Gay Sunshine Press, 1987.

Siegel, Adrienne. *The Image of the American City in Popular Literature: 1820–1870*. Port Washington, N.Y.: Kennikat Press, 1981.

Spann, Edward. *The New Metropolis: New York City, 1840–1857*. New York: Columbia University Press, 1981.

Spitzer, Leo. "*Explication de texte* Applied to Walt Whitman's Poem 'Out of the Cradle Endlessly Rocking.'" *A Century of Whitman Criticism*. Ed. E. H. Miller. Bloomington: Indiana University Press, 1969.

Stansell, Christine. *City of Women: Sex and Class in New York, 1789–1860*. New York: Knopf, 1986.

Steele, Jeffrey. *The Representation of Self in the American Renaissance*. Chapel Hill: University of North Carolina Press, 1987.

Stout, Janis. *Sodoms in Eden: The City in American Fiction Before 1860*. Westport, Conn.: Greenwood Press, 1976.

Stovall, Floyd. *The Foreground of "Leaves of Grass."* Charlottesville: University Press of Virginia, 1974.

Stuckey, Sterling, ed. *The Ideological Origins of Black Nationalism*. Boston: Beacon, 1972.

Sweet, Timothy. *Traces of War: Poetry, Photography, and the Crisis of the Union*. Baltimore: Johns Hopkins University Press, 1990.

Terdiman, Richard. *Discourse/Counter-Discourse: The Theory and Practice of Symbolic Resistance in Nineteenth-Century France*. Ithaca: Cornell University Press, 1985.

Thomas, M. Wynn. *The Lunar Light of Whitman's Poetry*. Cambridge: Harvard University Press, 1987.

Thoreau, Henry David. *Walden and Other Writings*. New York: Bantam, 1962.

Trachtenberg, Alan. "American Studies as a Cultural Program." *American Renaissance Reconsidered*. Ed. Walter Benn Michaels and Donald Pease. Baltimore: Johns Hopkins University Press, 1985.

Traubel, Horace. *With Walt Whitman in Camden*. 7 vols. New York: Various publishers, 1905–92.

Van Leer, David. "The Anxiety of Ethnicity in Douglass's *Narrative*." *Frederick Douglass: New Literary and Historical Essays*. Ed. Eric Sundquist. New York: Cambridge University Press, 1990.

Veblen, Thorstein. *The Theory of the Leisure Class.* 1899. New York: Penguin, 1979.

Versluys, Kristiann. *The Poet in the City.* Tübingen: Narr Verlag, 1987.

Volosinov, V. N. *Marxism and the Philosophy of Language.* Trans. Ladislav Matejka and I. R. Titunik. Cambridge: Harvard University Press, 1986.

Wald, Priscilla. *Constituting Americans: Cultural Anxiety and Narrative Form.* Durham: Duke University Press, 1995.

Walker, Cheryl. *The Nightingale's Burden: Women Poets and American Culture before 1900.* Bloomington: Indiana University Press, 1982.

Warren, James. *Walt Whitman's Language Experiment.* University Park: Pennsylvania State University Press, 1990.

Weisbuch, Robert. *Atlantic Double-Cross: American Literature and British Influence in the Age of Emerson.* Chicago: University of Chicago Press, 1986.

White, Morton, and Lucia White. *The Intellectual versus the City: From Thomas Jefferson to Frank Lloyd Wright.* 1962. New York: Oxford University Press, 1977.

Whitman, Walt. *A Child's Reminiscence.* Ed. Thomas Mabbott and Rollo Silver. Seattle: University of Washington Press, 1930.

———. *An 1855–56 Notebook Toward the Second Edition of "Leaves of Grass."* Ed. Harold Blodgett. Carbondale: Southern Illinois University Press, 1959.

———. *Complete Poetry and Collected Prose.* Ed. Justin Kaplan. New York: Library of America, 1982.

———. *Complete Writings.* Ed. Richard M. Bucke et al. 10 vols. New York: Putnam, 1902.

———. *The Correspondence.* Ed. Edwin Havilland Miller. 5 vols. New York: New York University Press, 1961–69.

———. *Daybooks and Notebooks.* Ed. William White. 3 vols. New York: New York University Press, 1978.

———. *The Early Poems and the Fiction.* Ed. Thomas Brasher. New York: New York University Press, 1963.

———. *The Gathering of the Forces.* Ed. Cleveland Rogers and John Black. 2 vols. New York: G. P. Putnam's Sons, 1920.

———. *I Sit and Look Out: Editorials from the "Brooklyn Daily Times," by Walt Whitman.* Ed. Emory Holloway and Vernolian Schwarz. New York: Columbia University Press, 1932.

———. *In Re Walt Whitman.* Ed. Horace Traubel, Richard M. Bucke, and Thomas Harned. Philadelphia: David McKay, 1893.

———. *Leaves of Grass: Comprehensive Reader's Edition.* Ed. Harold Blodgett and Sculley Bradley. New York: New York University Press, 1965.

———. *New York Dissected.* Ed. Emory Holloway and Ralph Adimari. New York: Rufus Rockwell Wilson, 1936.

————. *Notebooks and Unpublished Prose Manuscripts*. Ed. Edward Grier. 6 vols. New York: New York University Press, 1984.

————. *Prose Works, 1892*. Ed. Floyd Stovall. 2 vols. New York: New York University Press, 1964.

————. *The Uncollected Poetry and Prose of Walt Whitman*. Ed. Emory Holloway. 2 vols. Garden City: Doubleday, 1921.

————. *Walt Whitman of the "New York Aurora."* Ed. Joseph Jay Rubin and Charles Brown. State College, Penn.: Bald Eagle, 1950.

————. *Walt Whitman's Workshop: A Collection of Unpublished Prose Manuscripts*. Ed. Clifton Furniss. Cambridge: Harvard University Press, 1928.

————. *Whitman in His Own Time: A Biographical Chronicle of His Life, Drawn from Recollections, Memoirs, and Interviews by Friends and Associates*. Ed. Joel Myerson. Detroit: Omnigraphics, 1991.

Whittier, John Greenleaf. *The Complete Poetical Works*. Boston: Houghton Mifflin, 1894.

Wiebe, Robert. *The Opening of American Society: From the Adoption of the Constitution to the Eve of Disunion*. New York: Knopf, 1984.

Wilentz, Sean. *Chants Democratic: New York City and the Rise of the Working Class, 1788–1850*. New York: Oxford University Press, 1984.

Williams, Raymond. *The Country and the City*. New York: Oxford University Press, 1973.

————. *Marxism and Literature*. Oxford: Oxford University Press, 1977.

Wordsworth, William. *The Prelude: 1799, 1805, 1850*. New York: Norton, 1979.

Ziff, Larzer. *Literary Democracy: The Declaration of Cultural Independence*. New York: Viking, 1981.

Zweig, Paul. *Walt Whitman: The Making of the Poet*. New York: Basic Books, 1984.

INDEX

Aaron, Daniel, 73

Adams, Henry, 103

Addams, Jane, 103

Adorno, Theodor, 111, 183

Allen, Gay Wilson, 2

American literature, 38–41, 46, 53, 104, 142, 184; anthologies of, 42–43, 45, 52, 103, 191 (n. 25); canon of, 43, 163; pastoral in, 107–8, 112, 121; urban in, 108, 112, 121, 123–25, 128–29, 149; body in, 162–63; and women, 190 (n. 22)

Andrews, Thomas, 72–73

Arnold, Matthew, 1–2, 26, 39–40, 115–16, 189 (n. 17)

"As I Ebb'd with the Ocean of Life," 160

Aspiz, Harold, 130

Baker, Houston, 65

Bakhtin, Mikhail, 4–5, 24, 61–62, 105–6, 180–81; and notion of heteroglossia, 62, 112, 115, 129, 192 (n. 8)

Barthes, Roland, 4, 152

Baudelaire, Charles, 16, 116–17, 163

Benjamin, Walter, 148

Blake, William, 81, 94, 110, 116–17

Blodgett, Harold, 95

"Blood–Money," 85

Bloom, Harold, 7, 10, 23, 41

Blumin, Stuart, 124

Body, 4, 15, 24, 54, 80, 111, 144, 152–84; of slaves, 67, 70–71, 82, 87–90, 98, 168; and idiolect, 152–55, 164, 172;

and language, 153, 166–67, 178; in English literary tradition, 153, 162, 178–79, 181; of Native Americans, 168; and class, 179

Boime, Albert, 57–58

Bourdieu, Pierre, 3–4, 21–22, 24–25, 29–31, 165–67; idea of bodily hexis of, 4, 165–67, 169, 172, 179–80; notion of distinction of, 21, 27–28, 31

Bradley, Sculley, 95

Brasher, Thomas, 122

Brown, Charles Brockden, 162

Brown, John, 63, 78

Bryant, William Cullen, 7, 25, 30, 41–43, 45, 49–53, 63, 99, 112, 127, 182; poetics of, 46–48; "The Prairies," 47–48, 50–51; "Thanatopsis," 48–49, 51, 204 (n. 26); and urban poetry, 117–22

Bucke, Richard M., 149, 165

Buck–Morss, Susan, 156

Buell, Lawrence, 41–42, 52

Buffalo Free–Soil Convention, 63, 65

Burns, Robert, 25, 42

"By Blue Ontario's Shore," 160, 164

Byron, Lord, 25–26, 42

Calamus, 140, 160, 171–74

Cameron, Sharon, 162

Carlyle, Thomas, 115

Carnivalesque, 22, 24, 113, 115, 180–81, 188 (n. 10)

Chai, Leon, 41

Channing, William Ellery, 73, 83
Charvat, William, 37
"Child and the Profligate, The," 125
"City Dead-House, The," 128, 142-43,
    147
Civil War, 9, 63, 77, 138, 160, 163, 176,
    184
Class, 3, 16, 25, 31-33, 35, 61, 64, 169,
    179-80, 189 (n. 7)
Clough, Arthur Hugh, 115-16
Coleridge, Samuel Taylor, 26, 42, 44, 53
"Come Up from the Fields Father," 182
Conway, Moncure, 130-31
Crane, Hart, 116, 149
Creeley, Robert, 16
"Crossing Brooklyn Ferry," 9, 113, 129,
    135-45

Dana, Richard Henry, 36, 38, 42
"Democratic Vistas," 27, 31-33, 145
Denning, Michael, 124
Dewey, John, 103
Dickens, Charles, 115, 124-24
Dickinson, Emily, 14, 162, 186 (n. 15)
Donne, John, 116, 153-54
Douglass, Frederick, 65-66, 69, 94,
    193 (n. 12); Narrative of the Life,
    193-94 (nn. 12, 17)
Dred Scott decision, 63
Dreiser, Theodore, 103, 105, 149
Drum-Taps, 99, 104, 160

Eliot, T. S., 116
Emerson, Ralph Waldo, 7, 23, 25, 27-28,
    30, 36, 38, 41-43, 45-47, 63, 103, 117,
    143, 159, 162-63, 165; Whitman's 1856
    letter to, 11, 161, 167; and Romantic
    tradition, 23, 53; and nature, 24, 103,
    158; and slavery, 78-81
"Enfans d'Adam," 160, 162
Engels, Friedrich, 115

Erkkila, Betsy, 12, 15, 31, 60, 70, 78, 81
"Ethiopia Saluting the Colors," 98

"Faces," 111, 128, 130, 133-40, 142-43,
    147, 154, 184
Ferguson, Priscilla, 115
"Fireside" poets, 7, 26, 36, 41, 43, 45, 52,
    62, 102, 105, 118, 159, 163, 167,
    192 (n. 38)
Fisher, Philip, 143
Fishkin, Shelley, 19-20
Foster, George, 123-24, 131-33, 144,
    199 (nn. 21, 22)
Foucault, Michel, 168
Franklin Evans, 86-87, 124-25, 128, 136,
    200 (n. 24)
Freud, Sigmund, 163
Frost, Robert, 166
Fugitive Slave Law, 63-64, 77-78, 87
Fuller, Margaret, 29, 73

Garrison, William Lloyd, 73
Gay, Peter, 162
"Give Me the Splendid Silent Sun,"
    104-5, 107, 143
Glicksburg, Charles, 59
Goethe, Johann Wolfgang von, 42
Greenblatt, Stephen, 13-14
Greene, Albert Gorton, 122
Grossman, Allen, 81

Hardy, Thomas, 115
Hawthorne, Nathaniel, 22, 103, 129,
    162
Hollis, C. Carroll, 2
Holloway, Emory, 136
Holmes, Oliver Wendell, 34-36,
    190 (n. 21)
Homer, 27-29
"House of Friends, The," 85
Howells, William Dean, 103, 105, 149

Hugo, Victor, 116
Hunt, Leigh, 26, 43

Idiolect, 5, 7, 12–13, 49, 104; Whitman's, 5, 8–10, 13–14, 18–19, 25, 35–36, 50–51, 62–63, 69, 107, 112–13, 143, 151, 154–55, 157, 159, 179. *See also* Body, and idiolect
"I Sing the Body Electric," 67–71, 87–88, 93, 98, 100, 114, 135, 154, 160, 174, 176–80, 185 (n. 8)

James, Henry, 103, 105, 149
Jameson, Fredric, 12–13

Kaplan, Justin, 2
Keats, John, 25–26, 42
Killingsworth, M. Jimmie, 135, 163, 168, 172, 179

Leaves of Grass, 4, 8–9, 12, 14, 16, 23, 26, 29, 32–33, 38, 41, 46, 48–49, 62, 67, 82–83, 86, 101, 117–18, 122–23, 128, 139, 157, 169, 179–83; first edition (1855), 2, 18, 20, 25, 31, 34, 43, 51, 92, 135, 138–40, 145, 147, 151, 160, 164; second edition (1856), 11, 51, 160; fourth edition, 37; sixth edition, 95; third edition, 160
Leer, David Van, 65–66
Lincoln, Abraham, 63, 99–100, 184
Link, Jürgen, 56–57
Longfellow, Henry Wadsworth, 7, 25, 27, 36–45, 50–51, 53, 60, 63, 68, 82, 182; *Kavanagh,* 39–40, 53–54; *Poems on Slavery,* 81–85, 90, 94, 97
Lowell, James Russell, 36, 60, 63, 78, 81, 85

Machor, James, 112–13, 129
"Mannahatta," 146

Marx, Karl, 157
Marx, Leo, 107–8
McLuhan, Marshall, 10
Melville, Herman, 7, 22, 55–58, 103, 107, 129, 162–63, 181
Miller, Edwin Havilland, 89
Milton, John, 28, 40
Moon, Michael, 155, 164, 168

Nathanson, Tenney, 177
New York City, 4, 123, 125, 128, 130, 133, 136–49; as "American City," 108, 111, 116–18, 120
"New York Dissected," 80, 131–33, 145–46, 148
Nietzshe, Friedrich, 163
Norris, Frank, 103

"O Captain! My Captain!" 182–83
"Of My Poems," 35–36
"One's Self I Sing," 37
"Out of the Cradle Endlessly Rocking," 23, 51–52

Pearce, Roy Harvey, 36
Peeples, Ken, 59
Philadelphia, 120, 123
"Pictures," 48–51
"Play-Ground, The," 43–44
Poe, Edgar Allen, 22, 41, 52, 102–3, 162, 182
"Poem of Remorse," 86–87
Price, Kenneth, 12
"Primer of Words," 67, 166–67, 174–75

Rabelais, 22, 24, 180
"Reconciliation," 97–98
"Resurgemus," 85–86
"Reuben's Last Wish," 125–26
Reynolds, David S., 12, 15, 22, 79, 183
Ricks, Christopher, 153

Riffaterre, Michael, 5–10, 13–14,
186 (n. 12)
Rimbaud, Arthur, 16, 116
Rogin, Michael, 58
Romanticism, 5, 23, 25, 33, 41–53, 83,
104–5, 180–81, 183–84, 187 (nn. 17, 2);
and the urban, 113–14, 118, 139, 142
Rousseau, Jean–Jacques, 42

"Salut au Monde!" 154–55, 186 (n. 8)
Scarry, Elaine, 152–53
Scott, Sir Walter, 26, 42
Shakespeare, William, 27–29, 40
Sharpe, William, 140, 142–43
Shelley, Percy Bysshe, 47, 142
Shively, Charley, 165
Siegel, Adrienne, 123–24
Slavery, 4–5, 9, 14–15, 54–101, 153–54,
160, 193 (n. 10), 194 (nn. 12, 18),
195–96 (nn. 24, 25, 28, 30), 197
(n. 40); whale as symbol of, 55–56,
58, 91–93, 96; and discourse of
abolitionism, 63–64, 72, 82, 84
"Sleepers, The," 9, 16, 55–58, 65, 67, 71,
91–97, 100, 130, 135–36, 138, 140, 154,
160, 169–71
Smith, Alexander, 26, 45
Sociolect, 3–9, 12–13; Whitman's use
of, 4, 13, 55, 112, 186 (n. 15); Riffaterre
on, 6; American, 9, 38, 40, 56, 104; of
slavery, 60, 68–69, 83–84, 91–93, 153;
city as site of, 113, 115, 120, 123–24,
133, 143, 150, 154; and the body,
153–55, 158–59, 163, 174–76
"Song for Certain Congressmen," 85
"Song of Myself," 8–9, 67, 87–88, 97,
100, 105, 126–27, 129–30, 135–36, 138,
140, 146, 155–60, 165–66, 171, 183
"Song of the Answerer," 140–41, 150
"Song of the Broad–Axe," 160

"Song of the Exposition," 9, 33
"Song of the Open Road," 105, 108–12,
129
"Song of the Rolling Earth," 160, 183
Spann, Edward, 119–21, 136–37, 143, 149
"Sparkles from the Wheel," 143, 147
Specimen Days, 29–30, 147
Spenser, Edward, 40
Spitzer, Leo, 23
"Spontaneous Me," 160
"Starting from Paumanok," 160, 173
Stoddard, Richard, 165
Stout, Janis, 123–24, 129
Stovall, Floyd, 2
Stowe, Harriet Beecher, 79, 87
Sweet, Timothy, 104

Tennyson, Alfred Lord, 26, 45, 51,
115–17, 182, 184
Terdiman, Richard, 14–15
"This Compost," 160
Thomas, M. Wynn, 128, 130, 135,
143–44, 146
Thoreau, Henry David, 7, 81, 103, 108,
162–63, 171
"To a Common Prostitute," 142–43,
146–47
"Tomb Blossoms, The," 126
Transcendentalism, 11, 26, 36–37, 41, 46,
52–53, 103
Traubel, Horace, 45, 148, 165
Tupper, Martin, 51

Veblen, Thorstein, 4, 31–35, 111
Versluys, Kristiann, 128
Volosinov, V. N., 55–56

Warren, James, 95
Wendell, Barrett, 139–40
"What I Best See in Thee," 184

"When Lilacs Last in the Dooryard Bloom'd," 23, 99, 182–83
"Whispers of Heavenly Death," 183
White, Morton and Lucia, 103
Whitman, Walt: poetic development of, 1–2, 5, 12, 15, 19–20, 24–26, 34, 36, 43, 53, 63, 81, 101, 117, 124, 128, 148–51, 160, 183, 187 (n. 3); and American literature, 1, 3, 7, 11, 30–31, 36, 38, 40–41, 52, 184; and notion of distinction, 2, 4, 9, 28–37, 40, 61, 67, 78, 105, 107, 109, 113, 127, 148, 157, 164, 169–70, 179, 182–83; and high culture, 3, 27, 31, 36, 40, 61, 151, 182–83, 189 (n. 7); and urbanism, 3, 9, 54, 102–8, 110–13, 115, 117–18, 122–51, 160, 198 (n. 9); and the body, 3, 54, 153–84, 193 (n. 10), 202 (n. 7), 203 (n. 12); and race, 3-4, 54, 58–60, 64, 66–67, 71, 77, 80, 86–87, 97–99, 107, 154; poetic project of, 3-4, 6, 18, 23, 25, 62–64, 67, 112, 150, 183; notebooks of, 4, 16, 25, 28, 30, 66–68, 81, 86–87, 91, 134, 138–41, 174–75, 186 (n. 17), 204 (n. 23); and sexuality, 4, 9, 54, 153, 158, 160, 162–63, 165, 168, 172–75, 179–84, 185 (n. 2), 193 (n. 10), 203 (n. 19); and literary contemporaries, 7, 14–15, 18, 25–26, 36, 41, 44, 46, 60–61, 63, 90, 122, 165, 167, 181–82, 184, 189 (n. 6); and literary tradition, 7–8, 12–13, 19, 22–23, 25–28, 34, 38, 40–41, 43, 45, 53–54, 81, 100, 105, 116, 124, 159–60, 173, 182, 184, 187 (n. 2), 188 (n. 7), 191 (n. 29), 202 (n. 7); and popular culture, 10–12, 24, 29, 36, 61, 134; and journalism, 10–11, 19–21, 24, 29, 42, 76–77, 108, 117, 125–26, 133, 136, 148, 175, 187 (n. 3), 196 (n. 28), 198 (n. 2); political beliefs, 15, 60, 64, 77, 81, 145–46, 147–48, 163–64, 193 (n. 10); and language, 15–16, 186–87 (n. 17); poetics of, 20, 30, 61; readership of, 26–27, 40–41, 52, 61, 65, 150, 159, 184, 190 (n. 24); on Tennyson, 26, 45, 51; on Emerson, 27–28, 42, 45, 52, 189 (n. 9), 197 (n. 2); on Longfellow, 44, 51, 97, 189 (n. 6); on Bryant, 45–48, 189 (n. 6); on abolitionist discourse, 59–60, 68, 72–75, 77–79, 84, 93; as fiction writer, 73–74, 125–26; and working classes, 77, 165, 168, 180, 190 (n. 22); correspondence of, 98, 173; on Lincoln, 99–100, 182–84; urban–pastoral ideal of, 112, 129–30, 143; and New York, 125–26, 128, 130–31, 136, 145–49, 151, 198 (n. 6); as flâneur, 128, 132, 148; interest in medicine and health of, 161, 175–76, 178, 203 (n. 20), 204 (n. 23); on death, 181–84. *See also titles of specific works*
Whittier, John Greenleaf, 7, 30, 43, 52, 60, 63, 68–69, 78; anti–slavery poetry of, 81–85, 90; urban poetry of, 121–22
Wiebe, Robert, 168–69
Williams, Raymond, 28, 115–16
Williams, William Carlos, 116
Wilmot Proviso, 63, 74
"Woman Waits for Me, A," 160, 185(n. 8)
Wordsworth, William, 25–26, 42–43, 104, 113, 115–17, 142–43, 182; *The Prelude,* 105, 110, 113–14, 137–38
"Wound–Dresser, The," 99–100

"Young Grimes," 122, 126

Ziff, Larzer, 34
Zweig, Paul, 2, 130, 163